Living on a Time Bomb

Studies in Environmental Anthropology and Ethnobiology

General Editor: **Roy Ellen**, FBA
Professor of Anthropology, University of Kent at Canterbury

Interest in environmental anthropology has grown steadily in recent years, reflecting national and international concern about the environment and developing research priorities. This major new international series, which continues a series first published by Harwood and Routledge, is a vehicle for publishing up-to-date monographs and edited works on particular issues, themes, places or peoples that focus on the interrelationship between society, culture, and environment. Relevant areas include human ecology, the perception and representation of the environment, ethno-ecological knowledge, the human dimension of biodiversity conservation and the ethnography of environmental problems. While the underlying ethos of the series will be anthropological, the approach is interdisciplinary.

Recent volumes:

Volume 30
Living on a Time Bomb
Local Negotiations of Oil Extraction in a Mexican Community
Svenja Schöneich

Volume 29
Grazing Communities
Pastoralism on the Move and Biocultural Heritage Frictions
Edited by Letizia Bindi

Volume 28
Delta Life
Exploring Dynamic Environments Where Rivers Meet the Sea
Edited by Franz Krause and Mark Harris

Volume 27
Nature Wars
Essays around a Contested Concept
Roy Ellen

Volume 26
Ecological Nostalgias
Memory, Affect and Creativity in Times of Ecological Upheavals
Edited by Olivia Angé and David Berliner

Volume 25
Birds of Passage
Hunting and Conservation in Malta
Mark-Anthony Falzon

Volume 24
At Home on the Waves
Human Habitation of the Sea from the Mesolithic to Today
Edited by Tanya J. King and Gary Robinson

Volume 23
Edges, Fringes, Frontiers
Integral Ecology, Indigenous Knowledge and Sustainability in Guyana
Thomas Henfrey

Volume 22
Indigeneity and the Sacred
Indigenous Revival and the Conservation of Sacred Natural Sites in the Americas
Edited by Fausto Sarmiento and Sarah Hitchner

Volume 21
Trees, Knots, and Outriggers
Environmental Knowledge in the Northeast Kula Ring
Frederick H. Damon

For a full volume listing, please see the series page on our website:
http://berghahnbooks.com/series/environmental-anthropology-and-ethnobiology

Living on a Time Bomb

Local Negotiations of Oil Extraction
in a Mexican Community

Svenja Schöneich

berghahn
NEW YORK • OXFORD
www.berghahnbooks.com

First published in 2023 by
Berghahn Books
www.berghahnbooks.com

© 2023, 2025 Svenja Schöneich
First paperback edition published in 2025

All rights reserved. Except for the quotation of short passages for the purposes of criticism and review, no part of this book may be reproduced in any form or by any means, electronic or mechanical, including photocopying, recording, or any information storage and retrieval system now known or to be invented, without written permission of the publisher.

Library of Congress Cataloging-in-Publication Data

A C.I.P. cataloging record is available from the Library of Congress
Library of Congress Cataloging in Publication Control Number: 2022019180

British Library Cataloguing in Publication Data

A catalogue record for this book is available from the British Library

ISBN 978-1-80073-656-6 hardback
ISBN 978-1-80539-718-2 paperback
ISBN 978-1-80073-657-3 epub
ISBN 978-1-80073-743-3 web pdf

https://doi.org/10.3167/9781800736566

An electronic version of this book is freely available thanks to the support of libraries working with Knowledge Unlatched. KU is a collaborative initiative designed to make high-quality books Open Access for the public good. More information about the initiative and links to the Open Access version can be found at knowledgeunlatched.org.

This work is published subject to a Creative Commons Attribution Noncommercial No Derivatives 4.0 License. The terms of the license can be found at http://creativecommons.org/licenses/by/4.0/. For uses beyond those covered in the license contact Berghahn Books.

Contents

List of Illustrations	vi
Acknowledgments	viii
Introduction. Entering the Oilscape	1
Chapter 1. Theorizing Oil: A Conceptualization of the Oilscape	17
Chapter 2. A Mexican Oil Story: Historic Background and Contemporary Setting	41
Chapter 3. From Booms, Declines, and Time Bombs: Temporalities of Oil in Emiliano Zapata	73
Chapter 4. From an Ejido to an Extraction Site: Materialities of Oil in Emiliano Zapata	107
Chapter 5. Dealing with the Dragon: Social Dynamics and Ambiguity in Emiliano Zapata	143
Conclusion	181
References	192
Index	217

Illustrations

Figures

1.1.	Concept "oilscape" © Svenja Schöneich.	36
2.1.	Papantlas hilly landscape with orange orchards and an oil well, Papantla, Mexico, 2016 © Svenja Schöneich.	61
3.1.	The timeline of oil extraction in Emiliano Zapata by Svenja Schöneich.	75
3.2.	Construction workers in the 1970s/farmers in 2018, Papantla, Mexico, 2018 © Svenja Schöneich.	82
4.1.	A month-old seepage within the river, which awaits repairs, Papantla, Mexico, 2017 © Svenja Schöneich.	111
4.2.	Burning flame of one of three gas flares located in immediate proximity to human settlement, illuminating the main road during the daytime in Emiliano Zapata, Papantla, Mexico, 2018 © Svenja Schöneich.	112
4.3.	Decaying industrial installations—a pipeline and an unreadable sign—amid corn crops and orange trees, Papantla, Mexico, 2016 © Svenja Schöneich.	113
4.4.	Pipelines protruding in a field in Emiliano Zapata, Papantla, Mexico, 2017 © Svenja Schöneich.	118
4.5.	Abandoned processing plant at the cuartel in Emiliano Zapata where various decaying industrial installations and provision facilities for company staff are located, Papantla, Mexico, 2016 © Svenja Schöneich.	127
4.6.	Signboard by PEMEX at the fence of Emiliano Zapata's *telebachillerato*, which is renovated with money from the PACMA program, stating the exact sum spent and the number of beneficiaries, Papantla, Mexico, 2018 © Svenja Schöneich.	135

4.7.	Decommissioned pipelines used as ceiling joists of a house in Emiliano Zapata, Papantla, Mexico 2018 © Svenja Schöneich.	137
4.8.	A large, decommissioned pipeline used as a bench on a playground in the colony of San Andrés in Emiliano Zapata, Papantla, Mexico, 2018 © Svenja Schöneich.	138
5.1.	The colony San Andrés beside the main road, Papantla, Mexico, 2018 © Svenja Schöneich.	165
5.2.	Entrance of the primary school renovated by PEMEX and Oleorey in Emiliano Zapata, Papantla, Mexico, 2016 © Svenja Schöneich.	170
5.3.	Anti-fracking graffiti in Emiliano Zapata, Papantla, Mexico, 2016/2017 © Svenja Schöneich.	175

Maps

0.1.	The ejido Emiliano Zapata located in a region in Mexico, where fracking, as well as conventional oil extraction takes place © Orestes de la Rosa, used with permission.	8
2.1.	Contemporary Totonacapan with distribution of Totonac speakers in the area © Orestes de la Rosa, used with permission.	43
2.2.	Contractual area of the San Andrés oilfield with communities located within the area © Orestes de la Rosa, used with permission.	63
5.1.	The surface of the ejido Emiliano Zapata 2007, highlighting Plots and Parcels occupied, or affected by PEMEX Installations. Courtesy of the Comisariado Ejidal of Emiliano Zapata.	158
5.2.	OpenStreetMap of Emiliano Zapata highlighting the Colonia San Andrés © OpenStreetMap-Mitwirkende (www.openstreetmap.org/copyright).	162

Tables

| 2.1. | Community committees as institutional entities in Emiliano Zapata © Svenja Schöneich. | 68 |

Acknowledgments

This book is the product of many months of work through which I enjoyed the support of numerous colleagues, friends, and family members. I am deeply grateful for their comments, revisions, input, and moral support. I am especially thankful to Orestes de la Rosa for his support along the field research process and the informative maps elaborated for this book. Above all, however, the existence of this book is owed to the people of Emiliano Zapata. They took me into their homes and shared their sorrows, joys, and lives with me, which was an amazing gift that not only enriched this work, but also my personal life beyond words. I deeply admire their hospitality, patience, and humility, and I am grateful for every experience with them. I call myself fortunate to always have a home in Emiliano Zapata, and I wish its people all the best, whatever may come.

Introduction

Entering the Oilscape

The dust on the road stirs up every time one of the wheels hits a pothole on the brittle pavement of the country road as the bus approaches the community. The sweltering heat gushes onto the open windows when the bus slows down and supplants the notion of the last bit of a cool breeze created through the air blowing in at rapid speeds. Outside the dirty windows, the verdant stretch of lemon and orange trees standing in rows like soldiers increasingly supersede the different shades of the light green meadows that we passed after leaving the small city of Chote. It is almost six o'clock in the evening, yet the scorching heat remains as intense as it was in the morning, making me have a perpetual feeling of melting away. Before the bus passes the bridge, offering its passengers an impressive view over the valley of the Remolino River, the first apparently empty spaces within the landscape appear. The almost geometrical rows of citrus trees covering every inch of the hilly area, suddenly give way to square fenced lots of approximately 150 square meters here and there. At first glance, those lots seem abandoned, bleak and empty except for some thin spear-like metal trestles and white tanks, the contents of which are unknown. Many of them are in bad shape, since they have been abandoned by the company during the recent years of the oil crisis. However, at closer range, one can observe people moving between the installations, wearing overalls of the new foreign companies that came to the region during the last couple of years. We have reached the area with some larger boreholes, indicating that we are getting closer to the extraction sites of the oilfield San Andrés, where the community and ejido Emiliano Zapata is located.[1]

While the bus crosses the bridge, swerving rather than driving in a bid to avoid the pothole-pocked road, I glance at the old bridge, the original one, which was made of metal more than sixty years ago and is extremely rusty now. This bridge, which marked a turning point in the lives of many families on the other side of the river we are crossing at this very moment, is now cordoned off and serves only as a monument paying tribute to the early heady days of the oil boom. The bridge was built after the state-owned oil firm Petróleos Mexicanos (PEMEX), discovered large oil reserves in the area, as a measure to facilitate direct transportation from the oil city of Poza Rica de Hidalgo to the oilfields on the other side of the river. Before its installation, there was only an unpaved dirt road that connected the peasant communities on the other side with the city. With PEMEX came the steel, the asphalt, and the goods. With the recent crisis came the decay. And what comes after? Some changes have recently been palpable, when some of the old installations were revived and new people with fresh interests came to the area. Everything appears to be at a point of transition, fraught with uncertainty.

A few moments later, as we leave two villages behind, an unpleasant chemical smell from the nearby gas injection well suddenly rushes in through the window, coupled with the air. I get ready to grab my backpack and get up. The smell indicates that we have almost reached Emiliano Zapata, the community that has been my home for almost six months now. I have to hurry to get home before nightfall after having interviewed an oil worker in the city. The numbers of assaults and incidents related to drug violence have risen significantly within the last few years, and it is certainly prudent to get home before sundown. Houses start appearing on both sides of the road. Two of the facades present the passengers with a glimpse of graffiti protesting oil extraction, on houses built with compensation money from the oil firms, as I have come to know. The paintings show oil derricks surrounded by skulls and a Che Guevara looking unwaveringly into the future, while the slogan beneath his image condemns "fracking" in the name of the people. In particular, the extraction technique of hydraulic fracturing, called "fracking," has been a major issue that has come up in the wake of the implementation of the recent energy reform, which has caused a series of changes within the local setting.

More dust swirls up when the bus abruptly stops on the right side of the road. Getting off the little stairs at the back of the bus, I can see and hear the several meters high flame from the closest of the three gas flares in direct proximity to the settlement. The gas flare has become a symbol for the disturbances, pollution, and risks associated with oil extraction in the community, and many community members point to it when invoking the constant threat that oil extraction poses. "We are living on a time bomb" is a recurring expression in many conversations I had with community members. An elderly man on the other side of the road, carrying a machete and wearing a PEMEX jumpsuit, smiles and nods at me. When he passes by, I recognize him as Don Julio, coming back from his orchard. Like almost everybody in the community who works the fields, he wears old PEMEX jumpsuits to work because they are affordable, good quality working clothes. This creates the impression that I have entered a community of PEMEX workers, while ironically, nobody here has ever been part of the company staff. However, the work in the fields is hard and not very profitable, so many young people have already left the place to seek opportunities elsewhere—often finding them in the surroundings of the oil industry in other parts of the country. As I heave on my backpack and walk up the road, all those contradictions and the constant ambiguity almost physically engulf me, in addition to the first mosquitoes of the early dusk.

From Scapes and Time Bombs: Places Determined by Oil

The apparent contradictions regarding extraction in Emiliano Zapata not only reflect the historic processes and current circumstances at the national level but they are also linked to global forces behind oil production. The community provides a stage on which oil directs the plot development—and while it is not the focus, oil production seems to determine every part of community life. It is visible and tangible in the direct environment where the extraction takes place, in the landscape, and in the appearance of buildings, and it rules the sociocultural patterns of the community as well as the interactions among its members. It manifests itself in expectations and fears, in the hope for an improvement of life, but also in anxiety about the future, considering the uncertainty and the great risks associated with the extraction activities, which are often expressed with the idea of a "time bomb" by the people whose fate is interwoven with it. This book portrays the community Emiliano Zapata, which represents a place shaped by oil extraction and shows how the community members deal and interact with the extraction activities and uncertainty determining their lives.

The time bomb is not an uncommon concept within studies about resource extraction. In 1990, Colin Filer described a "time-bomb effect" for the process of social disintegration over time of landowning communities with respect to mining in Papua New Guinea (Filer 1990). Thereby, the resource extraction fails to meet expectations regarding economic possibilities and benefits for the local community, instead leading to major modifications on the territory. Resource extraction triggers a process of social disintegration where over time the reality regarding job opportunities, improved infrastructure, and compensation payments—or what is considered "development"—fails to meet expectations. Instead, the community members must live with major modifications on their territory; increased pollution of water, air, and soil; and move away from traditional ways of production and exchange toward the wage-based economy trade.

The time bomb image encompasses the uncertainty and anxiety concerning the future with extraction building on past experiences but also draws a lively picture of the collective imagination of a "spice of malice" lurking under the ground, ready to burst at any time. This phenomenon is also described by Frank Cancian for a Mexican community in Chiapas, where the development of the regional oil industry led to a process of increased renunciation of traditional farming economy and a movement toward wage labor, which changed the community's social patterns through the processual emergence of a worker's class (Cancian 1994: 3; 163). In 1996, Glenn Banks picks up the term "time bomb" again, when he asks, "Compensation for mining: benefit or time bomb?" and shows how compensation payments by the mining company for local residents foster social discordance instead of being the solution for a problem (Banks 1996). Lisa Breglia does not focus on the concept of a time bomb as such, but she inquires about the uncertainties of the oil crisis and post-peak futures in a fishing community in Campeche, engaging in the discourse about the local effect of global energy politics and the uncertain conditions it imposes on local residents (Breglia 2013). She thereby touches on an important aspect of the time bomb issue in resource extraction and particularly in the case of oil: its temporal particularities with regard to its uncertain but definitely unpleasant effects on local communities. In Emiliano Zapata, these effects have shaped the community and made it what it is today.

Oil as a resource is inevitably linked to temporal effects that generate a predestined course of wealth and economic growth, where oil is discovered at first and interlocked with a certain future ending. When the source is exhausted or the oil price drops, an oil crisis erupts. Yet, the exact moment in time when this will be the case remains elusive until it happens—thus featuring a resemblance to the idea of a time bomb. The bust then causes the economy to decline but the irreversible environmental impacts, which shaped the surroundings during the boom time, linger on. They continue to bedevil the local living conditions, compounding the crisis, until the oil price eventually stabilizes or alternatives for income are found. Therefore, the almost schizophrenic temporal dimension of an approaching and uncertain end, even in peak times, accompanies oil like no other resource, which has been widely acknowledged and described (e.g., Cepek 2012; Coronil 1997; Black 2000; Gilberthorpe 2014; Kaposy 2017; Limbert 2008; Weszkalnys 2014, 2016). This rhythmic sequence of abundance alternating with scarcity and an approaching finiteness links oil to a constant social and economic change, that is repeated worldwide in localities affected by oil extraction (Ferry and Limbert 2008: 3; Reyna and Behrends 2011: 5; Rogers 2015a: 367). These temporal features of oil thus also impact the material local environment of the places where it is extracted and processed. The material manifestations of hydrocarbons become inscribed into the surroundings over time, in the form of installations, infrastructure such as pipelines and transportation routes, through residues and fumes, and through the physical presence of industrial and company actors. Resources themselves are often regarded as the determinants of particular social and political outcomes. However, it is necessary to engage with the interplay of the complex local conditions with the resource and the corresponding extraction practices to enable a comprehensive understanding of the social processes that arise around the extraction (Davidov 2013: 487–88; Ey and Sherval 2015: 176; Gilberthorpe and Papyrakis 2015: 381).

Resource extraction in general severely modifies its immediate surroundings and consequently, the living environment of the involved people. The oil industry is no exception. In Emiliano Zapata, the extraction and industrial processing of oil and gas have profoundly modified the surrounding terrain, thus influencing the social and cultural practices of the people inhabiting those surroundings. I claim that the ejido territory of Emiliano Zapata has evolved into a space determined by oil including the particularities of extraction practices as well as social patterns emerging from the constellation of actors and materialities of extraction over time. In this book, this space is conceptualized as an oilscape in order to analyze the mechanisms of dealing with these uncertainties, considering the insights from research about the spatial dimension of oil, while paying attention to local particularities.

One approach for the analysis of extractive spaces, integrating material implications, as well as the processual character of the space emerging around extraction sites, is the concept of the "minescape," introduced by Melina Ey and Meg Sherval "as a way of conceptual mechanism through which to synthesize and integrate significant shifts in the way extractive processes and terrains are perceived" (2015: 177). The concept emphasizes the dynamic character of extraction spaces with complex sociocultural and material dimensions. The usage of scapes as an analytical entity was first introduced by anthropologist Arjun Appadurai and was not specifically used for a particular space, but rather emphasized the perspectival character of the construct "scape." Different scapes are determined by the actors, who experience, perceive, and navigate these scapes and thus construct them as multiple "imagined worlds" (Appadurai 1990: 296). Therefore, the suffix "scape" indicates a wider perspective than a territorially limited space. In the case of extraction, the minescapes are bound to a certain degree to a locally defined space where extraction takes place, but at the same time, it widens this scope through the integration of further dimensions. It offers a more comprehensive approach to understanding landscapes of extraction and their actors (D'Angelo and Pijpers 2018: 216; Ey and Sherval 2015: 178).

The term "minescape" was first used by the photographer Edward Burtynski (2009), who documented mining sites in Australia and first considered the physical inscription of the extraction into the landscape. Applied to terrains, where extraction physically takes place and also affects people's social practices, as carried out by Ey and Sherval (2015), the concept becomes more complex and describes an interplay of the sociocultural and the material dimension of space (D'Angelo and Pijpers 2018: 216). Yet, the concept "minescape" is, as the name suggests, mainly based on mineral mining and even though several aspects regarding social and economic effects of mineral and hydrocarbon extraction are comparable (Gilberthorpe and Rajak 2017: 186), oil as a resource bears a set of particularities. These particularities within the landscape are visible, for example, in the award-winning collection of photographs by the photographer David Gardner from 2020, which is entitled *Into the Anthropocene*.[2] The *New Scientist* wrote about the collection: "Surreal Californian Oilscape Wins Climate Change Photography Award" (Li 2020). The collection illustrates the unique material properties of oil. Oil extraction is linked to a different type of industrial installation and infrastructure than mining, which shape the landscape in a particular way. Furthermore, oil is linked to a particular type of temporal development, which can be understood as the temporalities of oil (see e.g., Kama 2020; Kaposy 2017 Weszkalnys 2014) and which is not expressly included as an important aspect in the concept of the minescape. Brian Black (2000) dedicates a chapter on the "The Sacrificial Landscape" of what he calls Petrolia—describing the transformation of Oils Creek as a space that turned from agriculture to oil industry basically overnight. He rightfully states: "A landscape is constructed of geology, hydrology, and biology; yet it also includes the creations of the humans or other beings that inhabit and change the environment. Where nature and culture meet, they construct a landscape" (2000: 61). In Emiliano Zapata, this landscape has been shaped in a special way that is unique to oil, just like in many other places with a history of oil extraction, since the underlying process always follows similar patterns. Therefore, a specific understanding of landscapes is required, as introduced by the concept of the minescape, but considering the particularities of oil. Such an approach helps to analyze the space constructed around oil extraction and processing sites, while also taking into account the particularities of oil production and the specifics of temporalities, which accompany the development of the oil industry. Myrna Santiagos (2006) approaches these particularities with the concept of "the ecology of oil," by looking at the impact of oil extraction on dynamics like land tenure as well as on social structures and distinctive forms of labor. All these dynamics, be they economic, social, or material in nature, are connected and shaped by the typical properties of oil extraction and production, I therefore introduce the concept of the "oilscape," which borrows the initial idea of the minescape and adapts it to the circumstances shaped by oil extraction. The concept emphasizes the material definition of the surroundings while considering the temporal dimensions of the processual inscriptions of oil into the living environment, as well as the constitution of the space as an outcome of social processes (see Löw 2008: 25). The oilscape thus represents a space within which oil extraction has become inscribed into the material manifestation of landscape, housing, fields, and infrastructure, as well as the social texture and behavior of the community members over time. It did so under the conditions of economic peaks and declines, related to oil as a resource of global demand. Hydrocarbons, often representing toxic and explosive substances, are considered dangerous assets, which form the oilscape in a particular manner by posing risks to human lives and health, as well as the environment, through which they cause a variety of uncertainties to lurk among the inhabitants of the oilscape.

Aside from the temporal and material components, the social dimension models the oilscape too. Oil and the extractive industries play crucial roles for the constitution of sociocultural patterns within the environment they are active in. Space is described by Löw as "subjected to analysis in the social sciences as a 'product of social action' or as a 'product of social structures'" (2008: 25) and the social component of space is taken into consideration as an essential analytical pillar when approaching the oilscape. The social dimensions of space are the result of content negotiation processes between different actors and actor groups, predicated on the hierarchies of power (2008: 26; Bourdieu 2018: 107). Through the actions and interactions taking place within the physical space, this space is shaped by social encounters and processes. The oilscape, therefore, undergoes a process of constant reshaping of the material and the social-cultural settings under the temporal conditions of oil as a resource. One of these conditions is the uncertainty perceived by the inhabitants of the oilscape due to immediate risk caused by extractive activities on the one hand and the extent of dependence on oil in the light of its anticipated ending on the other.

Welcome to Life on the Time Bomb: Oil in Emiliano Zapata

I first came to the rural community of Papantla in Veracruz named after the famous revolutionary Emiliano Zapata in early 2016 with the goal of conducting a research project on the impact of oil and gas extraction on

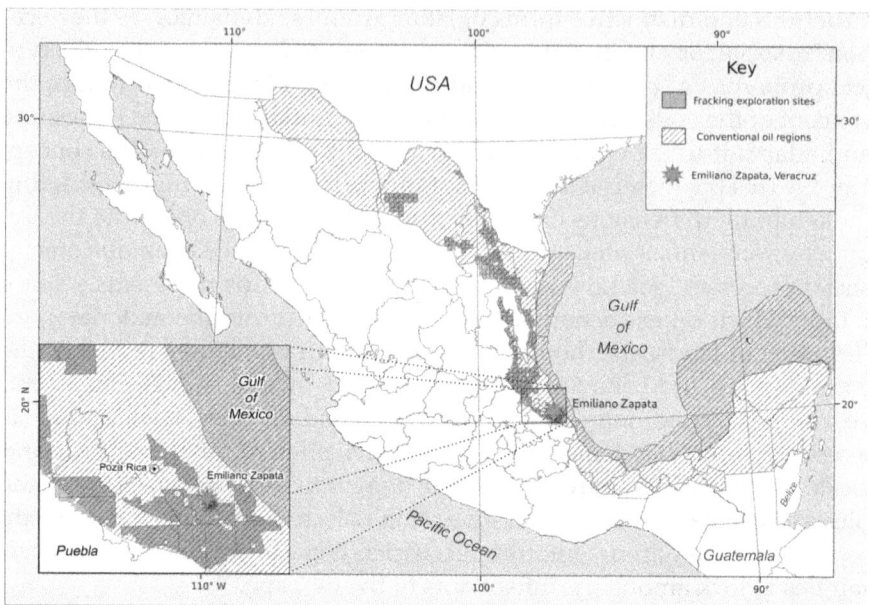

Map 0.1. The ejido Emiliano Zapata located in a region in Mexico, where fracking, as well as conventional oil extraction takes place © Orestes de la Rosa, used with permission.

people's lives. The community is located on the San Andrés oilfield, once one of the major oil producing sources in the region and a place where different forms of hydrocarbon extraction have been taking place since the 1950s (Chenaut 2017: 101). The community of around seventeen hundred inhabitants has more than fifty active oil wells and various industrial facilities on its territory and is also located in an area known for the first application of fracking in the country.

The story of the community itself, but also of Mexico as a nation, is inextricably linked to the story of oil and industrial development. In the context of the history of Mexico, since the nineteenth century and until today, oil and gas extraction came to play a crucial role for the economy and consequently for the national narrative (e.g., Breglia 2013; Checa-Artasu and Hernández Franyuti 2016; Santiago 2016). This holds especially true for the development of the oil industry after the nationalization of the oil sector in the aftermath of the Mexican Revolution (1910–20). The state-owned company Petróleos Mexicanos (PEMEX) was founded in 1938 and soon became one of the cornerstones of the national economy. For more than seven decades, the company wielded a monopoly on the exploration, extraction, and processing of hydrocarbon products, and thus became a symbolic entity representing development in the whole country. PEMEX, ever since was perceived as one of the main pillars of national wealth and established relationships with urban and rural communities, which is likely to be one of the reasons why the Mexican hydrocarbon sector used to be considered less conflict-driven than other extraction sectors in Latin America (see Viscidi and Fargo 2015: 6; Silva Ontiveros et al. 2018: 483). However, oil extraction in Mexico after the expropriation was certainly not conducted without protest or contestation by local communities (e.g., del Palacio Langer 2015: 130–31; Zalik 2008: 182).

The oil-rich territories in the north of Veracruz have been central for the Mexican oil sector since the advent of industry in the country (Brown 1993: 13). The oilfields of Poza Rica and San Andrés were discovered in 1930 and 1956 and represent important centers of Mexico's petroleum industry until this day. Moreover, the local economy was mainly driven by the booming oil industry since the 1950s (Cárdenas Gracia 2009: 31; Chenaut 2010: 60; 2017: 101). When the oil boom came to an end in the first decade of the twenty-first century, the oil economy was weakened because of the worldwide energy crisis and a drop in the oil prices in the second half of the 2010s. By 2014, Mexico's position as an oil producing nation and exporter of hydrocarbon products had already fallen to tenth place in international comparison, a considerable drop from the fifth place it once held in 2005. The crisis caused the sector to withdraw from its prominent position in the national economy. Consequently, the Mexican hydrocarbon industry was finally considered unable to compete, ultimately resulting in the dethroning of PEMEX as a symbol of the national oil bonanza (e.g., O'Connor and Viscidi 2015: 3; Sánchez Campos 2016: 307).

As a political response to the crisis, then President Enrique Peña Nieto launched a comprehensive liberal restructuring of the national energy sector, known as the Mexican energy reform 2013/2014. It included the reformation of three constitutional articles that enabled the opening of the hydrocarbon sector for private investment and thus halted PEMEX's seventy-six-year monopoly. It also changed the patterns of land use rights and opened the country to new extraction technologies such as seep water drilling and the application of hydraulic fracturing, also known as fracking. Fracking is a technique where water mixed with chemicals is injected at high pressure into a wellbore in the ground to create cracks in the deep rock layers through which natural gas and petroleum are released and start to flow so they can be extracted (de Rijke 2013: 13). By inviting foreign companies into the country and introducing the new extraction technology, it was expected that the country's oil wealth and prosperity would recover with the revival of oil revenues (see Seelke et al. 2015: 3; Viscidi and Fargo 2015: 6).

When I started the first research phase in 2016, the implementation of the energy reform and specifically the issue of fracking had become a controversial issue at both the national and international level (e.g., de la Fuente 2016; Hudgins and Poole 2014; Pearson 2013; Rabe and Borick 2013, Whitton et al. 2018). Emiliano Zapata then had earned a local and even national reputation because it had been the venue of a conference and various protest actions against the implementation of fracking, as documented by several newspapers and websites (see Administrador Regeneración 2015a, 2015b; Gómez 2015; Ramírez 2015). A conference called Encuentro Regional Norte-Golfo por la Defensa del Agua y el Territorio Frente a los Proyectos de Muerte organized by local NGOs that formed part of a wider network of anti-fracking activists, had taken place about six months previously. Even at the time of my arrival, several graffiti, visible at the community center and on the walls of several private houses, suggest that a lively resistance and open protest against fracking is still active. Yet, soon after my arrival, I noticed that most of the community members I talked to had a rather blurry idea of the concept of fracking. Furthermore, no actual protest was taking place anymore, apart from the traces left in the community by the June 2015 event. No marches, no blockades, no demonstrations took place during my stay, in stark contrast to what the newspapers had suggested.

I started to inquire about the issue explicitly during my interviews and asked what people knew about or associated with fracking. All my interview partners recognized the term but had varying ideas of what fracking actually means. Many associated it directly with the conference of June 2015 and the activists from Mexico City who visited Emiliano Zapata during the event. Don Ernesto, whose small convenience store is located right at the intersection between the main road and the smaller road leading directly to the community center, was present at the event and remembers the talks that were given that day. Yet, the actual technique and its implications remained unclear to him and he remembers the word "fracking" as mainly related to the group of activists who organized the event. Thus, when I asked him what fracking was, he suggested that the odd sounding word might have been the name of that group or NGO: "That are the ones who came here when the event took place," he said. "Some tall guys with long hair in ponytails. And we listened to what they had to say to support them like they came to support us. That's 'fracking,' the organization that came to support us."

Other community members also mentioned the event, but most of the residents I talked to mainly referred to environmental hazards and accidents with regard to fracking without knowing about the technological aspects and its implications. Doña Luisa, a housewife in her 30s, who lives up a little hill from the community center, where the noise of the gas flare is particularly loud, stated: "The 'fracking,' yes, I heard of that . . .," but then could not seem to remember exactly what the term implied. Yet, she knew that it was something potentially harmful and continued: "Well, it refers to the pollution, the accidents and the deforestation . . . well that is what I heard." The confusion surrounding the issue of fracking showed that, while the people seemed to have little knowledge about the technical aspects, they were certainly aware of the potential dangers that fracking entailed.

Almost everybody I spoke to about the extraction at first, mentioned the pollution, the accidents and the seepages that had occurred in the community during its long history with oil extraction. The oil industry, for most of the residents, is associated with constant anxiety with regard to possible accidents and health threats. Most of my interview partners therefore perceived their own community as quite a dangerous place to live and articulated qualms about something happening to them or their family, in addition to mentioning stories about such incidents. The common image of a time bomb on which the community members live is also taken up as an illustration by Doña Marieta, a woman in her fifties. She prepares food in the community kitchen once a week along with some of her female relatives. "Well . . . we already know that we're living on a time bomb." she said during a focus group interview, and adds: "Any minute everything here could explode and we would not wake up ever again." The other women in the group nodded in agreement. "You have to be aware and careful," she continued, "The loud noise of the gas flare scares us all, but most of all we worry about our children. We already have many diseases here from all the pollution." Meanwhile, the issue of fracking for many remained an unclear idea of something harmful and potentially dangerous, which became integrated into the catalogs of potential risks of everyday life imposed by the oil industry and its activities, rather than an independent concrete threat per se.

The community members of Emiliano Zapata are well aware of the situation of uncertainty and exposure to risk that they experience each day. During the course of the extraction activities on their territory, they were witnesses of the intensive industrial development that was triggered during the oil boom, and its questionable practices during the beginning, not to mention the oil crisis that led the oil company to withdraw and let many installations wither away. They have been a part of the local oil industry because of the community location on a contractual area of PEMEX, as well as through their active and passive participation in the industrial activities over a long period of time. Several accidents and seepages occurred over the years, while the oil boom, as well as the subsequent crisis, presented a variety of challenges to them. Today, the residents of the community are living with the constant uncertainty of potentially or probably harmful activities going on around them, even within the confines of their own homes. At the same time, they are apprehensive about the effects of the uncertain future of the oil industry after the crisis, the opening up of the energy reform and the possible application of fracking. Yet, they continue to lead their everyday lives. Despite the insecure future, the constant hazards, the severe pollution of air, water, and soil, which were expressed by many community members through the metaphor of living on a time bomb, the community found its own ways and means to make its life on a time bomb, if not desirable, at least possible. So, the question that determines the inquiry of the study at hand is: How do community members in Emiliano Zapata come to terms with living on a time bomb, an expression for a situation rife with constant uncertainties with regard to oil in their living environment?

Managing the Time Bomb

For the community members of Emiliano Zapata, who represent the main actors for this ethnography, the oilscape manifests itself in their living environment through a series of uncertainties that condense into the defining characteristic of the time bomb. These uncertainties underlie the conditions imposed by the oil industry and its temporal economic particularities, as also the social actions taking place within the oilscape. The concept of the oilscape can therefore be understood as an empirical approach to the realities in Emiliano Zapata, transformed into a generalizable framework that could help analyze the particular ethnographic settings in different parts of the world where oil extraction takes place.[3] An oilscape is a space emerging around oil extraction sites, within which oil extraction has become inscribed into the material manifestation, the social texture, and behavior of residents over time. The limits of this space are thus related to the spatial dimension of a certain location of the extraction site. Aside from the material dimension, it takes the temporal and specific social dynamic on the site into account but remains spatially bound to the place where the extraction is conducted. However, this space is also shaped by decisions, personnel, and material flows in and out as well as migratory movements, which are not particularly limited to a certain space. Hence the boundaries of the oilscape are permeable, but the analytical focus provided by the concept of scapes reflects a certain perspective of the actors on a topic—other examples are mines (Ey and Sherval 2015), coal (Portal 2018) or even water (Karpouzoglou and Vij 2017). The analysis in this book therefore represents a contribution to the body of literature on the anthropology of oil and resource extraction by representing a novel take on the broader category of "landscapes of extraction" (see e.g., Halvaksz 2008; Liesch 2014; Watts 2011; Wheeler 2014). The analysis is therefore meant to represent a certain perspective on oil and gas extraction from an actor-centered perspective, which has a territorial component, but is not limited to it. Instead, the relationship patterns and the social texture of the community members represent a crucial factor for the composition of the oilscape.

As a rural population living on the edge of an oilfield, the community members of Emiliano Zapata do not necessarily have a position of power within the hegemonic texture imposed by the national narrative, since PEMEX and the oil industry are essentially the main driving forces for wealth and "development." Yet, they continuously establish strategies that allow them to deal with the challenge of the uncertainty imposed by the predominant power of oil. Following the distinction between "coping" and "adapting," as Anthony Oliver-Smith proposed for crisis contexts, they do so through coping with the risks and dangers at the very instance of their appearance and adapting to the long-term conditions by making adjustments within their practices and sociocultural patterns (2013: 277). Therewith, they constantly and processually adjust to the conditions of the oilscape itself. The community members thereby actively participate in constructing the oilscape through their actions and interactions among themselves, with their surroundings or with other actor groups, as will be shown.

This ethnography contributes to the ongoing debate about the impact of oil on people's lives and the relationship between the extractive industry and human actors by showing how community members actively deal with uncertainties introduced by oil extraction in specific ways. It does so by taking the temporal matters and material implications of this resource into account, where each consolidates a dimension of uncertainty and thus leads to the advent of a situation perceived as the "time bomb." This book shows how local actors find innovative ways of dealing with and living amid this time bomb by creatively shaping patterns of behavior that allow them to successfully face the challenges by the presence of the oil industry. Thereby, they are part of the process of negotiating and shaping the appearance and limits of the oilscape. Thus, this work follows the claim of Emma Gilberthrope and Dinah Rajak who postulated recently about "bring agency back into the picture" as one of the most important tasks of anthropology addressing issues concerning resource extraction (2017: 200).

The ethnographic field research on which this book is based was carried out over the time of eleven months divided into two blocks from April until September 2016 and from September 2017 until March of

2018. I followed a mixed-methods approach with a focus on qualitative methods, including participant observation, grand tour, semi-structured as well as group and expert interviews. Furthermore I applied freelists to explore the domains of oil extraction in general and fracking in particular and conducted mapping exercises with community members of Emiliano Zapata where the participants drew individual maps based on a predesigned basic draft of the community. Additionally, I conducted a systematic survey within the community. The data was complemented by information drawn from local archives within the ejido itself, where large parts of the community's history is documented and stored as well as in historic archives in Xalapa and Mexico City.

Outline in Brief

In this book, I follow the trail of the "time bomb" by discussing the processual construction of the ejido Emiliano Zapata as an oilscape. The course of the discussion is divided into three main dimensions: the temporalities of oil, the materialities of oil, and the social dynamics within the oilscape.

The first chapter provides a brief overview of the theoretical approaches to oil in anthropology. I explore the issue of hydrocarbons as an anthropological topic, following the division of the two main analytical approaches of "temporalities" and "materialities," as proposed by Douglas Rogers in his overview of anthropology and oil (2015a). In the following subsection, I conceptualize the oilscape as an analytical framework for analyzing the situation of uncertainty with regard to the development of the oil industry in the case of Emiliano Zapata.

In chapter 2, the ethnographic circumstances in Emiliano Zapata are embedded into a national and regional context. The chapter begins with an account of hydrocarbon extraction in Mexico, where oil holds a special position in the historical development of the national economy and thus also in the national narrative (e.g., Breglia 2013: 5; Monreal Ávila 2008: 69; Suárez Ávila 2017: 8). The Mexican energy reform of 2013/14 thereby, represents the legal manifestation of an important turning point in national oil politics, which is crucial to understanding the case of Emiliano Zapata. After a general overview on the national scale, I will focus on the regional development of the oil industry in the northern area of Veracruz and the oilfield San Andrés on which the community is located. Subsequently, specific ethnographic details about the composition, economic background, and social texture of the community are presented.

Chapter 3 engages in the first dimension of analysis with an approach on the temporal properties of oil. They manifest in a process of peaks and valleys, therefore introducing certain patterns of social and economic change as well as anxiety about an imminent worsening of the given conditions (e.g., Cepek 2012; Coronil 1997; Kaposy 2017; Limbert 2008; Mason, Appel, and Watts 2015). Rather than a singular progress, the temporalities of oil are to be understood as multiple simultaneous processes that are determined by individual parameters of preconditions and settings (see Bear 2016; D'Angelo and Pijpers 2018; May and Thrift 2001; Munn 1992). Therefore, the analysis includes the diversity of the temporal processes of coping and adaptation mechanisms applied by local actors during the history of oil extraction in Emiliano Zapata.

In chapter 4, the analytical dimension of time is augmented by the dimension of material inscription, resulting in two aspects that are inevitably linked (Richardson and Weszkalnys 2014: 6). The section starts with the contextualization of the material dimension of the oilscape, within which the material modifications of the space act under the premises of the temporal particularities of oil. This approach aims at unraveling the material dimensions of oil extraction in Emiliano Zapata and their consequences on the lives of the community members without disregarding temporal matters or social implications. Thereby, it is shown how the community members develop the strategies and mechanisms that enabled them to deal with the altered environment and thus the inscription of uncertainty and risk onto the oilscape over time.

Chapter 5 focuses on the third analytical dimension of the oilscape, represented within the social sphere around oil extraction in Emiliano Zapata, which manifests within the relationships between different actor groups. In Emiliano Zapata, the constitution of the interrelation dimension of the oilscape is tied to the connections and dependencies the community members developed with the company, PEMEX, and its staff over a long time. This relationship is determined by conflicts on territory, as they are by the formation of multilayered sociocultural identities within the community itself. It will be shown how the changes introduced by the energy reform affected the social space, and consequently the oilscape, by the appearance of new actors and the reconfiguration of relationship patterns and power hierarchies.

In the closing and outlook, the results presented in this book will be discussed and merged to provide a comprehensive and innovative take within the conceptual approach of the oilscape and the manifestation of uncertainty through the perception of a time bomb. This discussion is followed by an epilogue explaining the situation of oil in Mexico after the induction of the new president, Manuel López Obrador, serving in office since 1 December 2018. The future of the energy reform in its original form and therewith, the future vision for the national oil economy is currently at stake under the new government and the economic challenges of the COVID-19 pandemic and a short description of the recent events will thus provide a concluding perspective for the "time bomb" of oil in Emiliano Zapata.

Notes

1. A form of communal landholding for small-scale agriculture in Mexico. The concept is laid out more in detail in chapter 2 of this volume: A Mexican Oil Story.
2. See https://www.lightight.com/into-the-anthropocene-1.
3. See, for example, the research project by Akin Iwalde at the University of Edinburgh, Africa's Oilscapes, which specifically looks at the role of youth and temporalities associated with oil extraction in Africa. Akin Iwilade, "Youth Temporalities in Africa's Oilscapes," *The University of Edinburgh*. Retrieved 2 April 2022 from https://www.research.ed.ac.uk/en/projects/youth-temporalities-in-africas-oilscapes.

CHAPTER 1

Theorizing Oil

A Conceptualization of the Oilscape

> Oil transformed everyday life in the twentieth century. In the twenty-first century, we are finally beginning to realize the degree to which oil has made us moderns who and what we are, shaping our existence close at hand while narrating us into networks of power and commerce far, far away.
>
> —Sheena Wilson, Adam Carlson, and
> Imre Szeman, "On Petrocultures"

Oil and fuel as one of its prior products, have been the primary resources that allowed countries to participate in a process of industrialization and thus the making of the global economy as it is (see Mitchell 2011). The overwhelming global dependency on oil remains until today: in the 2010s, access to fuel is still a crucial requirement for a functional economy. Despite global attempts for a turn toward sustainable "green" energy, the facts are unlikely to change any time soon. The two primary sources of any kind of fuel are natural gas and crude oil—a naturally occurring unrefined form of petroleum in the form of a combustible liquid that can be refined into gasoline. The availability and ability to safeguard access to these two substances are among the most important economic priorities of both industrialized countries and emerging economies (e.g., Love 2008: 3; Reyna and Behrends 2011: 3–4; Wilson et al. 2017: 3).

Even though anthropological studies on oil are rather limited compared to other social sciences, several significant anthropological approaches need to be considered here (e.g., Bille Larsen 2017; Black 2000; Cepek 2012; Coronil 1997; Fentiman 1996; Gilberthorpe 2007, 2014; High and Field 2020; Kama 2020; Limbert 2008; Perreault 2018; Reyna and Behrends 2011; Rogers 2015b; Weszkalnys 2014). Anthropologists researching oil have explored relationships of humans with this asset mainly under two viewpoints: first, the temporal dimension of oil as a finite resource linked to certain temporal processes of economic booms and declines, denominated as "temporalities," and second, the way extraction and production of oil materially shapes the environmental surroundings, thus impacting people's lives—referred to as "materialities" (Rogers 2015a: 366). For analyzing the oilscape of Emiliano Zapata, both approaches provide useful insights. The temporal as well as the material particularities of oil and oil extraction play a crucial role for the constitution of the community as it is today and continue to play a role in the everyday lives of the residents and their social actions and interactions. The oil-influenced surroundings and the interaction of the residents with their environment and with the actors of the oil industry, constituted the oilscape, while it constantly undergoes a dynamic process of reshaping. In Emiliano Zapata, uncertainty is a crucial aspect, characterizing the living circumstances beyond the moment in time, but nevertheless closely linked to temporal perception, as well as to the physical manifestation of risk introduced by the oil industry. The analysis in this book aims to link materialities and the temporalities of oil with a social sphere, while showing that these three mutually dependent aspects of the oilscape, produce a particular set of uncertainties that have to be dealt with by the inhabitants of the oilscape.

Oil and Anthropology

When dealing with oil, the anthropological literature stands between two approaches. First, the anthropology of energy, which mainly deals with oil as a source (e.g., Khalidi 2010; Lovins 2010), and second, the anthropology of extraction focusing on the accompanying conditions of oil exploitation due to its impact on local life circumstances (e.g., Breglia 2013; Behrends and Hoinathy 2017; Bille Larsen 2017; Fentiman 1996; Gilberthorpe 2007; Haller 2007; Vásquez 2014; Weszkalnys 2014, 2016). While energy studies rarely deal specifically with oil, there are many that focus on the extraction of oil and natural gas as natural resources and their effects on the environment. These have been and continue to be of great interest for anthropological inquiries (e.g., Appel 2012a, 2012b; Gilberthorpe 2006, 2014; Sawyer 2012; Stammler and Peskov 2008).

Studies in the broader tradition of an anthropology of extraction are at first sight dominated by an almost "traditional" anthropological interest in the mining sector remaining persistent until today within this field (e.g., Jacka 2018; Kirsch 2014; Pijpers and Eriksen 2019; Welker 2014). As Emma Gilberthorpe and Dinah Rajak (2017: 186) point out in their overview of anthropological perspectives regarding natural resources, mining represents an important starting point for topics like social and economic transformation, labor, exploitation, environmental damage or commodification. It does so, because of a strong territorial component, shaping the surrounding and therefore living environment of the people, thus offering approaches for ethnographic inquiries. At the same time, mineral extraction is closely associated with colonial structures of exploitation, and the destruction of nature for the sake of enriching the centers of the world economy (Jacka 2018: 62). Thus, in many aspects, it has become a symbol of the negative outcomes of modernity. Despite anthropology's dominant interest in mining, most of these theoretical implications, such as the close relationship between environmental impacts and social dynamics, are also applicable to hydrocarbons as natural resources, especially regarding their extraction. Therefore, many anthropological studies on oil draw on more general approaches to resource extraction that also apply to mining (Gilberthorpe and Rajak 2017: 186).

Current research on oil attempts to encompass the different interconnected elements of hydrocarbons and the way they shape the environment and hence people's lives. Here, some relevant contributions from other disciplines have had an important influence on the anthropological view of the subject. The geographer Michael Watts (2005, 2012) develops the concepts of "oil complex" or "oil assemblages" to fully capture the variety of impacts oil has on people's lives: from its extraction and production, its environmental impacts to its consumption and demand creating powerful collaborations. The economist Myrna Santiago (2006) uses her concept of the "ecology of oil" to place oil extraction at the center of the political, economic, and social dynamics of the Huasteca—an oil-producing region in northern Mexico. She disentangles the complex interplay of social change, nature, labor, and emerging local capitalist markets by starting from the perspective of oil extraction and shows how all of these domains interact, determined by this commodity. The political scientist Timothy Mitchell (2011) links energy production through fossil fuels to the greater whole, such as the development of democracy and the current world order. Moreover, an interdisciplinary research group on "Petrocultures" at the University of Alberta researches the multiple and complex impacts of the oil industry on different levels (Wilson et al. 2017). Anthropologists like Gisa Weszkalnys (2013, 2016), Andrea Behrends, Güther Schlee, and Stephen Reyna (2011), Emma Gilberthorpe (2007, 2014) and Hannah Appel, Arthur Mason, and Michael Watts (Appel et al. 2015a) develop more comprehensive models of oil by looking at how and where different sectors and living environments are entangled with oil and gas. Also, the authors of the Special Issue "Petro-Geographies and Hydrocarbon Realities in Latin America" of the *Journal of Latin American Geography* follow this approach (Fry and Delgado 2018: 10). In the edited volume *Indigenous Life Projects and Extractivism: Ethnographies from South America* many of the contributions also deal with the topic of oil extraction in Latin America and specifically look at politics of nature and ontological difference in the face of extraction (Vindal Ødegaard and Rivera Andía 2019: 1–2).

Oil has long been portrayed as a mixed economic blessing, as can be seen with the "resource curse" (e.g., Auty 1993; Ross 1999). Scholars researching the "curse" tried to explain why rich mineral and oil sources, whose revenues could be the cornerstone of economic growth and the improvement of living conditions—often summarized under the unclear and critically discussed term "development"—rather lead to the opposite situations including poor economic performance, high levels of corruption, ineffective governance and political violence. The oil curse seemingly strikes countries referred to as "petrostates," which are characterized by capital intensive oil exports, economic dependence on oil rents, and an enclaved production model. For the first time during the 1970s oil boom, those petrostates, often located in the Global South and considered lacking "development," hoped for an improvement of the economic and social situation for all segments of their societies through petrodollars. However, it turned out that in many cases the opposite happened and instead of gaining broad prosperity, the wealth in resources led to an impoverishment of parts of the society, fostered inequalities, the fragmentation of society and often violent conflicts (Reyna and Behrends 2011: 5; Gilberthorpe 2014: 93). In the 1990s, the economic performance of these states declined significantly and authors like Michael Ross (2001) claimed that authoritarianism was more likely to be found in petrostates, in addition to substantial internal and external conflicts (e.g., Klare 2002; Ross 2001; Omeje 2008). This resource curse has been picked up mainly by political scientists, while, as mentioned earlier, it has received less attention in anthropology with its focus on mining (Gilberthorpe and Rajak 2017: 187; Reyna and Behrends 2011: 19–20). More recently, anthropology also became involved in the discourse regarding the oil industry and its global as well as local impacts (e.g., Behrends, Park, and Rottenburg, 2014; Di Muzio 2010; Gilberthorpe and Rajak 2017; High and Field 2020; Rogers 2015b; Weszkalnys 2016), opening up important new perspectives in the debate on the potential for conflict that the industrial usage of oil bears. Recent works also target questions of responsibility for social and environmental impacts and respective mechanisms to mitigate risks by implementing corporate social responsibility (CSR) measurers following a decolonializing approach by involving the local level and implementing an actor-centered approach (see e.g., Dolan and Rajak 2016; García-Chiang 2018; García-Chiang and Rodríguez 2008; Uwem 2019)

Anthropological studies on hydrocarbon extraction or mining have shown that it is important to consider the effects of resource extraction at a local level in order to understand its immediate social and cultural impact. Furthermore, a critical approach to social and historical specificities from a perspective that focuses on agency can challenge abstract theories such as the resource curse as well as its underlying notions of modernization and development, and may require more appropriate conceptual tools to adequately solve the puzzle (Gilberthorpe and Rajak 2017: 191, 201). This ethnography contributes to the body of literature on anthropology of oil and thereby to the understanding of "oil's magic" (Weszkalnys 2014) by revealing social and cultural implications of oil from a local perspective by presenting a detailed ethnographic study of a community shaped by hydrocarbon extraction in many ways.

The Temporalities

The sky is cloudy today, and it looks like the rain is going to start any minute, which is why we are sitting inside around a table in the community kitchen. Besides me, there are five teenagers from the community school that I asked to talk about their lives in Zapata this afternoon. When I first invited them, they seemed rather puzzled. Usually adults, and especially the elderly, are the focus of attention when journalists or other people from outside the community ask about the troubles with extraction. "I don't know what to tell you," Nayelly, one of the girls I asked to interview, answered first. "I could take you to my grandmother, she has lived here all her life and can tell you more about the accidents and spills of the past." I assured her, that what grandmother had to say was very interesting as well, but that I also would like to talk with her and her friends about their perspective as young people and their expectations about the future.

Now they are sitting here with me, sipping their Coca-Colas and still looking mildly confused about what is expected of them. I asked them what they would like to change in their community if they could. They are now looking rather indifferent. "Well," one of the two girls begins. "I think I would prefer it here if there were more jobs, like there used to be. Me and most of my friends will go and study somewhere—maybe in the city of Veracruz—and study accounting. I would like that." The other agree, nodding silently.

"None of your friends want to work in agriculture?" I ask, anticipating the answer.

"Not really," she responds. There isn't enough land, and the land there is already very polluted and dried out, I don't think we can work here."

"And don't you think that maybe there will be new opportunities in the future?"

She shrugs. "I don't really know. My parents and grandparents tell me that there were good times when there was a lot of industry, but they also say that there were so many accidents, and they complain about the pollution a lot. The noise of the gas flare is also really disturbing, I guess. I don't know what it was like before, but I don't think it will be any better here anytime soon. We have to see where we can study and work and then maybe have a nice house here."

What Nayelly describes is a very common phenomenon in Emiliano Zapata—young people leaving the community to work and send remittances to their families for a bigger house that they will one day return and live in. Many of these houses are bare brick and remain in a constant state of being under construction, as their owners have built lives and founded families elsewhere. The younger generation in Zapata is well aware of that fact, yet plans to continue this practice. Even though everyone accepts the process of out-migration, most people seem and want to keep the option of returning. Just in case.

In the social sciences there is a tendency to view the economy and society in terms of spatial change rather than temporal aspects, and studies concerned with resource extraction generally follow this trend (D'Angelo and Pijpers 2018: 215). Yet, thinking about resource extraction and in this case oil as a "complex set of multiple temporal processes" (2018: 215) enables a level of understanding, which expands beyond the assumption of the singular dimension of space as an analytic entity (e.g., May and Thrift 2001; Munn 1992). Anthropological studies have shown that the imperative of a single homogeneous timeline that capitalist modernity builds on, and history as the one-dimensional internal logic of the nation-state are to be questioned (Bear 2014; Eiss 2008; Pedersen and Nielsen 2013). Therefore, some scholars refer to this trend as "the temporal turn" (Bear 2016; Hassan 2010), which has generated more research on the issue of time and its different dimensions in the field of extraction (e.g., Behrends 2008; Ferry and Limbert 2008; Halvaksz 2008; Peña and Lizardo 2017; Salman and Theije 2017). Regarding extraction sites and practices like drilling for oil, conceptions of time can only be understood in their plurality of cycles, durations, and velocities. These not only have social and cultural implications, but also emerge as products of socially and culturally constructed spaces intertwining and creating overlapping levels of times. These levels have been called "timescapes" by some scholars and therefore include the frictions and conflicts emerging around and within them, and are not limited to the extraction processes but also relate to national politics or even global discourses about resources and nature (e.g., Adam 1998; Bear 2016; Ingold 2011).

Extraction creates settings that are inseparably linked to the temporal requirements of a market-driven economy and produces certain temporal conditions of the present as well as notions of the past and future for the residents of these extraction sites (e.g., Gilberthorpe 2014; Ringel 2016; Smith 2015). Hence, a comprehensive analysis of the temporal process of cause and effect is particularly important concerning extraction. Anthropologists contribute extensive ethnographic material to the analysis of the processual shaping of narratives, and therefore offer important insights into the construction of and the navigation of situations of uncertainty, especially when dealing with natural resources (e.g., Behrends and Schareika 2011; Cooper and Pratten 2015; Pijpers 2018; Schritt 2018). In this context, studies often consider one of the most dominant properties from a social and cultural science viewpoint: the perception of a predetermined process of scarcity followed by abundance tied to a finally approaching finitude (Ferry and Limbert 2008: 3; Rogers 2015a: 367). Oil as a resource has a particularly strong temporal connotation, which is why anthropological studies about oil often refer to the perception of past, present, and future. The perpetual knowledge of the approaching end of oil in local contexts affected by oil extraction leads to an ever-present fear of a soon-to-come change of economic and social conditions, paired with the hopes and dreams associated with anticipated economic prosperity (e.g., Behrends 2008; Cepek 2012; Schritt 2018; Weszkalnys 2014). The almost schizophrenic temporal dimension of a predetermined process of wealth and growth followed by economic decline and always linked to an approaching yet uncertain end accompanies oil like no other resource. The obvious link to global energy production allows oil to develop its own temporal logic and complexity (Kaposy 2017: 390). Even the mere anticipation of the disposability of oil in the near future can have impacts on social, economic, and political dynamics (Behrends 2008; Schritt 2019; Weszkalnys 2014) and the transformation of a country into an oil nation changes society and even national narratives (see Gledhill 2011; Kaposy 2017). During its position as part of the economic foundation of a country or region, the actual decline of oil revenues—as well as only the anticipation of them—also leads to social and cultural outcomes (see Apter 2005; Salas Landa 2016). Therefore, the temporalities of oil become increasingly laden with expectations, anticipations of environmental damage, and anxieties about crisis and curses in the light of current modernization projects (Rogers 2015a: 369). With the changing post-crisis panorama and the development of alternative income generation strategies, or the possible recovery of the industry, the physical attributes of communities, extractions sites, and the surrounding landscape are changing again (see Breglia 2013; Filer 1990; Pijpers 2016).

This process is represented in the well-researched phenomenon of "boomtowns," which has been explored in social science, mostly in the United States in the 1980s, where boomtowns emerged due to rapid industrialization and population growth induced by the discovery of natural resources (e.g., England and Albrecht 1984; Gramling and Brabant 1986; Freudenburg 1981). On the one hand, the resources then become the driver for the local economy, which prospers at first due to higher salaries, and more money spent locally. On the other hand, prices and rents rise with increasing demand, as do the prices of labor. Immigration of workers and other people seizing the economic opportunities created around the extraction, bring greater diversity and different lifestyles with diverging values, some of which may create tensions with former community norms. This spiraling process of local economic and demographic growth is then usually put to an end by a predictable bust, when the resource runs out or loses value on the market. Consequently, employment opportunities decline, followed by rapid emigration and the decline of the local service sector with it, while irreversible environmental impacts of the industrial development have already affected the surroundings. Therefore, the boomtown model was seen rather as a problem that emerged with the resource boom and inevitably ended in an abrupt deterioration (Gramling and Brabant 1986: 179–80). However, some newer studies indicate a "boom-bust-recovery" cycle in which problems induced by very rapid growth are resolved over time (e.g., Brown, Dorins, and Krannich 2005; Smith Rolston 2013; Stedman et al. 2012), creating a sequence of "social stages of boomtown development: enthusiasm-uncertainty-panic-adaptation" (Willow and Wylie 2014: 225). Even if boomtowns as such do not necessarily develop everywhere where oil extraction takes place, the main features of the phenomenon are usually visible in the surroundings of major hydrocarbon extraction sites in many parts of the world (2014: 225–26; Black 2000: 124).

Meanwhile, environmental impacts and pollution, boomtowns, economic growth related to construction, money and goods, as well as decay and deterioration in times of crisis strongly point to the inseparability of the temporal and the material dimension of oil (e.g., Breglia 2013; Limbert 2008; Zalik 2009). Thus, the temporal properties of oil are inextricably linked with the material manifestations of oil and its extraction.

The Materialities

I lean over the bridge railing to get a better look at the muddy ground beneath me. The water in the small riverbed has almost dried up, but a small rivulet makes its way under the bridge where I stand with Don Rosalio.

The rivulet shows shiny black streaks and dark spots can be seen everywhere in the mud. "Look Gürea, do you see the leak back there?" I bend over to see what it looks like behind the barrier further up in the riverbed. There is an old pipeline sticking out of the embankment, but it is difficult to identify the details.

Don Rosalio points to the barrier. "They've sealed it off now, but nobody has cleaned it up yet. We've told the *ingenieros* already, but they're taking their time, as always." Don Rosalio is part of the community water committee. When any of the bodies of water around here are polluted he has to take care of it, as in this case. Until then, the water supply for the community is cut off and the company brings clean water with tankers.

"Is that really oil?" I ask him. Whether this is really the expensive heavy crude oil that leaks drop by drop or some other kind of industrial waste product, I cannot tell.

"I don't know what it is exactly, but one thing's for sure: I don't want to take a bath with it." Don Rosalio remarks ironically. "Come on, let's go."

We walk back to his truck on the side of the road. Such minor leaks are not uncommon here in Emiliano Zapata and most people have seen and experienced them in various forms. For me, this was the first encounter with the substance I came here for some weeks ago, and as unspectacular as the blackish trickle may seem, it was a strange experience to actually be physically close to the substance after so many weeks of talking about oil. Installations for extraction and processing are omnipresent in the appearance of the community and pipelines are impacting the community everywhere, but it almost feels like something special to actually see the substance at stake.

The material presence of oil as a substance itself is unpleasant at first sight—sticky, smelly, and in many ways harmful to human life, flora, and fauna. Coming from the under the ground, the substance requires a variety of processing techniques for which certain technologies, knowledge, and facilities are needed and these techniques represent a significant intervention in the environment with oftentimes harmful consequences. Hence, one important aspect of the materialities of oil are the hazards to an environment and ecosystem. The dangerous and harmful potential of oil, such as the conflicts and frictions emerging between actors around these risks, has been widely acknowledged and extensively studied from an anthropological point of view (e.g., Appel et al. 2015a; Behrends et al. 2011; Fabricant, Gustafson, and Weiss 2017; Vásquez 2014). Importantly, the risk analysis takes into account present oil not only as a commodity and producer of petrodollars and economic growth, but also as deeply entangled in the social fabric of the actors involved—residents, oil workers or company staff—with particular potential for dispute (Weszkalnys 2016: 127). In her analysis of "oil's material powers," Gisa Weszkalnys frames oil as a form of "distributed materiality that spans this substance's physical and chemical constituents as well as the specialist equipment needed for its extraction, the practices of abstraction and valuation that go into its making, and the people doing the extracting, contesting, and transforming of oil." (2013: 267) This approach allows oil's materiality to be seen as a set of material inscriptions in an environment shaped by oil extraction and processing.

The material itself but also the machinery required for extraction onsite, the chemicals and industrial apparatus used for processing crude oil into petroleum, are the enablers of economic and perceptive transformation. In particular, oil infrastructure in the form of pipelines, streets, and moving vehicles, but also in the form of housing, shapes the environment surrounding extraction sites, which means severe modifications of the landscape through the industry. Therefore, the infrastructure relating to oil is one aspect of oil's materialities, which is to be regarded as part of the structural patterns of oil in general. Considering oil in the context of its infrastructure allows for a broader view of the resource and its idiosyncrasy regarding its wider impact on social and cultural dynamics. Infrastructures as the material representation of oil are highly political matter "that spatialize and temporalize capitalism, and moreover, make it eventful, indeterminate, and never completely knowable" (Appel et al. 2015a: 253). Infrastructure therefore represents an analytical link between the spatially determined local research arena and the socio-political dimensions of oil. It thus a crucial factor in understanding the material dimension of oil and extraction in Emiliano Zapata.

Infrastructure has emerged as a topic of interest for anthropologists in recent years, who started to investigate the issue as a focus of ethnographic study, rather than just as conceptual tool (Appel Anand, and Gupta 2018: 4). Nevertheless, infrastructure in anthropology remains part of the systemic analysis of a larger setting, which can be considered a strength rather than a weakness, as Brian Larkin points out, because it contributes to the construction of a more holistic picture (2013: 328). Infrastructure as a form of material culture is central to the reproduction of states and their goals and is connected to ideologies of progress and social equality (Baptista 2018: 527). Roads are generally considered the main manifestation of infrastructure and as such act as a symbol and carrier of modernity and connectedness. As Dimitris Dalakogulu and Penny Harvey put it in their overview of roads in anthropology: "they could arguably be taken as the paradigmatic material infrastructure of the twenty-first century" (2012: 459). Roads determine the mobility of people, commodified goods and labor, and therefore act as enablers of "development," in particular regarding extractive economies of developing nations that depend on the circulation of such goods and labor (2012: 459; Harvey and Knox 2012: 523). However, the ways actors use the public infrastructure and often reinterpret it, also reveals the agency of local agents who resist an undesired state narrative, only realizable by careful consideration of social and cultural patterns and networks (see Melly 2013). This also holds true for the emerging body on anthropological scholarship on energy and infrastructure, which mainly focuses on different social groups and their engagements with resources (e.g., Anand 2011; Dalakoglou 2012; Strauss, Rupp, and Love 2013; von Schnitzler 2008). Infrastructure has the power to make energy and energy flows tangible and therefore reveals power structures and social inequalities that otherwise could not be grasped (Firat 2016: 81). Responding to a request for more anthropological inquiry on infrastructure, Nikhil Anand, Akhil Gupta, and Hannah Appel provide a comprehensive compilation of work addressing the topic from an anthropological perspective in their book *The Promise of Infrastructure* (Anand et al. 2018). In the introduction, Appel and her co-authors distinguish between "hard" and "soft" infrastructure, where "hard" means the tangible constructions, pipelines, and roads, but also concrete arrangements like payment systems, while "soft" infrastructure comprises the ontological forms, such as political systems or capitalists' circuits. Hard infrastructure is directly related to sociality and the way people interact and negotiate social and cultural patterns, making it a recurrent topic for anthropologists (Appel et al. 2018: 4–5). The research of oil infrastructure is linked to an attempt to paint a holistic picture, since it encompasses the "hard" in form of rigs and pipelines as well as the "soft" with oil as the "fuel for capitalism" and the "motor of modernity" (Appel et al. 2015a: 258).

In connection to spatiality, oil infrastructure becomes the essence modification force within the arena and oftentimes the starting point for the process of shaping the oil landscape. Oil infrastructure is closely connected to politics and also to the general structure of labor. Because of its nature as a fluid and a transportable asset, oil as the primary energy source changed the supply situation and questions the role of the worker in the twentieth century (see Rogers 2015a: 372). Thereby, the pipeline appears as the incorporation of oil infrastructure and is often a key protagonist of conflicts related to extraction. It also connects different arenas in which these social entanglements in different spaces can be linked and brought together to form a terrain that can be analyzed (see Le Billon 2005; Reyna 2007; Valdivia 2008). Oil therefore has become an "anchor for the grievances of an array of local and global actors" (Weszkalnys 2013: 12), which makes pipelines welcome pegs for anthropological inquiry (e.g.,

Appel 2012a; Barry 2013; Gelber 2015). The material aspects of pipelines, in the sense of their physical embodiment in space, are part of the way politics is made and policies are implemented (Appel et al. 2018: 15; Barry 2013: 27; Leonard 2016: 112). This makes infrastructure and the conjoined physical installations of oil, which also interfere in the most concrete sense with their environments, useful reference points for anthropological analyzes. In their works on pipelines as a part of oil infrastructure, Lori Leonard (2016) and Hannah Appel (2012b) have shown how oil infrastructure has affected people's lives in ways not originally intended by the industry, and then triggered a rearrangement the patterns of local social organization. Oil infrastructure such as roads, pipelines, and buildings have physically shaped the environment of the community Emiliano Zapata and thereby also contributed to the arrangement of the social texture of the community. While residents of the community benefited to some extent from infrastructure expansion, it did not primarily serve the development of the locality, but rather was part of a larger ideal of development on a national scale. It will be shown how the local actors not only adapted to the infrastructure, but appropriated its material manifestations to use them in the ways they preferred, and even partly repurposed material installations to their advantage.

New Ways and Old Issues? Anthropology and Fracking

Despite all of the recognized problems of fossil fuels, global demand is still increasing because of a lack of alternatives for energy generation and the increased hunger for energy in developing countries. Reaching Hubbert's peak does not mean that the reserves are depleted, but rather that a point has been reached where the largest amount of near-surface oil that could be easily extracted with conventional methods has already been removed. Oil and natural gas from regions that have not been entirely exploited like Latin America will thus continue to be an important driving force of the global economy in the future. At the same time, the predictable scarcity is the reason for extended investments in renewable energy on the one hand, and intensifying the search for undiscovered oil sources and new technologies to access those which have been difficult to extract in the past on the other. This point in time is characterized by the fact that the oil and natural gas required for the global economy are more difficult to extract and therefore more expensive (Haarstad 2012: 1; Svampa 2015: 66).

One example for such a new technology is hydraulic fracturing, which is mainly used to extract "shale gas." It has been under development since the mid-twentieth century, but until recently was not commercially viable. "Shale" is a type of sedimentary rock composed of mud that is a mix of flakes of minerals, especially quartz and calcite. It is characterized by breaks along thin laminae or parallel layering or bedding, and it is the most common sedimentary rock. The term "hydraulic fracturing" refers to the practice of fracturing the subterranean rock deep below the surface to extract oil and/or gas by injecting water mixed with chemicals under high pressure. Hydraulic fracturing, also called fracking, entails vertical drilling several kilometers deep for the injection. Once pierced, a steel pipe called casing is placed, at the bottom of the well. Between this pipe and the wall of the reservoir, there is a space in which a certain type of cement is placed, which prevents the additives from mixing with the soil (Aguilar Madera 2014: 9; de Rijke 2013: 13).

The technique of fracking holds great uncertainty about environmental impacts, which have been widely acknowledged by scholars of many different formations and also popular media within the last decade (e.g., Brasier et al. 2013; Feodoroff, Franco, and Martinez 2013; Smartt Gullion 2015; Hays, McCawley, and Shonkoff 2017; High and Field 2020; Pearson 2013: Willow et al. 2014). Local fracking is discussed by local scholars describing the conflicts and negative impacts induced by this new extraction technique (Aguilar León 2018; Checa-Artasu and Hernández Franyuti 2016; Silva Ontiveros et al. 2018). Allegations of air pollution, groundwater contamination, or even causing earthquakes accompany the launch of fracking projects all over the world. Due to the novelty of this technique long-term studies are not available so far and further research will be necessary (Feodoroff et al. 2013: 2; Willow und Wylie 2014: 223). Indigenous populations especially are often described as vulnerable with respect to possible negative effects of fracking projects, considering their mostly rural location and their reliance on an intact environment in order to survive through farming, fishing, or hunting. Local actors often benefit the least while taking the highest risks and suffering the most from environmental and social impacts (Whiteman and Mamen 2002: 1).

Currently, fracking draws the public's attention and increasingly becomes a topic for anthropologists. It mainly concerns gas extraction for energy production rather than oil and is therefore primarily discussed within the context of energy anthropology (e.g., Cartwright 2013; Espig and de Rijke 2018). Nevertheless, the material consequences are similar to the circumstances induced by oil extraction facilities. It thus presents a topic for scholars looking at practices of extraction under the premise of peak oil and an inevitable finitude, as well as theoretical implications for the global energy supply and cultural dimensions of energy consumption and production. Appel, Mason, and Watts (2015b: 2) characterize fracking as another "boom story" within the history of fossil oil, which already generated a high resonance in the (comparably short) history of oil and gas extraction. Currently, more studies on this topic are published while the topic becomes one of the latest contemporary challenges within the debate about conflictive fossil fuel extraction. Although the current focus of fracking research is still based on quantitative survey methods rather than qualitative ethnographic fieldwork, some ethnographic studies have been published, mainly in the United States but also in the UK that document conflicts and protests against fracking projects (e.g., Bradshaw and Waite 2017; Cotton 2016; Smartt Gullion 2015; Simonelli 2014; Willow et al. 2014). Therefore, further anthropological studies on the matter are urgently needed (Willow and Wylie 2014: 236).

Currently, the literature on fracking is being broadened with ethnographic case studies in other parts of the world where fracking has been applied recently or will be applied in the near future, like in China or many parts of Latin America (e.g., Delgado 2018; Riffo 2017; Silva Ontiveros et al. 2018; Yu et al. 2018). Thereby, fracking is mainly discussed in relation to the environmental-human relationship and risk perception. Due to a relatively short period of implementation and deficient dissemination of information, scholars face a shortage on long-term studies regarding the environmental impacts and health hazards. Thus, risk perception becomes one of the key features of fracking, which has been widely acknowledged (e.g., Ashmoore et al. 2016; Brasier et al. 2013; Cartwright 2013; Clarke et al. 2015; Schafft, Borlu, and Glenna 2013; Whitmarsh et al. 2015; Williams et al. 2017).[1] Kathryn Brasier and colleagues (2013: 109) developed a model for risk perception along three lines: (1) perceived knowledge of effects, (2) institutional trust on managing risk, and (3) demographic and geographic characteristics of the actors. Anthropologist Elizabeth Cartwright examines eco-risk and fracking while framing risk as a "particularly lived understanding of in this case, the dangers of fracking" (Cartwright 2013: 204). She sees eco-risk at the intersection between fear, the ability to visualize or diagnose, and the legalistic structure for protection (2013: 214). She also draws attention to the health risks of fracking and calls for addressing local knowledge and the political discourse fracking is embedded in, while also attending to technologies of quantification and regulation (2013: 211). Fracking confronts participating actors and therefore also the scholars with a particular set of properties that require consideration as to fracking's connection to environmental risk regarding water distribution (e.g., Finewood and Stroup 2012; Jorritsma 2012) and uncertainties of risk measurements due to the novelty of the technique (e.g., Brasier et al. 2013; Cartwright 2013; Silva Ontiveros et al. 2018). Research on different actors involved in this system of energy production is required for a more comprehensive understanding of this recent topic. Research on the spatiality, socioeconomic landscapes shaped by fracking and discursive approaches of fracking, uncertainty and risk can add to this undertaking (de Rijke 2013: 14). Within this work, fracking is considered a new challenge within the complex of hydrocarbon extraction in a broader sense by presenting a case where concerns about fracking fit into a complex picture of various forms of oil and gas production in a community setting.

Spaces of Oil and Uncertainty: Conceptualizing the Oilscape

Oil is found in a certain space underground (and sometimes under the sea). Therefore, its extraction and its production take place in certain locations that are not only determined but are also shaped by the industry. The places where oil is found, extracted, and processed are geographically restricted areas of different types—extraction sites, factories, also boomtowns and cities where the asset and its revenues are produced and distributed. In this way, oil, as well as many other natural resources, when coupled with extraction and processing, establishes enclaves. These are spaces where wealth and power linked to the idea of modernity are concentrated, while its frontier-style setting provokes cultural encounters enforcing inequalities—with regard to oil-sector workers and local residents as a classic example (Rogers 2015a: 371). Oil enclaves emerging as hotspots or boomtowns are places with special material conditions, where global neoliberal capitalism encounters local realities and the different actors participating in this process shape them in a way that often differs significantly from the rest of the country (e.g., Ferguson 2005; Sawyer 2004). Oil and its extraction in particular, therefore, are linked to a specific spatial dimension in terms of geographically bounded locations (Rogers 2015a: 371). The ejido Emiliano Zapata represents such a space to a large extent, where oil extraction is interlinked with local particularities and negotiated among local actors. Therefore, I developed a framework for analyzing such spaces by introducing the concept of the "oilscape," in which oil is deeply entangled with both the environment and all spheres of political, social, and cultural life.

Spaces emerging around oil extraction in particular and resource extraction in general are constructed via an interplay of industrial standards, national policies, local material properties and the involved actors (see D'Angelo and Pijpers 2018: 216; Ey and Sherval 2015: 176–77). In combination with the element of time a complex construct emerges, which I will approach via the oilscape as an analytical tool. In order to provide a comprehensible operationalization of the concept, I will first provide a brief introduction to the concepts of "space" and "scapes" with regard to extraction. Besides the aspects of temporalities and materialities of oil, the social dimension plays an important role in negotiating the appearance, composition, and even spatial boundaries of the oilscape. Therefore, particular attention will be paid to the questions emerging around the social element of space, or social spaces, as this approach provides a more comprehensive notion of space, which exceeds its material dimension as a singular requirement. In Emiliano Zapata, a distinctive concomitant phenomenon of the formation of an oilscape is the creation of a situation marked by constant uncertainty, so I conclude with a discussion on uncertainty as a possible compelling element of the oilscape.

"Spaces," "Scapes," and Their Social Construction regarding Oil Extraction

The spatial dimensions of oil and its extraction are continuously relevant for anthropological analyses, or as Rogers puts it in his overview on oil and anthropology: "The geography and geology of the earth's oil deposits have lent a basic, if constantly morphing spatial shape to the oil industry" (Rogers 2015a: 371). Hence, the geographically bound dimension of extraction, and the industry calls for a close look at the spatial dimensions of oil. In fact, studies on extraction often gather around production sites and regions, which Rogers considers an "artifact of the vertical integration of the oil industry in capitalist contexts" (2015a: 371) through which he sees a reflection of the oil industry's focus on reserves and technology. Despite this legitimate critique, studies that take the spatial dimension of oil extraction into account, have shown how local particularities significantly influence the process of shaping a living environment on, or close to, extraction sites and therefore, provide valuable contributions to the anthropological literature on oil. Instances that show how extraction-shaped spaces turn into or overlap with local living environments that are constructed via an interplay of local conditions and consequences of the extractive industry are, besides the already-mentioned work of Myrna Santiago (2006), for example, the works of Brian Black, Lisa Breglia, or Patricia Vásquez. Black (2000) describes the daunting landscape of Oil Creek Valley, an oil town in Pennsylvania, where the oil boom of the late nineteenth century is reflected in the local social, cultural, and political life. Breglia (2013) demonstrates how the Mexican oil industry, and more specifically the declining oil production in the Cantarell oilfield after 2004, is directly linked to a decline of the local fishery close to the offshore production. Vásquez (2014) examines oil-extraction-related conflicts in the

Amazon region, which despite their political and international dimension, are closely bound to the regional specificities of the Amazon as a geographically limited space and its actors.

Space within studies on resource extraction is often displayed as the product of contestation and negotiation processes between actors and actors' groups. Indigenous people and nation states as adversaries in the struggle for land and territory have, for example, been a topic for a whole variety of studies (e.g., Haller et al. 2007; Merino Acuña 2015; Savino 2016; Svampa 2015, 2019; Vindal Ødegaard and Rivera Andía 2018). Those studies illustrate the importance of the spatial dimension of resource extraction, while emphasizing space and its limitation as the outcome of social negotiation processes. Suitable examples for that are the territorial struggles of indigenous people, who managed to establish their status as "indigenous" in the national legal framework and thus manifest their rights to certain spaces (e.g., Fabricant and Postero 2019; Nolte and Schilling-Vacaflor 2012; Schilling-Vacaflor and Flemmer 2015).

Despite the dominance of a spatial approach in many anthropological studies on extraction, the dimension of space is often difficult to grasp. Questions of "space" and "place" as theoretical constructions have often caused difficulties for anthropologists in the past, since it is challenging for ethnographers to discuss these categories without confining the inhabitants (Low 2009: 21). Therefore, the ethnographic conception of place and space, which reduces the ethnographic endeavor to a location and thus confines people to a certain geographical boundary, has been criticized by different scholars (e.g., Rodman 1992; Low 2009). Setha Low proposes to solve this problem by acknowledging "that place and space are always embodied" (2009: 22). Thereby, she understands embodied space as "the location where human experience and consciousness takes on material and spatial form" (2009: 26). This understanding implies the interconnection of several dimensions within the concept of space, such as the physically located aspect with a discursive and socially constructed materiality. Space must therefore be understood as a social construct of the people who live and interact in it, rather than just a geographically limited area (Low 2009: 22; Rodman 1992: 641).

In social science, space is considered "subject to analysis as a 'product of social action' or a 'product of social structures'" (Löw 2008: 25). At the same time, social space is always linked to a tangible outcome (e.g., Low 2009). The production of space thus includes social, economic, and ideological factors that lead to the physical creation of a material setting. The space is then constantly in a state of transformation through human practices such as memories, feelings, and interactions of the actors. The creation of a social space is thus often a conflict-riddled process over economic and ideological resources (Low 2014: 35). Space thus must be understood as "process-oriented" and "person-based and allow for agency" (Low 2009: 22) to facilitate a comprehensive anthropological approach to it. The space of Emiliano Zapata must therefore be contemplated under these premises in order to obtain a comprehensive understanding of the processes involved.

The ejido Emiliano Zapata is a certain geographic location and thus a material space. But at the same time, this space is constantly negotiated by its human actors in the context of geographic boundaries as well as in terms of its physical appearance and shape. For the analysis of this space, it is useful to take the geographic boundaries of the ejido territory as reference points for physical localization, while understanding space as multidimensionally constituted and formed in a processual manner by constant renegotiations and reconfigurations through the social dynamics of its actors (see Bourdieu 1985, 2018; Lefebvre 1991). Hereby, the social element of the construction of space is highlighted in order to avoid a unidimensional understanding of space as a physical locale.

When studying such specific spaces where resource extraction takes place, for example, scholars often resort to "landscapes" as an analytical framework (e.g., Grund 2016; Halvaksz 2008; Liesch 2014). The landscape functions as a form of modified environment, and thus a specific and geographically determined space as well. The perspective of mining environments as landscapes (and thus nature) that are altered by extraction activities offers an approach to the interplay of the sociocultural and the material dimension and can reveal conflictual aspects of extraction (D'Angelo and Pijpers 2018: 216). The relationship between landscape and time within the context of modernity has been researched, for example, by Barbara Adam (1998), Barbara Bender (2002), and Pamela Stewart and Andrew Strathern (2003). Their works show that human interventions, such as industrial settlements or resource extraction, shape the socioenvironment as a landscape in a way that alters the perception and usage of nature (see also Hofmeister 1997: 310). Here, the suffix "scape" indicates a wider perspective on space, which facilitates the integration of temporal and sociocultural, and often the conflictual processes of its construction and negotiation (D'Angelo and Pijpers 2018: 216). In the sense of "timescapes," for example, it emphasizes the interplay of the temporal dimension with the spatial dimension within a mining site (Lanzano 2018: 2).

"Scape" was introduced in anthropology by Arjun Appadurai (1990), who used it as a concept to analyze the dimensions of global cultural flows. He thereby, uncoupled the suffix from the term "landscapes" and applied it to a wider range of diverse scapes like "ethnoscapes," "ideoscapes," or "technoscapes." The scape thereby, emphasizes the fluidity and multiplicity of the shapes of certain terrains, which are under constant modification and function as "deeply perspectival constructs" (Appadurai 1990: 33). Understanding spaces from the perspective of scapes enables a more comprehensive approach incorporating several dimensions, which contribute to the constitution of these spaces. The environmental geographers, Melina Ey and Meg Sherval (2015) take up this approach and develop an analytical tool for researching extraction sites, which they call "minescape." In doing so, they aim to "draw together significant insights concerning the extractive sector, which are increasingly being deployed when representing extractive spaces" (Ey and Sherval 2015: 176). The authors understand "minescapes" as "material-discursive terrains imbued with sociocultural significance" (2015: 177), which thus transcend the site of mining and integrate further aspects of the construction of the mining site's environment (2015: 177; D'Angelo and Pijpers 2018: 215; 217). However, the concept was developed with regard to the circumstances of mineral mining, and even though the extraction of subterranean substances referred to as resources, which comprise various kinds of minerals and hydrocarbons, includes to some extent comparable conditions, each substance holds certain particularities. Oil as a resource is determined by certain material and temporal particularities, as discussed in the previous section, and these aspects should be considered when analyzing oil extraction sites and their surroundings. Thus, I introduce a new category of minescape—the oilscape, which is customized to the space where oil extraction takes place and becomes part of the local living environment, as is the case in Emiliano Zapata.

The oilscape is introduced as a tool for the analysis of spaces, where oil extraction takes place and is based on the concept of the minescape by Ey and Sherval (2015), which "situates resource extraction as a dynamic, contested terrain with complex sociocultural, material and discursive dimensions." (2015: 177). The oilscape draws on this conceptualization by emphasizing on the interplay of a material and a sociocultural dimension of oil extraction, but furthermore adds the temporal particularities of oil as a third main aspect, while the discursive dynamics are rather understood as part of the sociocultural category. An oilscape is thus understood as a space within which oil extraction has become inscribed into the material manifestation of landscape, housing, fields and infrastructure, as well as the social texture and behavior of the community members over time. The construction of the oilscape is a process of constant transformation determined by three main factors, namely the material implications and the temporal particularities of oil, as well as the sociocultural dynamics that arise within this space. All three aspects are mutually affected by each other and collectively influence the processual formation of an oilscape.

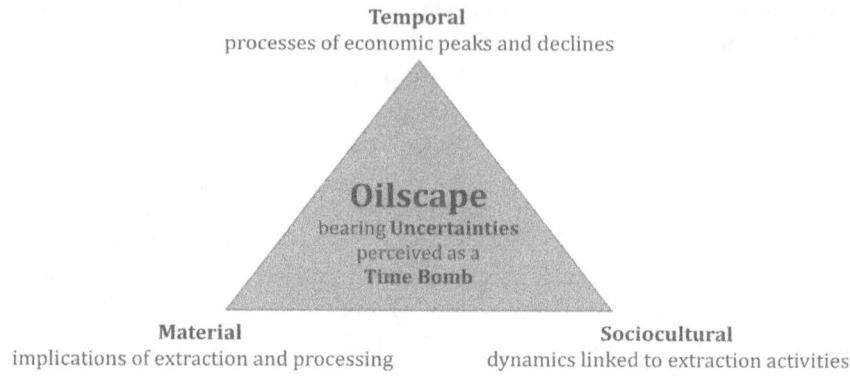

Figure 1.1. Concept "oilscape" © Svenja Schöneich.

As pointed out before, an important part of the particularities of oil is that it carries certain material and temporal risks, some of which are comparable to, but not identical, to those of other types of resources. Hydrocarbons, often representing toxic and explosive substances, are considered dangerous assets, which furthermore underlie specific temporal processes that incorporate the elusive and terminable character of the benefits generated through its extraction. Consequently, the perception of risk and the anticipation of economic and sociocultural changes accompany oil like no other resource (Weszkalnys 2014: 215). The experiences of crisis and the perceptions of risk form the oilscape in particular ways, creating a variety of uncertainties among the actors of the oilscape. In Emiliano Zapata, the perception of this uncertainty has led to the notion of a "time bomb," which reveals uncertainty as a feature of the oilscape.

Uncertainty as a Feature of the Oilscape

The dynamics in which people navigate circumstances created by the extraction of raw materials are decisive for how the social and cultural conditions in those spaces are shaped. Oil extraction generates a variety of uncertainties for local actors, which become embedded in the environment as well as in the living conditions of the individual actors with a permanent character (Pijpers 2018: 29). Uncertainty is usually considered something that results from exposure to a potential risk or danger, but there is a wide spectrum of what is considered a risk. In the anthropological literature, risk and risk perception are generally identifiable but not central themes (Alaszewski 2015: 205). One branch of risk perception mainly focuses on crises (see, e.g., Vigh 2006), disasters (e.g., Faas 2016; Hoffman and Oliver-Smith 2002; Oliver-Smith 1996), or hazardous natural environments (e.g., Reno 2011; Torry et al. 1979). While uncertainty as such is not necessarily directly related to a disaster, it may also arise from a situation that is perceived as unpredictable in a broader sense. Uncertainty can thus have many causes, be it working conditions or insecure income (Archambault 2015; de L'Estoile 2014), medical conditions such as illness or pregnancy (Beckmann 2015; Reynolds and Etyang Siu 2015), or drastic changes in the social and physical environment, as in the cases of actors who migrate (Di Nunzio 2015).

In his work *Contaminated Communities* ([1988] 2018), Michael Edelstein analyzes how communities within a toxic environment deal with exposure to pollution and risks for health and life. Edelstein defines a contaminated community as "any residential area located within or near the identified boundaries for known exposure to pollution" ([1988] 2018: 9). These can be places exposed to chemicals, toxic waste, or affected by a strong environmental pollution. With regard to the extraction of oil and gas, the accompanying exposure of the immediate environment to polluting substances is generally assumed to be part of the extraction and production processes. This has already been demonstrated in the extensive literature on pollution and conflicts over contamination through resource extraction throughout the world (e.g., Auyero and Swistun 2008; Bavinck and Lorenzo Pellegrini 2014; DeCesare and Auyero 2017; Engels and Dietz 2017; Gilberthorpe and Hilson 2014; Omeje 2008). Apart from contamination with substances toxic to humans, extraction is characterized by its massive interference with the structure and nature of the environment, which provides water and soil as the basis of livelihood for its inhabitants. Furthermore, they shape the landscapes of extraction through their secondary impacts, such as the construction of related infrastructure, as well as the social structure in these environments through the flow of workers and exposure to novel goods and lifestyles (e.g., Black 2000; Breglia 2013; Santiago 2006; Sawyer 2004; Shever 2012).

Especially in areas with extractive activities, the determination of a possible health risk is made procedurally rather than abruptly. The population in the immediate vicinity of extraction projects is usually not aware of the risks to health, the environment, or their vital and social space from one moment to another but has incorporated the knowledge of the dangers existing in their daily lives over the course of time. This risk knowledge is generally composed of diffuse information about actual and detailed risks to health and life and a relativization of perceived risks related to the lack of alternatives and/or a means to reduce risk perception. This could be done, for example, through a system that guarantees benefits and economic security as a tradeoff (e.g., Breglia 2013; Nash 1979; O'Faircheallaigh 2013). With the collapse of risk mitigation facilities, the damages and hazards triggered by the extraction, the perception of risk may change significantly.

In their article "The Social Production of Toxic Uncertainty," Javier Auyero and Debora Swistun (2008) show how the social production of environmental uncertainty by the residents of contaminated areas is based on the confusion that results from ignorance about the sources of pollution and their effects, which in turn leads to obstacles in organizing responses to them. The authors identify two factors that favor this process. The first is "relational anchoring" (Auyero and Swistun 2008: 374) of risk perceptions. "Relational anchoring" is understood as a crucial process in shaping the collective schemes that residents use to assess hazards, which is manipulated by material and discursive powers. The perceptions of risk are rooted in the interactions and routines that characterize a particular place. The second factor is the "work of confusion" by powerful external actors who generate diffuse information about the origins and effects of extraction and its consequences (2008: 374). A common strategy of actors, such as companies, is to try to neutralize the damage done. Then, the latency period between the start of extraction or industrial production and public recognition of negative environmental impacts can create a period of perceived certainty that ultimately culminates in an uncertain temporality of risk (Kirsch 2014: 138, 145).

In the case of oil extraction, the factors that determine uncertainty and risk perception arise primarily from exposure to toxic substances and from accidents. Furthermore, another level of uncertainty comes into play, which is embedded in a predetermined process of booms and declines, in which economic benefits offer a fast improvement of individual living conditions, followed by decline and disenchantment. The temporal character of this relief creates a boom that must inevitably end and lead to a crisis, either when the oil prices drop or when the source is exhausted (see e.g., Kaposy 2017; Limbert 2008; Weszkalnys 2016). Since it is impossible to predict—certainly not from a local perspective—exactly when the tide will turn, the unpredictability of the market leads to a number of challenges that take the form of uncertainty as a persistent condition in which people are forced to continuously adapt and renegotiate their conditions over and over again (see Appel 2012b; Limbert 2010; Weszkalnys 2014). The book at hand draws on previous findings in uncertainty research, by contextualizing the condition of uncertainty as a consequence of industrial pollution and as a result of the boom and bust inherent in oil as a resource. However, the question that remains is how people respond to the uncertainties of life when they live in the vicinity of an oilscape.

Conclusion: Analyzing the Time Bomb

The community and ejido Emiliano Zapata has been deeply impacted by oil extraction and its accompanying effects for more than six decades. Thus, it is also inseparably linked to the national and global history and consequences of oil and gas extraction, which are reflected in the local environment of material formation and in temporal and social dynamics. To understand these entanglements, I present the concept of the "oilscape" as a useful analytical tool. It considers the circumstances of extensive, long-term oil extraction, which follows the temporal characteristics of oil as a resource and causes economic booms and declines (see Ferry and Limbert 2008: 3; Reyna and Behrends 2011: 5; Rogers 2015a: 367). An oilscape is thus understood as a space where industrial oil extraction has inscribed itself over time in the material manifestations of landscape, housing, fields, and infrastructure, as well as in the social texture and behavior of the local residents. Uncertainty plays an important role as a feature of the oilscape, reflected in each of the three dimensions described.

As discussed above, oil bears certain particular properties, which distinguish it from other resources for extraction. These particularities are best illustrated by looking at the temporal and material characteristics of oil and their interaction with social and cultural dynamics. I therefore elaborate on the temporal as well as on the material particularities of oil and oil extraction. Recent studies of oil extraction are increasingly attempting to unravel the complex internal structures of multinational production projects, and current oil research is trying to grasp the various interrelated elements of hydrocarbons and their impact on the environment and people's lives. However, the places where oil is found and extracted are usually geographically restricted areas. In this way, oil, like many other natural resources linked to extraction and processing, forms enclaves. These are spaces where the wealth and power associated with the idea of modernity are concentrated, while their proximity provokes cultural encounters that reinforce inequalities with oil-sector workers and residents as a classic example. Emiliano Zapata represents such a space, where oil extraction is interlinked with local particularities and negotiated between local actors. In relation to oil extraction, each of these dimensions provokes a set of different uncertainties, accumulating in the oilscape, which community members expressed with the metaphor of "living on a time bomb." The following chapter shows how these uncertainties are inscribed in the oilscape and how Emiliano Zapata's community members deal with them.

Notes

Epigraph: Wilson, Carlson, and Szeman (2017: 3).

1. See Reno (2011) for a comprehensive discussion on risk perception.

Chapter 2

A Mexican Oil Story
Historic Background and Contemporary Setting

> In Mexico, oil holds a very special place not only in the popular imagination but also in the national budget. Mexican oil is a foundation for the economy and the cornerstone of nationalism.
>
> —Lisa Breglia, *Living with Oil*

In this statement, Breglia illustrates the twofold nature of oil in Mexico. Oil is indeed a strategic economic resource that, despite the dropping oil price and the oil crisis of first decade of the twenty-first century, funds up to 40 percent of the national budget through its revenues. Within the years of 2013 and 2016 the country ranked tenth in the world with regard to crude oil reserves and fourth in natural gas reserves in the Americas (Sánchez Campos 2016: 292). But oil is also keenly discussed in questions of national resources sovereignty and political organization and has therefore come to play an important role within the construction of Mexican identity (Checa-Artasu and Hernández Franyuti 2016: 7; Monreal Ávila 2008: 69; Seelke et al. 2015: 2). An understanding of the context of oil in Mexico is vital for engaging with the particularities of oil extraction at the local level, since the national and even global entanglements of the hydrocarbon market result in a wide array of local outcomes. The example of Emiliano Zapata illustrates the local impacts of national and international decision-making processes in the oil sector, for which a brief contextualization of oil in Mexico and its linkages to the regional and local levels will be provided.

From Vanilla and Oil: The Formation of Totonacapan

Looking at the tropical evergreen surface of the hilly landscape of the municipality of Papantla, an unaware visitor might not notice the fortune hidden under the surface of the area at first sight. Papantla is part of a geological feature called Paleocanal de Chicontepec in northern Veracruz, a 3,815 square kilometers accumulation of Palaeocene-age sediments. It was explored for extraction in 1926, with the commercial production beginning twenty-six years later in 1952. Even though the expectations regarding its prospects have been lowered recently, it currently represents the largest PEMEX asset. With 139 billion barrels of oil in place, and considerable gas deposits, it is expected to extend Mexico's peak beyond declining production of the former major oil field Cantarell, especially because of the assumed potential of its unconventional gas deposits (Fry and Delgado 2018: 12; Sígler 2016). The municipality of Papantla once belonged to the larger cantón de Papantla, which comprised about 3,500 square kilometers until it was divided by the Constitution of 1917. It is located in a region with coastal plains—the Llanura Costera and the Sierra Papanteca, a strongly vegetated hilly area crossed by river valleys. A variety of climatic conditions as well as different infrastructure developments in the past have also led to diverse economic development in the Llanura Costera and the Sierra Papanteca. The coastal region is also called *tierra caliente* (hot soil) because of its warm climate, tropical rainforest, and high humidity. Together with its exceptional rainfall, this is the reason for Papantla's particularly fertile soils, which allow two corn harvests per year without supplemental irrigation, thus facilitating the agricultural base of many rural communities (Kourí 2004: 38–40). However, while the oil deposits of the Llanura Costera enabled rapid industrialization, accompanied by a shift to cash crops and monocultures, the cultivation of maize for local consumption and more traditional cultivation patterns persisted for a longer period of time in the Sierra Papanteca (Velázquez Hernández 1995: 39–42).

The city of Papantla de Olarte is the capital city and governing authority of the municipality, covering a territory of about 1,200 square kilometers, with 376 localities, out of which only three are classified "urban." The municipality has a total population of about 166,000 with a high percentage (68.5 percent) of the population considered "poor"[1] (SEFIPLAN 2016). More than 40 percent of citizens in Papantla speak an indigenous language, and it is thus recognized as an "indigenous municipality" by the Comisión Nacional para el Desarrollo de los Pueblos Indígenas de México (CDI) (CDI Catálogo de Localidades Indígenas 2010). The dominant indigenous language is Totonac. The Totonac people are officially the eighth biggest group of indigenous peoples in Mexico with approx. 213,000 speakers, concentrating in the northern parts of Veracruz and Puebla (Chenaut 2010: 47). Papantla is therefore part of an area known as Totonacapan (realm of the Totonacs), which today consists of several municipalities in the states of Puebla and northern Veracruz, with Papantla

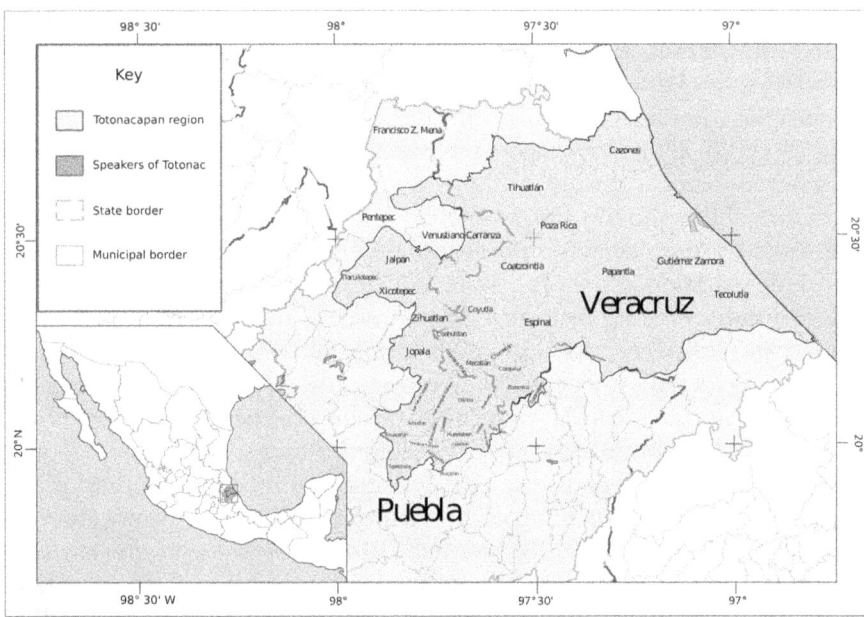

Map 2.1. Contemporary Totonacapan with distribution of Totonac speakers in the area © Orestes de la Rosa, used with permission.

being the vastest among them (Masferrer Kahn 2004: 22–23; Valderrama Rouy 2005: 188).

The extension of today's Totonacapan is different from its historical expansion the Spaniards found at the time of the Conquista. In its heyday during the post-classical period from 1200–1540 CE, it stretched from the Cazones River in the north to the southern Papaloapan River, and from the western coast to the region that today is known as the northern highlands of Puebla. The city of Papantla was probably already an important trading spot during that time (Kasburg 1992: 12–13). After the takeover by the Spaniards, many Totonacs escaped into the hilly region of the north, which was covered with dense rainforest and therefore more difficult to access, to escape repression and turmoil induced by the colonial intruders. The expropriation of the indigenous population at the end of the sixteenth century caused even more Totonac people to flee further to the north. Here, they were able to continue living relatively unhindered in their preferred circumstances, thus preserving the system of communal land and family parcel ownership. This was mainly possible because of the subsistence-oriented agriculture (*milpa*)[2] and dispersed settlement patterns, facilitating a certain local independence and enabling many Totonac communities to maintain their traditional lifestyles until the twentieth century. In general, the colonial authorities showed only minor interest in the territory of Papantla that remained commercially insignificant before the onset of commercial vanilla production in the nineteenth century (Kasburg 1992: 25–27; Kourí 2004: 2). Nevertheless, Papantla was the scene of several violent uprisings in the wake of the Bourbon Reforms and, in particular, the monopolization of tobacco in the mid-seventeenth century with riots by Totonac communities that were in an increasingly difficult economic situation at the time (see Frederick 2016).

Papantla has a long history with commercial oil extraction, which has shaped and influenced its rural areas in distinctive ways. Northern Veracruz maintains not only one of the most important regions for oil and gas extraction nationwide today, but hydrocarbon products have been known and used by the population since precolonial times. The Olmec people, who were the first users of crude oil, are often said to be the earliest major "civilization" in Mexico, referring to their organization of society, their art and craftwork (e.g., Diehl 2004; Grove 2014). They settled between 1500 BCE and 400 BCE at the Gulf coast area in the south of today's state of Veracruz and in Tabasco and were the first ones in Mesoamerica to collect and process *chapopote*—a form of petroleum also known as asphalt or bitumen, whose texture is highly viscous and liquid or semi-solid. It consists of a mixture of natural hydrocarbons, oxidized products and residues of certain crude oils. It was used by the Olmec to seal aqueducts and boats, for decoration, as construction material or glue, as well as toothpaste or chewing gum (Carreón Blaine 2007: 25). To improve its usability, the Olmec people also processed the *chapopote* through boiling, which became known as refining later in the nineteenth century. They also commercialized the *chapopote* so it was used by other ethnic groups in Mesoamerica as well, such as the Aztec people in today's state of Veracruz, who gave the substance its contemporary name. *Chapopote* stems from the Nahuatl word *chapopotli*, deriving from *tzauc* or *tzouctli* (glue, cement, rubber) or *chiáhuatl* (fat) and *popochitli/popochtli/poctli* (smoke, odor, perfume) (Gerali 2013: 240; Santiago 2016). In the fifteenth-century Huasteca region, the Teenek also started using *chapopote* they had gathered from natural springs. There is no evidence that the pre-Hispanic ethnic groups extracted the oil from the ground with technical procedures, but rather gathered it where it surfaced naturally. Oil extraction as it is known today therefore did not start until the twentieth century. As different ethnic groups in precolonial Mexico gathered and used *chapopote* where it was accessible, it is very likely that also the Totonac of northern Veracruz used the substance according to their cultural circumstances (García Martínez 2005: 69).

After the Conquista, *chapopote* was first mentioned by the Spanish Franciscan missionary Bernardino de Sahagun in 1547, reporting that the local population of the Gulf coast collected big uneven patches of *chapopote* floating on seawater. The Spanish colonizers used the *chapopote* as varnish or as sealant repairing leaks in their ships, while the tar pits were also regarded as hazardous for the livestock of the colonial settlers at the Gulf coast. Soon Spanish merchants began to export the Mexican crude oil but only in small quantities and limited to the Iberian Peninsula. In 1783, oil was recognized as a mineral resource by a decree of King Charles III of Spain, with the Spanish crown holding the exclusive right of exploitation, even though it maintained a low value (Gerali 2013: 241–42). The industrial usage of petroleum started in the second half of the nineteenth century when crude oil could be converted into kerosene for lanterns, which led to commercial interest in the deposits. However, the tropical vegetation and climate created a difficult terrain for extraction and prevented early exploitation of the Gulf coast deposits in Veracruz at first.

Beginning in the mid-nineteenth century, the exponential increase of vanilla production induced a series of transformations even in regions where social patterns had been dominated for many decades by *milpa* economy and the corresponding social organization. Traditionally, vanilla is an indigenous crop, which has been cultivated in the region since precolonial times by the Totonac. Later on, the Spaniards exported vanilla to Europe on a regular basis during the eighteenth century. In the early nineteenth century, the usage of vanilla in Europe, especially France, started to increase significantly and the scarce commodity, only growing in very distinct climatic circumstances of the Gulf coast, experienced a high demand. At that time, Papantla was still relatively isolated from the commercial centers and dominated by traditional indigenous settlements based on subsistence agriculture. The rise of the vanilla economy initiated the most important process of social and economic change in nineteenth- and early twentieth-century Papantla. Papantla soon became the most important vanilla-producing region worldwide, triggering a variety of local socioeconomic changes (Kourí 2004: 80–83). Several land tenure conflicts developed primarily at the local or regional level, with the emergence of vanilla and Papantla became directly involved in the capitalist logic of domestic demand and export trade. It produced global pressures on the control of production and trade of the spice and therefore introduced massive changes within the economic organization and land tenure (López Vallejo 2020: 23–24).

With the vanilla boom, a class of entrepreneurs and merchants of European descent emerged who changed the economic and social pattern of the whole region while the easy money that could be made with vanilla also brought tensions and social stratification to the Totonac localities. The land gained value through its aptitude for vanilla cultivation, which led to increasing pressure toward its privatization. Large parts of the area were viewed by the state government as "underpopulated" and "unexplored," which then intended to specifically invite European settlers to further develop the commercial vanilla economy. In 1826, a decree issued by the state congress had already defined the dissolution of indigenous communal landholdings and their transformation into private property. However, due to a lack of administrative power, the decree was not put into practice for more than fifty years, but when the land values rose, the state government increasingly pressed for the dissolution of communal lands. Some plots were sold to the same community members who had previously worked the land from communal landholding, causing discontent among the communal land right holders. Other areas were given to European settlers with the goal to establish a vanilla-producing hacienda. On these haciendas, the cultivation of agricultural products was most often strictly oriented toward commercialization, with new forms of optimizing production processes, such as the artificial pollination of vanilla. This process of land distribution was highly conflict-ridden and led to various violent local uprisings, particularly in the late nineteenth century. As a response, the government aimed for partial privatization rather than none, and permitted the establishment of so-called *condueñazgos*, private landholding associations. Within these, each *condueño* owned a share of the land that could be bought or sold individually and was subject to property taxes. Yet less than ten years after their establishment, it had become evident that these joint stock associations of landowners had not displayed solidarity but rather deepened the tensions that had started with the increasing use of the land for commercial vanilla cultivation (Kourí 2004: 104–8; Skerrit Gardner 1994: 162–64).

Despite continuing endurance of ancient practices of *milpa* agriculture and a social organization marked by the dispersion of settlements, the rural landscape at the end of the nineteenth century reflected the emergence of viable profit-oriented enterprises and haciendas. Certain syncretistic practices emerged on cultural level, where the European settlers were confronted with local customs and Mexican cultural patterns (see Serna 2008; Skerrit Gardner1994). The diversification into commercial vanilla production, cattle ranching, tobacco growing, coffee farming and newly discovered oil wells competed with the *milpas*. Soon unregulated logging and other more destructive forms of land use took over and led to gradual deforestation in the area. The *condueñazgos* were dissolved in the later years of the nineteenth century, accompanied by social unrest and considerable bloodshed. Former vanilla barons had become big landowners, occupying large holdings in the region, who bought and violently grabbed even more land after the dissolution of the *condueñazgos*. Uprisings caused by this appropriation of mostly Totonac territory in 1887, 1891, 1896, and 1906 were brought to an end through violent interventions from the government (Chenaut 2010: 56–57; Kourí 2004: 108).

When petroleum increasingly gained economic value in the United States in the years following 1900, US companies began to explore the promising deposits on the Gulf coast and the first regional oil booms began (Breglia 2013: 33; López Vallejo 2020: 46). The first drillings with the purpose of oil extraction in Mexico took place in the years 1858–69, but it still took until the turn of the century to start the commercial production of crude oil in the country. In that year, a small group of Anglo-Americans, who worked for the British Mexican Railroad Company (Mexico City–Veracruz route) for the first time started the attempt of exploring an oil deposit 40 kilometers southwest of the town of Papantla known by the Totonac population as Quhax, later renamed by the Spaniards as Cuguas. The attempts were initially unsuccessful, as unpaid debts, lack of diplomatic relations, and poor exchange rates prevented the first companies from obtaining the necessary funds from Europe. The first successful attempt to drill for oil started in 1907, when the British businessman and oil pioneer Percy Furber recognized the economic potential of the Cuguas area, and La Constancia became what is known as the Furbero oilfield today. Due to abundant yields, national oil production increased significantly. A few years later, Furber sold the rights to the influential US oil firm Compañía Mexicana de Petróleo El Águila SA, also known as El Águila, which henceforth conducted all commercial extraction and exploration activities in the area. The company operated the fields mostly with their own personnel, rarely benefiting the local population (Garner 2011: 82; Gerali and Riguzzi 2013: 77–79).

In the following years, Mexico became the third largest producer of oil in the world, with companies mostly exporting to the United States. Although oil production was not entirely free from conflict and violence in 1910 when the Revolution began, it remained relatively stable due to high international demand and the protection of labor by US companies. Oil production continued until 1915 when oil workers began to increasingly organize strikes. Working conditions had become a contentious point by then and the imbalance between the conditions of Mexican personnel and US staff had caused further discontent among the Mexican workers (Brown and Knight 1992: 2–5).

The 1917 constitution promised more rights for workers and obligations for employers and created an additional basis for protest movements claiming those rights and responsibilities. In the aftermath of the constitution turmoil and conflicts among the oil workers arose and continued until the year 1920, when the demand and thus also the price of oil decreased. Meanwhile, the Carranza regime was overthrown by General Álvaro Obregón, who established taxes and regulations that weakened the role of foreign investors. The imposition of Article 27 established the separation of the ownership of the land and the subsoil and endows the nation with dominion over the latter. With this act, oil became subject to national mining, and the inalienable and imprescriptible dominion over hydrocarbons was consecrated to the nation. The constitution secured a permanent and inalienable right of the natural resources to the Mexican government for the first time and therefore weakened the property claims of foreign oil companies. Its practical application and regulation with foreign extractive companies caused much political tension between investors and General Álvaro Obregón, and later with the successor president Plutarco Elías Calles (Cárdenas Gracia 2009: 20; Rippy 1972: 34).

Foreign investment in the sector and the rights and interests of foreign oil companies in Mexican oil remained a major subject of political debate in the 1920s when Mexico had become the second largest oil producer in the world. In the 1930s, El Àguila explored the Poza Rica oilfield located on the territory of the municipality of Coatzintla, only about seventeen kilometers from Papantla. The discovery of this large oil deposit caused a major upswing of the hydrocarbon industry in the region as well as on a national level. The situation and tensions about foreign investment worsened further in the course of the 1930s, when oil revenues began to suffer from the Great Depression and the Mexican government's share of the profits still declined further. Due to constantly falling wages unrest rose among Mexican workers (Brown and Knight 1992: 20–23). At the beginning of the presidency of Lázaro Cárdenas, whose political goal was the final implementation of the promises of the constitution of 1917, the union Sindicato de Trabajadores Petroleros de la República Mexicana (STPRM) was established in 1935 and demanded the rights the constitution had promised. Posta Rica already had a local union, but it was the STPRM that gave the region its collective strength. This led to a strong cultural unification among the workers, paired with certain distancing from the demands of the campesinos[3] of the same area, whose troubles and demands were structurally different. In 1937, the Poza Rica oilfield produced 40 percent of the national crude oil, and the STPRM became particularly powerful in the region (Olvera Ribera 1992: 66–69). They rapidly gained organizational strength, and when several lawsuits were filed in labor disputes and a national strike by oil industry workers put the economic functioning of the country at risk, the Mexican government was forced to take drastic measures. Thus, President Cárdenas decreed the expropriation of foreign oil companies on 18 March 1938. This expropriation is understood as a nationalization of the hydrocarbon sector because the expropriation of company properties functioned as a direct measure to the change the economic structure of the whole country rather than an individualized action. With this act, the Mexican state received the domain of exploration, production, refining, and distribution of oil and natural gas, and the production and sale of petrochemical products (Cárdenas Gracia 2009: 31;; Rippy 1972: 286–87). The same year on 7 June, President Cárdenas created the company PEMEX. Since then, the firm has been in charge of the production, distribution and commercialization of Mexican hydrocarbons. Thus, the oil industry became the lever of national development at that time and laid the foundations for the formation of an economic model of import substitution. PEMEX also took over the Poza Rica oilfield and its prosperity (Cárdenas Gracia 2009: 31). With the intensification of the extraction and production of hydrocarbon products, a new industrial era dawned. Attracted by the infrastructure and economic wealth provided by PEMEX, many people from all over the country started to settle in and around Poza Rica in the following decades and modified the sociodemographic structure of the region significantly (Kourí 2004: 127; Velázquez Hernández 1995: 175).

Oil and the Ejido: Between Two Pillars of the Mexican Revolution

Oil and Mexico's economy at the time of the Revolution was mainly based on agriculture, and despite its prominent position as an oil producer, the bonanza was contributing little to the national income. An important outcome of the Mexican Revolution was comprehensive land reform with the purpose of redistributing the land, of which overwhelmingly large parts were in the hands of *hacenderos*—a great landowner, mostly of European descent in Latin America. In Mexico, the majority of the Mexican territory was owned by *hacenderos* before the Mexican Revolution (see Storck 1986). This reform introduced the concept of the ejido, a unique figure of communal landholding for agricultural communities not only in Latin American but also on a global scale enshrined in Article 27 of the 1917 constitution. After the Revolution came to an end in 1920, large holdings of wealthy landowners were expropriated and distributed to landless peasants to be administered as communal land by a community of ejidatarios with equal rights and responsibilities. The territory demarcated as the ejido was to be governed by recognized members of the ejido and could not be rented out or sold. At first, after the Revolution, ejido territory was reluctantly given out, yet under President Cárdenas from 1934 onward, it was extensively distributed in the whole country and persists until today (e.g., Nuijten 2003: 4; Schmidt 2007: 526–29).

Legally, the ejido lands are owned by the federal government, but the ejidatarios are endowed with the usufruct rights to farming parcels on the territory. These land use rights were granted until the death of an ejidatario and then transferred to one single successor or reverted to the community for redistribution. The governing body of each ejido is the comisariado ejidal, which is elected by the general assembly of all ejidatarios. Land conflicts within the ejido territories are mostly resolved internally. The ejido strengthened the legal position of peasants to a degree previously unknown and therefore played a crucial role within the constitution of an indigenous peasant identity in Mexico. In contemporary Mexico, slightly more than half of the national surface belongs to ejidos and agrarian communities allowing for a certain level of self-determination in regard to governance of the endowed territory (Castañeda Dower and Pfütze 2013: 5; D. Smith et al. 2009: 176).

When the Mexican Revolution started, social unrest in the region increased as it did in the whole country. Many Totonac farmers migrated further north to more remote places to escape revolutionary violence. After the end of the Revolution, some of the areas further south were resettled by the Totonacs, so that today's Totonacapan—consisting of the municipalities of Cazones de Herreras, Coahuitlán, Coatzintla, Coxquihui, Coyutla, Chumatlán, Espinal, Filomeno Mata, Gutiérrez Zamora, Macatlán, Papantla, Poza Rica de Hidalgo, Tecolutla, Tihuatlán and Zozocolco de Hidalgo—was formed in the 1920s and 1930s (Kasberg 1992: 27; Masferrer Kan 2004: 22–23). In the aftermath of the Revolution, a new form of communal landholding was established, which forms an important distinctive element in the turbulent history of Mexican landownership figures. With the ejido, a form of communal land holding was re-established in Mexico. Its roots lay in the ideal of a precolonial times communal organization that was based on an idea of joint land governance by rural communities for agricultural purposes. As one of the agreements after the Mexican Revolution, large parts of private landholdings were expropriated and granted to agricultural communities in the whole country. The figure of the ejido in Mexico underwent a series of modifications during its history but it endures until the present day (see Schmidt 2007; Vázquez Castillo 2004). Two concepts can be considered the main pillars of a postrevolutionary national project. The first one is the ejido as the expression of a nationwide redistribution of land for agricultural purposes for communal management through agrarian reform, and the second one is the industrialization as well as the nationalization of strategic industries such as the hydrocarbon industry. However, they have rarely been analyzed as complementary parts of the same redistributive force causing conflicts and frictions over property within the oil areas of Mexico (del Palacio Langer 2015: 130–32). Ana Julia del Palacio Langer makes an attempt to analyze the land distribution as ejido and the nationalization of the hydrocarbon sector as two corresponding parts. She thereby shows how the industrialization of the nation through the oil industry opposed sometimes with the distribution of land for agricultural purposes. Even though ejido land was inalienable by its invention, Article 27 of the constitution of 1917 encompassed the possibility of expropriation of strategic resources for "the common good" but guaranteed indemnifications. These rules came into play especially with respect to the interests of PEMEX: after the hydrocarbon sector was nationalized in 1936, PEMEX expropriated large parts of ejido territory in the country aiming at extracting for the common good of national development. Although the ejidos were compensated accordingly, this process was often conflictual in practice (del Palacio Langer 2015: 22, 138).

Until the 1940s, many communities in Papantla held titles as ejidos, but in some areas community members obtained farming and housing plots as private property rather than applying for the ejido status. That time, many small-scale farmers continued to grow vanilla for an international market. At the same time oil became the main source of income for the country and with it, PEMEX conquered its place as the nation's main company, as it was also the largest taxpayer. During the following decades, PEMEX remained successful and, ending up with a monopoly on oil and gas extraction, as well as its processing and production of petrochemicals. The STPRM managed to negotiate particularly favorable conditions for the workers, and besides a certain prestige, the PEMEX workers soon came to enjoy a number of advantages compared to workers in other sections, campesinos, or even workers on temporary contracts (see Olvero Ribera 1992; Quintal Avilés 1994) Until today, being a *petrolero* and the state company itself plays an emblematic role within Mexican nationalism (Seelke et al. 2015: 2; Suárez Ávila 2017: 8; Monreal Ávila 2008: 69).

PEMEX: Patrimony and National Emblem

At first, the oil workers who began to strike in 1937–38 benefited only little from the nationalization. The unions' demands were rejected by the government, which attempted to directly manage the industry. Nevertheless, wages began to rise, and the work week was limited to forty hours. When the unions kept demanding the full implementation of the rights granted by the constitution in 1940, PEMEX's general manager Vicente Cortés, accused the workers of lacking discipline and appropriating company equipment. President Cárdenas then called on the workers to be patient and to allow the labor to be suspended until the industry could pay off the losses of indemnification money to the expropriated companies (Maurer 2011: 611).

Soon, the awaited economic development of the oil industry brought the desired progress. The oil industry became the economical lever of the nation and the national budget began to build up on petroleum. PEMEX then became the most important national company, also due to the fact that it generated the major part of tax revenues at the time. The emerging oil city of Poza Rica became an important factor for national revenues as well as for the regional development in the 1930s, which attracted migrants from different parts of the country. This process rearranged social life in the former rural area of Poza Rica and consolidated the formation of a working class, forging new identities like that of the oil worker, which challenged the foremost rural agriculture-based indigenous and campesino identity of the area (Chenaut 2017: 95; Olvera Ribera 1992: 66–67). By the end of the decade, the Mexican government had managed to negotiate several pacts with Western nations enabling the flow of capital, material, and know-how, so that PEMEX could enter its "golden age" in the 1950s (Brown and Knight 1992: 203). The industry managed to unfold a variety of activities within a short time period and started to produce diesel, gasoline, liquid gas, asphalt lubricants, paraffin, dry gas, and later also petrochemicals. This helped PEMEX to further professionalize and independently advance their activities. The company then started to train its own engineers and material experts and began to fund its own research and development of material, technology and laboratories (Cárdenas Gracia 2009: 35).

The next president, Ávila Camacho, continued to negotiate the indemnification payments with the expropriated foreign firms. The negotiations took until the year 1947, when a final settlement was reached. During the negotiation process, the government under President Ávila Camacho allowed foreign involvement in the exploitation of fossil fuels in Mexico through a special contract form with very limited scopes. Under the governance of President Miguel Alemán in the second half of the 1940s, the first contracts were signed between PEMEX and small US firms who agreed to explore in limited areas over the course of ten to fifteen years. In a document of the president's campaign, it was expressed that foreign investment should be marginal and that the most important deposits should not be touched by foreign firms, as for the refining or commercialization of fuels. In addition, it became clear that at no time the state property on the deposits would be touched. In the end, these contracts did not turn out to be beneficial for Mexico as they did not generate the external resources that had been expected. However, it took several years until the legislation was modified again (Cárdenas Gracia 2009: 37–40).

In 1960, under the mandate of President López Mateos, Article 27 was reformed once more, determining the prohibition of contracts with foreign companies for the extraction of oil, reaffirming the dominance of the Mexican state over all resources. This strategy generated many benefits for PEMEX and strengthened the national industrialization model backed by import substitution until the crisis in 1973, when oil prices were rising due to the US oil embargo imposed by the member countries of the Organization of Petroleum Exporting Countries (OPEC). In the early 1970s, petroleum production had become increasingly important for Mexico, but was still not the dominating sector, a fact which helped to deal with the oil shock in 1973. During the President Luis Echeverría administration (1970–1976), more investments were made in the petroleum industry, leading to overproduction of crude oil and making Mexico an oil exporting country, with the United States as its main partner. But at the same time, these loans generated an external debt of more than $19,000 million that left Mexico in a deep economic crisis. At this point, the country had undergone a constant process of modernization, but by the beginning of the 1970s, the agricultural sector also fell into a crisis. Until then, the sector had served as a financing pillar for the industrialization. The economic crisis of 1976 was overcome by an ascension of the oil revenues, as PEMEX managed to deal with the shock in a productive manner that transformed into the Mexican oil boom a few years later (1978–1979). The boom raised the expectations for a better and wealthier future through the expansion of the oil industry (Cárdens Gracia 2009: 43;). The oil industry and the commercialization of agricultural products during the boom years 1970–90 has shaped the landscape of coastal Totonacapan until today. In the 1950s and 1960s, this changed with the fall of the vanilla price by the rapidly increasing competition and the industrialization of the sugar production in other parts of Mexico, which displaced manually processed sugar. A dropping coffee price in the 1980s added on to the increasing hardship in small-scale agriculture. This finally led to a rapidly advancing impoverishment, especially of the highland areas (Kasburg 1992: 19–21, Kourí 2004: 198–99).

While the highland of Totonacapan is characterized by a stronger Totonac identity and by keeping traditional communal farming patterns and certain community customs until today, commercial agriculture and wage labor are more common in the lowlands. This division is the result of political trends to foster a national industrialization and the economic development in the rural areas of Mexico, which has been conducted more intensely in the lowlands. These include less remote and more populated towns, such as Papantla de Olarte or Gutiérrez Zamora. They have facilitated the execution of governmental power due to a better infrastructure than the hilly highland communities, which are difficult to access. An important factor for the establishment of this infrastructure was the emergence of the oil infrastructure mainly limited to the lowlands. Many of the roads, as well as the flow of capital and goods is directly connected to the PEMEX activities in the area and has changed the sociodemographic patterns in the lowlands during the oil boom more than in the sierra, where no larger extraction had been undertaken (García Martínez 2012: 78; Popke and Torres 2013: 218).

The Mexican oil boom reached its peak between 1977 and 1981 and even though several fields had been discovered in the meanwhile in other parts of the country, like the extremely productive Cantarell field in 1976, the oil wealth around Poza Rica continued. In times of the oil boom, PEMEX relished a prestigious status around the country and became the major driver for national industrial development. During that time, the company further developed its internal infrastructure, building its own schools, hospitals and leisure facilities for its staff. Higher PEMEX staff gained the privilege of company-provided housing and medical service, as well as high pensions and guaranteed workplaces for their children. The STPRM, which had always been deeply entangled with national politics, continuously gained more power. Since at least the time of the boom and its aftermath in the 1980s, the status of PEMEX as a national symbol for political sovereignty, wealth and progress was established (Suárez Ávila 2017: 8). This also provided economic benefits to the communities around the city and the wider area. During the 1990s, the wealth of the area did not increase further but remained mainly stable until the oil crisis hit the country in the first decade of the twenty-first century (see Sánchez Campos 2016). By 1980, the peak of the oil bonanza was over. In the following years, the external debt situation worsened, and although Mexico based the national economy on petroleum and became the fourth largest exporter in the world, the low price of oil resulted in the declaration of the moratorium on the payment of foreign debt in 1982 (Cárdenas Gracia 2009: 43–44).

Crisis and the Neoliberal Turn

Due to the debt crisis, the Mexican government was forced to change the economic model even more toward integrating neoliberal ideas in order to strengthen the market economy. In the beginning of the 1980s, 40 percent of the national budget came from oil resources, and PEMEX remained an indispensable actor for the national economy. The government then began to disintegrate and limit the company following the measurements suggested by the World Bank to reduce public investment. The leaving president López Portillo as well as the 1982 installed President Miguel de Madrid took measurements to open up some national sectors to foreign investments to revive the economy. (Brown and Knight 1992: 257–59; Cárdenas Gracia 2009: 51–52). Despite these political tendencies, at the beginning of the president de Madrid's term of office in 1983, a constitutional reform was adopted to determine hydrocarbons and petrochemicals as a strategic area of the national economy. The production and processing of hydrocarbons then was assigned exclusively to the public sector. However, the criterion of maximizing oil production as an export good and as a guarantee for obtaining international loans was reaffirmed. Under the political pressures of the United States to limit the monopoly of PEMEX, in 1986, President de Madrid authorized the import of petrochemical products that PEMEX could not produce. Also, the privatization of some PEMEX subsidiaries was promoted, together with regulations for opening to the international market (Breglia 2013: 218; Cárdenas Garcia 2009: 47).

Under the term of the next president, Carlos Salinas de Gortari (1988–1994), more foreign companies entered due to contracting in the petrochemical sector and the role of the oil workers union, the rights and benefits of Mexican oil workers. The pressure of privatization in Latin America at the time also affected Mexico as part of the Washington Consensus, which consisted of a set of neoliberal reforms including trade liberalizations, tax reforms and deregulation, and a liberalization of property rights (Breglia 2013: 216). The financial crisis of 1995 was the trigger for the solicitation of international support by the Mexican government. To obtain a loan from the International Monetary Fund, President Ernesto Zedilla, successor to Salinas de Gortari, signed an agreement with the United States in which he guaranteed the payment of the debt with hydrocarbons. In the agreement he also committed to deliver all strategic information of PEMEX to the United States. Once again, the Regulatory Law of Article 27 of the constitution was amended to exclude exclusivity from transportation, storage, distribution, sale, and foreign trade of natural gas from the petroleum industry, which remained public in general. It also opened up the petrochemical industry to private initiatives (Cárdenas Gracia 2009: 51;Wood 2010: 858–60).

Apart from a reform of the oil sector, through a comprehensive reform of the agrarian law in 1992, the redistribution of land eventually came to an end and promoted the privatization of the ejido land. In times of neoliberal modernization, the ejido incorporated notions of backwardness and rural mores, opposed to any kind of development or economic ambition. The reform aimed at giving private ownership of house plots and the prospect of private ownership of demarcated farmland to individual ejidatarios if the general assembly and the comisariado ejidal, agreed to it. Through the reform, ejidatarios could then lawfully mortgage, rent, or sell their plots. The reform was recognized by several scholars as of tremendous significance for the structure of land ownership in Mexico under the premises of a wider set neoliberalization policies and thereby characterized as a counter reform, as its tendency toward privatization counteracts the initial premise of a movement toward communal governance (see Vázquez Castillo 2004). As a key instrument of privatization, the Programa de Certificación de Derechos Ejidales y Titualción de Solares Urbano (PROCEDE) program was introduced as an initiative to certify the communal lands. The program was voluntary and designed to survey external boundaries and internal divisions of tens of thousands of ejido territories on a national level since 1993. It was conducted and administered by three different state entities and followed the final goal to promote investment in the rural sector and increase agricultural productivity. Yet, the process of implementation was often linked to internal conflicts about the exact dimensions as well as present and future distribution of the parcels (D. Smith et al. 2009: 181, 187).

With the entry of President Vicente Fox (2000–6) in 2000, the uninterrupted governmental period of the Partido Revolucionario Institucional, which had begun after the Revolution, came to an end with the first president from the opposition party Partido Acción Nacional (PAN). The former Coca-Cola executive Fox brought an even more intensive neoliberalist vision to the country and thereby to PEMEX. As part of his campaign, Fox had called for the privatization of PEMEX but backpedaled upon the negative reaction this aim had provoked among many Mexicans. Nevertheless, the neoliberalization trend intensified significantly under the new PAN president. Despite his nationalistic rhetoric, which also concerned the administration of PEMEX and oil in its role as national patrimony, the private sector became increasingly involved in the oil industry. Multiple service contracts were allowed in the hydrocarbons sector, which in the strict sense of the constitution were illegal. Especially in the sectors of the liquefied natural gas industry and the distillate of hydrocarbons, PEMEX lost several territories for extraction (Breglia 2013: 219).

During the presidency of Felipe Calderón (2006–12), this trend not only continued but intensified, and multiple contracts became possible to an extent that PEMEX granted private companies the entire network of oil pipelines and pipelines in the southern region through a service contract.

Calderón was working toward an energy reform that also included the administration of PEMEX. He attempted to privatize electricity and made an effort to change the constitution accordingly. After a dispute with the PRI and discussions in congress, a modified PAN energy reform bill was passed that maintained the national ownership of oil and PEMEX's status as a state-owned company but included other amendments concerning PEMEX's autonomy. Mexico's oil sector was still maintained as the de jure national patrimony while at the same time de facto participation of the private sector was expedited (Breglia 2013: 225; Cárdenas García 2009: 55). A continuing decrease of the oil production in Mexico during the 2010s had a substantial impact on the urban as well as the rural areas of Papantla and Poza Rica. Also, the supremacy of PEMEX was seriously threatened when it became increasingly obvious that the state firm had become unable to compete on an international level (O'Connor and Viscidi 2015: 3; Sánchez Campos 2016: 307). The decreasing oil production affected the city of Poza Rica as the "oil capital" and the adjoining rural area heavily. The job market decreased, poverty, delinquency, and the influence of the organized crime increased (see de la Fuente et al. 2016: 64; Hernández Ibarzábal 2017: 367–69).

The Energy Reform 2013–14

Mexico was still classified as the fourth largest oil producer in the world, but recent developments in oil policy greatly impacted the hydrocarbon sector. In 2014, Mexico's position as an oil producer had already fallen to tenth place when crude oil production was at its lowest point since 1986. Mexico's oil production then continued to decline, and exports were decreasing. In other words, the oil bonanza came to an end, and the sector began to withdraw from its position as the main pillar of the national economy (Breglia 2013: 25–26; Sánchez Campos 2016: 292; Viscidi and Fargo 2015: 6). As a result, the hydrocarbons industry in Mexico was finally considered to be capable of competing, a result of which PEMEX was ultimately dethroned as a symbol of the national oil bonanza (Gómez 2015: 7; O'Connor and Viscidi 2015: 3). However, to this day the state company continues to hold an emblematic position within Mexican nationalism and is often still regarded as an image of national wealth in the days of economic prosperity (Monreal Ávila 2008: 69; Suárez Ávila 2017: 8).

In order to take advantage of international demand and to revive the national economy, in his campaign for the 2012 elections, current president Enrique Peña Nieto (2012–18) announced a reformist agenda that intended to improve Mexico's competitiveness. It included a reform of the energy sector, again aiming at privatizing the oil sector, as attempted by several of his precursors. This reform consists of the modification of the Articles 25, 27, and 28 of the Constitution of the United Mexican States, the creation of new laws and a modification of twelve existing ones. It was approved on 20 December 2013, which inter alia included the following key elements: The hydrocarbon resources of the subsoil in the country remain in state ownership, but private companies can appropriate the resources at the time they are extracted and reserve them for accounting purposes. Four new types of contracts were created to involve private companies, including contracts to obtain ownership of the resources after the payment of taxes. In addition to changing the legal status of PEMEX to a "state productive enterprise," an autonomous budget was facilitated and a board of directors, excluding representatives of the unions was installed. This new figure seeks the provision of greater technical and operational autonomy but changes the budget regulations of the company. In addition, the Agencia de Seguridad, Energía e Ambiente (ASEA) was created through the new Law on the National Agency for Industrial Safety and Environmental Protection of the Hydrocarbons Sector. This body acts independently of the Secretaría de Medio Ambiente y Recursos Naturales (SERMANAT), responsible for the regulation and supervision of oil and gas activity in environmental matters, industrial and operational safety (de la Fuente et al. 2016: 9; Seelke et al. 2015: 3).

Through the reform, hydrocarbon exploration and extraction activities are declared social interest and public order, which means that the activities will have "preference over any other activity that involves the use of the surface or subsoil of the lands"[4] (Nueva Ley de Hidrocarburos 2014, Articulo 96). Through them, priority is given to activities related to the extraction of hydrocarbons. In theory, this regulation prohibits the expropriation of rural communities by companies. However, a constitution of a legal tenure of lands under which the respective hydrocarbon source is found can be promoted through a federal executive. This applies in cases of lacking an agreement between assignees or contractors and the owners of the land or property, including ejidos or communal rights. The figure of legal servitude existed before the reform within the Federal Civil Code, but with the reform, its application is allowed for a wider range of types of works and greater territorial occupation (Vidal Cano 2016: 4).

However, Article 118 of the Hydrocarbons Law establishes the guarantee of the principles of "sustainability and respect for human rights of the communities and people in the [affected] regions"[5] (Nueva Ley de Hidrocarburos 2014, Articulo 118). This regulation represents the tendency of the legal reform to prioritize the business interests, where criticism is mainly directed at the insufficient implementation of mechanisms of participation of the population. The implementation of "social impact studies" and "social impact assessments" have been criticized as insufficient at first due to the lack of a specific format, which allowed for companies to carry them out as they best saw fit. They therefore have been developed further in cooperation with Mexican universities (García-Chiang 2018: 5). Yet they continue to be criticized by scholars and the media for lacking considerations of sociocultural implications, as well as a limited participation mechanism for the public and indigenous stakeholders (see Huesca-Pérez et al. 2018: 488; de Montmollin 2018). Prior to granting contracts, the Secretaría de Energía (SENER) together with the Ministry of the Interior must carry out a social impact study. The study is presented to companies interested in conducting an exploration or extraction project. Afterward, companies must carry out a social impact assessment and submit it to the SENER, which issues a resolution and gives recommendations. To conclude the process, the SENER resolution must be presented to the ASEA (de la Fuente et al. 2016: 65). These studies do not foresee the participation of the population, nor their information on the measures. In this regard, the absence of an efficient mechanism for the implementation of prior consultation according to the right to free and informed consent is mentioned in accordance with the provisions of convention 169 of the International Labor Organization (ILO) signed by Mexico in 1990. Since then, the legal implementation of prior consultation has been debated and could not be solved (de la Fuente et al. 2016: 68–67; Viscidi and Fargo 2015: 6)

A further source of uncertainty is the promotion of an intensified exploration of unconventional oil and gas sources via fracking. Former explorations of unconventional gas in Mexico have been conducted since 2001 and hydraulic fracking has been implemented to a limited extent since 2003 (Silva Ontiveros et al. 2018: 482). The major concern is an expansion of fracking through the government auctioning unconventional gas sources to the private sector, which is allowed by the energy reform (Castro Alvarez et al. 2018: 2; Hernández Ibarzábal 2017: 364). The uncertain situation of the extent to which fracking is already taking place and the future prospect of its increasing implementation has initiated an oppositional social movement joined loosely under the organization Alianza Mexicana Contra el Fracking (AMCF). The activists organize events and talks in several parts of the country that might be or might become affected by fracking in order to inform the local population and also possibly support them with regard to the articulation of protest (Silva Ontiveros et al. 2018: 482).

Emiliano Zapata is a case of a community located in an area where national NGOs suspected fracking activities have been taking place without being able to access official data confirming the conjecture at first. Even though the energy reform has already been adopted into law since 2014, the first official bidding process for shale gas sources was conducted until 2018. The local communities that might be feel negative effects in terms of health or environment were not consulted by an official process beforehand. Apart from the uncertainty related to possible environmental and social damages that an intensified usage of fracking could imply, there is great uncertainty regarding the exact geographical location of the wells, the technical specifications, and the boundaries of the oilfields. The prospect of communities being affected by fracking activities without being informed how and where these activities are carried out, nor what would be the possible consequences, has caused major concerns within society (de la Fuente et al. 2016: 64; Hernández Ibarzábal 2017: 367–69; Silva Ontiveros et al. 2018: 482).

Sitting on Oil:
Setting and Community Organization in Emiliano Zapata

The example of the community Emiliano Zapata illustrates the described processes in Totonacapan in many ways while, like any locality, it maintains its particularities. Today, most of the rural communities in the municipality of Papantla earn their living from a variety of income-generating activities. The cultivation of corn for auto-consumption is widely practiced but rarely the only livelihood. Most families support themselves through a variety of smaller revenues at the same time. They include part-time wage work, agriculture for auto-consumption, the sale of agricultural produce or handicraft products and small businesses like tailoring or selling everyday items in community stores (Chenaut 2010: 60–61; Valderrama Rouy 2005: 208). Today, in addition to the extraction of hydrocarbons, about 89.8 percent of Papantla's surface area is used for agriculture and livestock, with the main crops being citrus fruits and corn.

The name of the community Emiliano Zapata is at the same time also the name of the ejido, which was demarcated in 1936. It is located twenty-five kilometers to the southeast of the municipality of Papantla in an area known as El Llano.[6] The term derives from *llanura*, which means "plain" or "prairie" and represents a commonly known name for a region in the coastal area of Totonacapan, within the municipality (see Aguilar León 2018: 34; Hoffmann and Velázquez Hernández 1994). It encompasses several communities determined by cattle ranching and citrus fruit production, and social and cultural patterns perceived as campesino rather than indigenous. The area is locally known as stricken by poor infrastructural development and economic disadvantages. As PEMEX is operating in or close to several of the Llano communities, the oil industry and its environ-

Figure 2.1. Papantlas hilly landscape with orange orchards and an oil well, Papantla, Mexico, 2016 © Svenja Schöneich.

mental and economic implications play a role in many of them (see Redacción el Heraldo 2018; Velázquez Hernández 1995: 104). Emiliano Zapata fits this broad description of the Llano area in several aspects. Besides part-time or temporary wage labor in the agricultural or service sector relating mostly to the oil industry, the major income-generating activity in the community is the cultivation of commercial agricultural products. Remittances generated by transnational migration have become an increasingly significant source of income for the community of the Llano in recent years. Economic opportunities for young people are often pictured as difficult, especially in rural areas. The alternatives to agricultural occupations are scarce and many young members of rural communities search for an improvement of their status and income in the nearby towns or bigger cities further away. The increasing violence in the region through the emergence of drug cartels, a rising delinquency, as well as the increasing criminalization of human rights activism play an important role for the perception of hardship and decision for migration (see e.g., Chenaut 2010, 2017; Popke and Torres 2013; Silva Ontiveros et al. 2018).

Emiliano Zapata is located on the San Andrés oilfield (Bloque San Andrés), which is exploited by PEMEX as an Área Contractual (AC). It covers an approximate area of 209 square kilometers within three municipalities in the north of Veracruz: Papantla, Gutiérrez Zamora, and Tecolutla. The San Andrés oilfield was discovered in 1956 and consists of 356 wells, out of which fifty are in operation today. The production peak of the oilfield reached 44,870 bpd in the year 1965 and maintained its productivity for many years until it decreased in the first decade of the twenty-first century, with a new low point of 950 bpd in 2011. This oil area occupies a large part of the municipality of Papantla, and therefore one of the main centers of the Totonacapan region. Forty-six settlements are located within the contractual area of the Bloque San Andrés, accumulating a total population of about 16,600 inhabitants according to the last census of 2010 conducted by the Mexican Instituto Nacional de Estadística y Geografía (INEGI). Ten of these communities are particularly close to extraction installations, Emiliano Zapata being one of them. The total number of inhabitants on the contractual area has been declining continuously since 1995 when 20,073 inhabitants were counted. This demographic development, caused by a composition of several different factors related to neoliberal political trends and the economic decline of the oil sector, reflects a general trend in Totonacapan (Checa-Artasu and Aguilar León 2013: 2; Nejapa García 2018: 9–12; Popke and Torres 2013: 220–21).

The communities located on the Bloque San Andrés rely on a variety of different occupations for the generation of income, but the main source has remained agriculture. This includes *milpa* economy for subsistence, the production of commercial produce such as citrus fruits and corn, cattle farming practiced on ejido as communal landholdings, as well as small-scale farming on independent private land holdings. The resulting "messy patchwork of crops and land tenure systems" (Popke and Torres 2013: 216), which is visible in the composition of the communities within the borders of the San Andrés contractual area, characterizes the contemporary Totonacapan landscape. Social frictions about access and usage rights to land are also mirrored within the conflicts that have emerged about environmental damages caused by the oil industry. Lately, a growing body of literature and studies on environmental conflicts have emerged, which reflects the conflictive situation of local farming communities struggling with the impacts of hydrocarbon extraction (e.g., Aguilar León 2018; Checa-Artasu and Aguilar León 2013; Nejapa García 2018).

While the topic has been known for a longer period of time, the issue has gained popularity—in the whole country and therefore also in Totonacapan—through the implementation of the energy reform and the aligned modifications in national law and extraction practices (Viscidi and Fargo 2015: 6–7; García-Chiang 2018). The issue of fracking has been

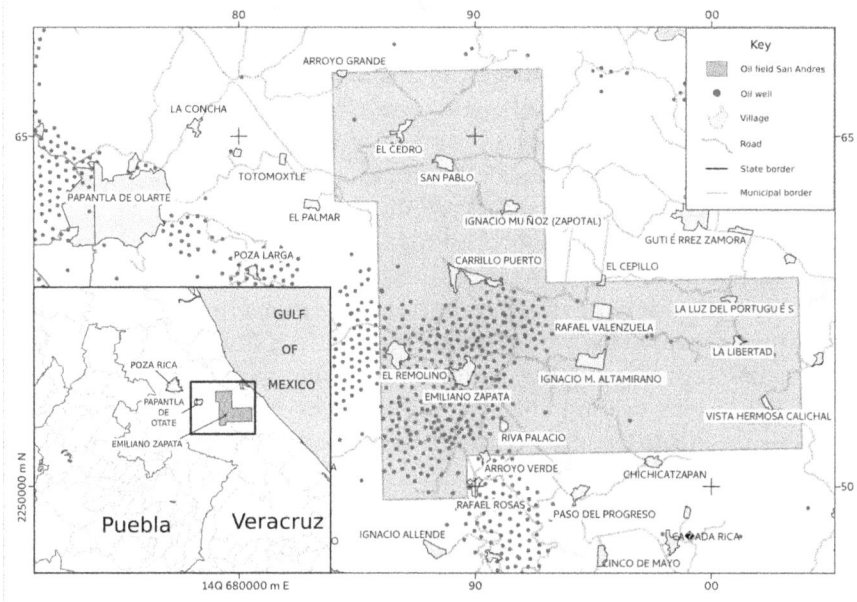

Map 2.2. Contractual area of the San Andrés oilfield with communities located within the area © Orestes de la Rosa, used with permission.

discussed recently as Veracruz is the state with the highest number of operating fracking wells so far. Furthermore, large parts of the state territory are integrated in the bidding rounds for foreign direct investments, who want to operate Mexican oil sources. Where PEMEX already maintains many extraction facilities, new companies are often hired as subcontractors. In 2012, Pemex Exploración y Producción (PEP) launched rounds of bidding for contracts for exploration for the three contractual areas for the first time. The result of this process was the entry of private companies as PEMEX's partner. During the second bidding round on 19 June, PEMEX and twenty-eight other companies participated to obtain integrated contracts for exploration and production of mature fields for the north region of Veracruz and Tamaulipas, among them the Bloque San Andrés. The company Oleorey SA de CV, belonging to Monclova Pirineos Gas was awarded the San Andrés oilfield (García-Chiang 2018: 4–5). The local communities within the oil-rich areas of the state, such as the communities located on the Bloque San Andrés, are therefore affected by the regulations of the energy reform in several different ways and hence largely concerned about its future implications (Chenaut 2017; Cruz 2018; SENER 2015).

Administration, Social Structure, and Local Politics

Emiliano Zapata holds the status of an ejido with areas for human settlement, which entails the implementation of certain political institutions accountable to the municipal or state government, like the establishment of an agencia municipal and a comisariado ejidal. These two governing bodies are compulsory by law, as are their composition and term period for the respective incumbents. The total surface of the ejido territory is about 662 hectares,[7] from which 11 percent is endowed as *asentamiento humano*, which can only be utilized for human settlement. Approximately 7 percent are occupied by infrastructure like roads, a storage tank, and three small rivers, representing the community's water supply. Of the ejido territory, 192.37 hectares are currently officially expropriated for extraction purposes by PEMEX reducing the surface disposable for the community members to 469.62 hectares.

The community has a system of public education from kindergarten to high school, where students can obtain a university entrance degree. Several different forms of businesses are present in Emiliano Zapata, such as grocery stores, small pharmacies, mechanical workshops and a car wash, a hairdresser, gas stations, stationers, and three internet cafés. Furthermore, several small family businesses provide street foods and snacks, or sell bread around the clock. The lack of a potable water system and the deplorable condition of many roads is perceived as one of the biggest shortcomings, and the community members have attempted several times to receive financial support for the construction of both. So far, they have not been successful. Even though a garbage collection system exists, transporting the garbage to the closest official dump via truck, most of the community members do not regularly use this service since the truck is perceived as unreliable and the frequency of the service as insufficient. Therefore, the majority of the households continue to burn most their garbage themselves.

Emiliano Zapata is equipped with a rather well-developed economic infrastructure compared to other communities of the same size in the area. Nevertheless, the community is characterized by official means as an agricultural community with a high degree of marginalization (CONAPO 2006). Similar to many marginalized communities, Emiliano Zapata receives support from several different government programs. One of them is PROSPERA,[8] which currently includes about 250 families in the community and supports many rural localities in the area. A community kitchen constructed as a joint program with support from the Ministry of Social development's Secretaría del Desarrollo Social (SEDESOL)[9] and PEMEX. The government keeps providing aliments on a regular basis, while volunteering community members—only women—prepare breakfast and lunch in shifts for only seven pesos a meal. The women who work there do not receive a salary but have access to additional food supplies, they are allowed to take food home for themselves and receive an expense allowance every Christmas. Many of the women are wives or widows of migrants working abroad or in other parts of Mexico to maintain their family through remittances. Many community members seize that service. Furthermore, a community store[10] selling subsidized products for basic needs has been operating in Emiliano Zapata since 1983.

Most households in Emiliano Zapata depend at least partly on income from agriculture. Despite the commercialization of products, the profit from small-scale farming is considered to be rather low in comparison to wage labor activities. The most important crops are citrus fruits, banana leaves, and corn, while some farmers also maintain small numbers of cattle. Another important source of income for many is day labor employment as farm hands, who earn about 120 pesos working from seven o'clock in the morning until two o'clock in the afternoon. During harvest season, farm hands are required by most farmers. Most male community members permanently living in the community engage in the cultivation of crops, even if the majority does not hold the ejidatario title. To obtain plots for cultivation, they have to negotiate the distribution of land parcels with the comisariado ejidal and the ejido council.

As an ejido, the ejidatarios in Emiliano Zapata remain the governing entity of the territory and decide about the distribution of land among themselves and for any other resident. The main governing bodies of the community are therefore the agencia municipal with regard to public responsibilities and political representation, and the comisariado ejidal regarding all issues concerning the government of the ejido territory. Moreover, different committees exist, which are responsible for certain public tasks. Those committees are part of the governmental bodies of all communities in the wider area, but their exact organization and structure differs locally according to the needs and preferences of every community. All local political entities comprise a president, a secretary, and a treasurer and are elected by the group of people they represent within the community. In the following, the individual local political entities will be listed and briefly introduced.

Agencia Municipal

The community is headed by the agencia municipal, which is accountable to the council of the municipality, in this case, the city of Papantla.[11] The agencia is constituted by a president, a secretary and a treasurer, and three respective deputies, accompanied by a surveillance committee (*comité de vigilancia*), which monitors all activities of the incumbents. The agencia is elected every three years by all community member over the age of eighteen. The agente municipal summons general assemblies every month, which require the attendance of at least one member of every household of the community. All public issues are discussed in the assemblies, where all important public political decisions are taken by vote. The agencia also organizes the community service (*faenas*) that all adult community members are expected to serve on a regular basis. The service usually involves cleaning and maintenance of public buildings and areas within the community.[12] If a compulsive assembly or the community service is not attended, the respective individual must pay a fine.

Comisariado Ejidal

The comisariado ejidal represents all ejidatarios and administers the communal land in terms set by the assembly of all members. It distributes and administers all of the territory within the ejido endowed as communal. The comisariado is also monitored by a surveillance council to hinder corruption. The comisariado convenes the ejido council consisting of all ejidatarios, has the responsibility to conduct the agreements taken within the assembly, and is elected by its members every three years. In Emiliano Zapata, there are only fifty-eight ejidatarios in total, while sixteen of them are currently in the process of approval after inheriting the title from their predecessor. The governmental agency corresponding to the comisariado ejidal is the Registro Agrario Nacional (RAN), where the ejidatarios must file and administer their titles and all political decisions regarding the ejido lands.[13]

Table 2.1. Community committees as institutional entities in Emiliano Zapata © Svenja Schöneich.

Name of the committee	Tasks	Representing	Notes
Comité de junta de mejoras	Organizes the maintenance of public places and the construction of buildings and infrastructure for the public good	All community members	Re-election every three years aligning with the agente municipal

Comité del agua	Organizes the distribution of water via a pump from one of the streams, which is the main water source for the community	All community members	
Comité de la casa de salud	Organizes working shifts for a nurse who regularly comes to the community to care for patients within the "casa de salud," administer the distribution of medicaments	All community members	Every representative has a vice representative
Comité de la ambulancia	Organizes the maintenance of the ambulance and its operations in case of emergency	All community members	Sometimes facilitates the ambulance to neighboring communities in need
Comité de la primaria	Intermediation between teachers and parents, representing the interests of parents before the school directory	All parents who have children attending primary school	
Comité de la preparatoria	Intermediation between teachers and parents, representing the interests of parents before the school directory	All parents who have children attending secondary school	
Comité del telebachillerato	Intermediation between teachers and parents, representing the interests of parents before the school directory	All parents who have children attending telebachillerato	

Comité del comedor	Organizes the groups of chefs, administers the salaries and supplies for the community kitchen	All women participating as chefs	
Comité rural de abasto	Organizes the supply of the community store	All community members	
Comité de la iglesia católica	Organizes the masses, administers the collections for certain religious events	All individuals of Catholic faith within the community	
Comité de fiestas patronales	Organizes festivities within the community	All community members	
Comité del drenaje	Organizes the drainage of the sanitation facilities since the community lacks a sewage system	All community members	Campaigns for the installment of a sewage system

Conclusion: A Community Built on, with, and around Oil

Among the states with a high conflict potential is Veracruz, a state rich with oil, which has been one of the main sites for hydrocarbon extraction since the beginning of the industry in the country. The region around the city of Papantla was already explored with the purpose of oil extraction since the 1860s (Brown 1993: 11). The city of Poza Rica de Hidalgo, founded initially as an oil camp in 1932 and as a city in 1951, has been a strategic center of Mexico's petroleum industry until today. It looks at a differentiated local identity deeply interwoven with oil and PEMEX (see del Palacio Langer 2016; Olvera Ribera 1989; Quintal Avilés 1994). This long and intensive history of oil and gas extraction has affected in a variety of ways the indigenous and peasant communities in the area of the field research for this study (Chenaut 2010: 60).

The history of Mexico's oil is inseparable from the history of the Mexican Revolution and its aftermath upon which the political history of the nation reflects and has been constructed. Within the process of the nationalization of natural resources after the Revolution, the state-owned company PEMEX was founded, which held a monopoly of extraction and processing of hydrocarbon products for seventy-six years. The company therefore plays an emblematic role within Mexican nationalism. It was and mostly still is the determining authority for everything related to oil in the country, but also an important factor for regional development wherever PEMEX did business. In the beginning of the 2000s, Mexico's oil bonanza decreased significantly. Mexico is considered to have passed peak oil in 2004, which first went unnoticed, because of the oil price rising at the same time (Ferrari 2014: 27; Fry and Delgado 2018: 11), yet the decline became palpable in a decrease of oil revenues from 3.8 million barrels per day to 2.5 million barrels in 2013. Mexico's hydrocarbon industry had finally proven to not be able to compete on an international level anymore (Gómez 2015: 7). As a counter measure, the oil industry was thought to be revived through political reforms, first and foremost through the amendment of three articles in the constitution, known as the Mexican energy reform 2013–14. The reform opens the hydrocarbon sector to private investment and thus ended the seventy-six-year monopoly of PEMEX, changing the perspectives for PEMEX employees and oil workers, but also for related sectors and local residents who had dealt with a single responsible entity until this point. Furthermore, the reform included the implementation of new technologies such as fracking to revive the national economy (Seelke et al. 2015: 3; Viscidi and Fargo 2015: 6). The work at hand takes place at a point in time where the reform was being implemented, and the uncertainties about the economic and environmental consequences were topic of a lively national and international debate.

The historical overview at the national, regional, and local level has shown that the history of oil in Mexico is inextricably linked to the situation in Emiliano Zapata. Oil extraction impacts local and regional infrastructure, land tenure and distribution, and social dynamics. Zooming into the region, it becomes clear how the composition of the community reflects its sociodemographic development in connection with the oil industry. As part of the overall affected coastal region of Veracruz, Emiliano Zapata is a representative example of the transformation into an oilscape, where the different nuances of everyday life have been determined in one way or the other by the presence of oil and its extraction. As the following analysis along the lines of temporalities, materialities, and social dynamics in the community will show, viewing Emiliano Zapata as an oilscape contributes to the understanding of the various uncertainties that arise in from a time bomb.

Notes

Epigraph: Breglia (2013: 5).

1. "Pobreza: Una persona se encuentra en situación de pobreza cuando tiene al menos una carencia social (en los seis indicadores de rezago educativo, acceso a servicios de salud, acceso a la seguridad social, calidad y espacios de la vivienda, servicios básicos en la vivienda y acceso a la alimentación) y su ingreso es insuficiente para adquirir los bienes y servicios que requiere para satisfacer sus necesidades alimentarias y no alimentarias" (SEFIPLAN 2016: 10).
2. The traditional economic basis for most Totonac communities was the practice of the *milpa* system. This form of small-scale farming has existed since precolonial times and represents a form of subsistence economy that guarantees a relatively high diversity of crops cultivated through slash-and-burn agriculture. Its basis comprises corn, beans, and chilies, which are cultivated in polyculture following a certain crop rotation system, which includes further types of edible plants. This agricultural system is practiced until today by several rural Mexican communities. The *milpa* includes communal control of natural resources and the reciprocal work of the whole community. Slash, burn, and sow in work groups formed by several community members through mutual assistance. This support system goes beyond agriculture and influences many other aspects of social life, which is linked to the local mythology and the festivities of the seasons that are generated by the circle agricultural activities, such as sowing and harvesting, as well as local ecological knowledge (Gónzalez Jácome 2007: 173; Govers 2006: 199).
3. The term campesino in Mexico and most of Latin America is laden with a certain ideological implication that exceeds the denotation "farmer." Today's notion of campesino has its roots in the aftermath of the Mexican Revolution, when the entire rural population of Mexico was included in the juridical category of campesino. With this term, the revolutionary elite created a homogenous clientele group with the purpose of denominating the criterion of land ownership in the postrevolutionary order. Before 1910, the term campesino was mainly used in the sense of a small proprietor. At that time, this property category, which shaped many political structures in the country, disappeared. The campesino became a common term for the landless population of the countryside, which is hardly reflected upon even by agrarian historiography until today. The right to own land in Mexico used to be attached to the conditions of its effective use, according to which the land belonged to the one who was working it and the category of the ejdio—a form of communal landownership granted for agricultural purposes for communities of campesinos emerged. The concept of the campesino differs from the concept of indigenous peoples because it does not include an indigenous identity but rather refers to a certain attachment to their farmland, even though several of the landless peasants after the Revolution were indigenous people. Over time, the campesino became an important figure in agricultural policy and social science. It represented a class of small-scale farmers struggling against unequal and

unfair land distribution in favor of the big landowners, politically favored during a long episode of agricultural politics in Mexico and other Latin American countries (Schmidt 2001: 537–38).
4. "preferencia sobre cualquier otra que implique el aprovechamiento de la superficie o del subsuelo de los terrenos afectos" (Nueva Ley de Hidrocarburos 2014, Articulo 96).
5. "sostenibilidad y de respeto de los derechos humanos de las comunidades y pueblos de las regiones" (Nueva Ley de Hidrocarburos 2014, Articulo 118).
6. The name Llano appears to be a locally known term, which largely corresponds to the regional concept of the "Llanura Costera" (see Hoffmann and Velázquez Hernández 1994).
7. An official report from 2012 published by the federal government defines the total surface of the ejido with 604.91 hectares, which would contradict the official endowment numbers (338 hectares in 1936 and additional 324 hectares in 1944 summing up to a total of 662 hectares) (Secretaria de la Reforma Agraria [SRA] Cuaderno de Alternativas de Desarrollo y Retos del Núcleo Agrario "Emiliano Zapata," Papantla de Olarte, Veracruz, Marzo 2012). It is possible but not ensured that the missing approximately 57 hectares have been excluded from the count as settlement area of the San Andrés colony, which appears as an individual locality in the INEGI census in 2005 and 2010, despite its administrative affiliation to Emiliano Zapata. The sometimes-contradicting numbers from different official sources reflect the discordance in questions regarding land ownership and management, which is very prominent in Emiliano Zapata.
8. PROSEPRA is a conditional cash transfer (CCT) program to foster social inclusion. It was launched in 2014 following its predecessors *Solidaridad* (1988–1997), *Oportunidades* (2002–2014) and *Progresa* (1997–2002). The households are elected by an application proxy, based on the survey Encuesta de Características Socioeconómicas y Demográficas de los Hogares (ENCASEH), based on a socioeconomic and demographic household survey answered by one person of the household. Once accepted in the program, the participating families must comply with a set of health- and education-related responsibilities, where they are registered with the authorities from their community in charge of checking the compliance. In the year 2014, more than six million households all over the country were receiving payments from the program (see Dávila Lárraga 2016).
9. In 2018, the Ministry was renamed Secretaría de Bienestar.
10. The community stores are supported by a government-related company providing supply programs (DICONSA, previously CONASUPO), establishing points of sale for products of basic needs for a reduced price.
11. The Mexican states are divided into municipalities, which emerged as administrational entities after the Mexican Revolution. Its citizens elect a "president" (*presidente municipal*) who heads a municipal council (*ayuntamiento*) responsible for all public services. A municipality includes at least one, but usually several, settlements (*localidades*), where the largest is usually the seat of the *ayuntamiento*. Other *localidades* elect representatives who are accountable for

their town or community to the *ayuntamiento*. In Veracruz, they are usually called agencia municipal. The agencia is the political representation of the respective community (see González Minchaca 2011).
12. In case the public area in question falls within the remits of a certain group of people and therefore a specialized committee (for example, the school, where only parents of students are responsible), the corresponding committee organizes the *faenas*.
13. For more information about the legal circumstances and role and tasks of the *comisariado ejidal*, see Barragán (2019).

CHAPTER 3

From Booms, Declines, and Time Bombs
Temporalities of Oil in Emiliano Zapata

> Living in Emiliano Zapata is like living on a time bomb. We can't know if anything's going to happen to us tomorrow and we'll explode. We're exposed to that kind of danger because of the place we live in.
>
> —Doña Isabel

The time bomb metaphor, as expressed by Doña Isabel in this quote, was frequently used by community members of Emiliano Zapata representing their feelings of anxiety and vulnerability. The oil industry has been conducting extraction and to a lesser extent also processing of hydrocarbons in the immediate proximity and on the territory for more than sixty years. It left its traces everywhere in the living environment—a process through which the space of Emiliano Zapata has been converted into an oilscape over time. The particularities about the temporal implications of oil are closely linked to the processes of wealth and growth while anticipating a certain but still not predictable decline interlocked with hopes for a new upswing. The temporal logic and complexity of oil thereby depends on the rhythms of global energy production and influences local circumstances. For localities dealing with the oil industry this implies a widening set of opportunities related to economic growth at first, as it links the upswing to a perpetual knowledge about an approaching end. At the same time, the presence of the oil industry changes the environment over time and exposes the residents and their surroundings to constant health risks. The peaks and declines of oil introduce certain patterns of social change, as it provokes fear of a soon-to-come worsening of economic and social conditions, again linked to change. Hence, they are closely interlinked with time as an analytical dimension (e.g., Cepek 2012; Kaposy 2017;

Weszkalnys 2014, 2016). Because the temporalities of oil are inseparably linked to its material and social outcomes, the temporal dimension of the oilscape is difficult to disentangle.

The temporal process of oil is not to be exclusively understood in the sense of a singular headway, playing out identically in different spaces but instead rather acts as a texture of multiple temporal processes depending on individual parameters of preconditions and settings (see D'Angelo and Pijpers 2018; Watts 2005, 2012). For a comprehensive analysis of the temporalities of oil in Emiliano Zapata, it is therefore necessary to incorporate the diversity of temporal processes of social change and cultural adjustments that play out during the history of the community with oil extraction. The approach of a temporal analysis enables a level of understanding, which goes beyond the assumption of the singular dimension of space in as a valuable analytic entity (e.g., Bear 2016; May and Thrift 2001; Munn 1992).

Due to its interlinkage with hopes and despair in relation to growth followed by a hard-to-predict crisis onset, the temporalities of oil thereby come with an undeniable dimension of uncertainty. For localities connected with oil extraction, it furthermore entails the exposure to the heteronomy of oil as a global commodity (e.g., Behrends, Schlee and Reyna 2011; Coronil 1997). In Emiliano Zapata, uncertainty characterizes the living circumstances beyond the particular moment in time, but nevertheless particularly tangible at the current turning point represented by the changing conditions after the energy reform. The community members face constant challenges for dealing with these uncertainties. In his work on "Disaster Risk Reduction and Climate Change Adaptation," Anthony Oliver-Smith (2013) identifies an important distinction between "coping" and "adaptation" in cases of catastrophes and disasters. He claims that coping mainly refers to the context of novel crises and are developed as short-term reactions to drastic change, adaptation refers to long-term adjustments within knowledge and sociocultural patterns of the affected population (2013: 277). This chapter explores the temporal dimension of the relationship of the community members with uncertainties, booms, declines of oil, which accordingly are met with the development of local coping and adaptation strategies, through which the uncertainties can be faced and partly overcome.

For a better understanding of the chronology, I introduce the following timeline, which is intended to help the reader follow the flow of oil temporalities in Emiliano Zapata. I divided the history of the community since the foundation of the ejido until the current date into phases portrayed above the timeline. They represent the characteristic course of crisis and hardship followed by the preparations for the upswing and then boom of

From Booms, Declines, and Time Bombs | 75

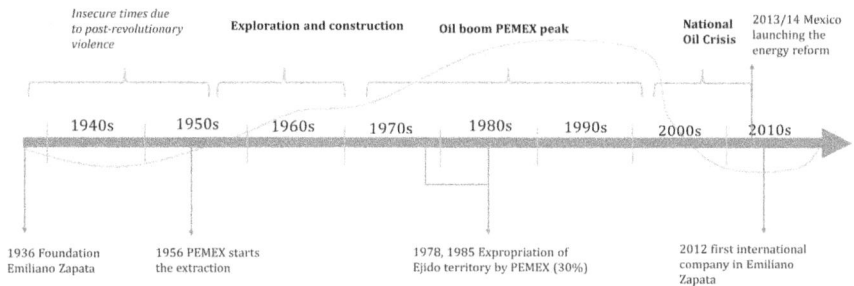

Figure 3.1. The timeline of oil extraction in Emiliano Zapata by Svenja Schöneich.

the oil industry, followed by the decline of the oil industry playing out as local crisis and the subsequent novelties introduced by energy reform. Important events, representing markers for each phase are depicted above.

Starting the Oil Story: The Before and the Beginnings of the Boom

"And here I am at the compound where the big compressor is today. Do you know which one?" Don Ramón pushes another photo in my direction, and I look at it with fascination. Finding old photographs from everyday life situations is very rare in this part of the country, where people did not have their own cameras for domestic use until the 1990s. Apart from rare shots of weddings or baptisms when a photographer was paid, there are hardly any private photographs of the 1970s and 1980s in rural areas. I am sitting in the living room, which also serves as a kitchen in a wooden house at the big family table and Don Ramón unpacked the old paper box where he keeps his treasures.

I have been waiting to see these photos for several weeks now, since he had told me already that he had them but could not find them or was not at home when I came over to see him. His house is in San Andrés, the colony of Emiliano Zapata, which is located very close to the entrance of the extraction site called Pozo San Andrés and therefore takes about twenty-five minutes to walk in the relentless sun from my host family's house.

Don Ramón's wife Doña Geralda appears behind the curtain representing the backdoor of the house. She brings two cups of hot water and puts them on the table together with a can of instant coffee and a big jar of sugar. "Do you want milk in your coffee?" she asks, but responds to her question herself immediately, "You better take some milk, otherwise the coffee will be too hot!" She vanishes again behind another curtain probably looking for a milk carton. Doña Geralda is somehow related to my host family—like almost every person here, as I have learned within the last months. She also introduced me to her husband who worked for the oil company as a day laborer for many years and who told me about the photos I am now here to see.

Don Ramón takes a small spoon from the little plastic basket on the table and puts coffee powder in his cup. I do the same and both of us start stirring while we are looking at the photos lying on the table. They always show Don Ramón himself in the 1970s and 1980s in different poses, such as standing in a freshly dug gutter where he and two other men are letting in a pipeline, on the back of a truck laden with rocks or in front of different types of heavy machinery. "I liked working in construction! My father already did the same, and he always took me with him, following the oil company wherever they would go. They would always want a new road, or a new pipeline and it was easy to find work," he said and fishes another photo out of the box, showing him on a yellow cargo bike with two plastic food containers on each side going up the road. "Look, here I'm selling lunch to the *ingenieros*[1] at the compressors. This was when I had already settled down here. They were always very kind to me, they let me come to the compound even though technically nobody except company staff was allowed in." A boyish smile appears on his face when he adds: "and sometimes they even invited me when they were having some beers up there."

"But you never wanted to be one of them?" I ask taking the last photograph of him on the bike. He laughs while looking for more photos in the box but does not seem to bother to answer. "I mean, did you ever want the company to hire you as a proper oil worker?" I insist. "Technically you have been working for them for a long time, right? Always in the form of constructing something but only on those short contracts."

He looks at me with skepticism. "No, of course not. They do not hire someone like me. I didn't go to one of those schools, and in my family, we aren't oil workers—we are laborers." With that, everything seems said.

Don Ramón, like many others who came to Emiliano Zapata during the oil boom. His family were landless peasants and the oil company-provided opportunities to make a living for untrained laborers. Many people came here during the boom years, settling close to the extraction site, earning their living with hard labor. Some founded a new family with daughters of the resident peasants, like Don Ramón. The community changed a lot during these years. "And maybe your son?" I revisit the topic. "Like, one day, maybe, he could go to one of their schools and become a proper employee."

"Maybe," he says, but but it sounds rather dismissive.

The First Settlers: Building a Community

What constitutes the community of Emiliano Zapata today emerged at the beginning of the twenty-first century from a loose settlement of farm workers and their families on the haciendas that held the property of the land in pre-revolutionary times. There is not much known about the exact numbers of inhabitants or the living conditions of this settlement because the landlords did not keep track of that kind of census data, or if they did, the documents are not available anymore. It is certain though that when the ejido was founded by a couple of Totonac families, who had been laborers on the San Andrés hacienda before, the community was rather isolated from the urban centers and relied on subsistence economy. Many of the laborers came to the hacienda looking for work and a place to stay in times of insecure property structures of land for indigenous people and the therefore shifting demographic pattern of contemporary Totonacapan. Considering the loose structure of the settlement, the low population density, and the long distance between the homesteads as was common in the area (see Kourí 2004: 48–49; Valderrama Rouy 2005: 198–99), it is very likely that a rather undefined identity existed with vague social strings to form a community. The settlers were mostly dependent on the good will of the landowners, but they were also protected by them to some extent when they stayed on their territory.

The dwellers had certain independence concerning the practice of subsistence agriculture, but they were prohibited to own their own land. On the other hand, they benefited from the cultivations set by the *hacenderos* and had access to basic goods that would otherwise have been only accessible on the market in one of the larger cities, difficult to reach. Some people from the older generation of inhabitants still remember vaguely how life was before PEMEX entered the community, and they shared with me the stories of their parents who lived on the hacienda territories.

Don Emilio is an elderly inhabitant in his eighties who was brought up in Emiliano Zapata. He recalls the stories his father and uncle told him about the life before the foundation of the ejido. At that time, most of the Totonac settlers practiced subsistence *milpa* economy, but the *hacenderos* sometimes offered goods to them they could not produce themselves.

"In those years the landowners installed a little shop. Back then we were poor, and only a handful of people. In the shop you would buy, salt or whatever you wanted to buy . . . and the landowner would give you credit." In these stores mentioned by Don Emilio, basic provisions were exchanged for vanilla during harvest season. If the quantity of vanilla vines did not match the price for the goods, the settlers came into conflict with the landowner. However, due to the clear hierarchical structure on the hacienda, the intervention possibilities of the farm workers were quite limited. When the hacienda territory was partly expropriated in the aftermath of the Revolution in the year 1936, the ejido was founded by thirty-three heads of households and their families and named Emiliano Zapata, after the famous revolutionary hero. During its foundation the ejidatarios who managed the settlement and usage of the territory established a political organization, and for the first time, the community was governed independently by its inhabitants.

The violence of postrevolutionary Mexico during the 1930s and 1940s also shook Emiliano Zapata (see Santoyo Torres 2009). The community remained rather isolated from other communities and towns in the area except for a primary school founded in the community in 1938 where teachers were sent to from Papantla. A few years after the ejido was granted an extension in the mid-1940s, conflicts with a band of armed bandits arose as usual during the postrevolutionary years and caused further imbalances of power. The violent actions of robbery in which community members were killed, aroused fears causing many inhabitants to escape to neighboring communities. The school closed for several years until 1952 since the teachers, who were employed by the government, refused to travel to the community.

The situation became so critical that finally the military had to intervene and bring the region back under state control by the end of the 1940s. After the troops left, the area was again open to armed civilians or ex-revolutionary fighters who had brought parts of the rural areas of Totonacapan under their de facto control. Most of today's inhabitants have family members who had to flee and relocate during this period. The community's original structure was set during those turbulent times. The ejido had been founded only a few years ago and now the social circumstances of the area were shaped by insecurity, fear, and danger. People were living on what they could gain from their subsistence agriculture and often tried to cultivate some vanilla. As the plant was expensive and highly in demand for consumption and export in the city centers, the peasants were unable to protect their cultivations properly and a lot of vanilla was stolen by armed gangs who killed people for their yield. Selling crops on the market was also a risky endeavor.

The roads to the closest market or Santa Rosa were in a bad shape, people had to walk, carrying their goods themselves or with donkeys without any protection against possible assaults on their way. To get to Papantla, where they would get good prices on their products, especially vanilla, the people of Emiliano Zapata had to cross the river Remolino in small boats called *pangas,* which complicated the journey even more. Consequently, administrative and commercial ties to the capital and other communities minimized during those years. People then avoided going to the city if they did not have to and many farmers decided not to engage in the cultivation of vanilla anymore. Most community members lived from subsistence agriculture, producing everything they needed themselves. Therefore, despite the described risks, some of the community members describe these bygone times as an ancient era, with a nostalgia of "simpler times" and a romantic transfiguration of the past. They associate it with times when people still spoke the indigenous language and followed the traditional way of life in addition to being independent and leading a simpler but honest life in undisturbed nature, which offered them what they needed to survive. Among them was Don Clemente, an elderly community member, who remembered the old times when he was a child: "Back then, our lands were clean. There was no pollution, and we gathered our food from the surroundings. There were plenty of animals to hunt and in the creek, there was plenty, plenty of shrimp and macaw . . ."

Yet the majority of the inhabitants who lived during that time also paint a disturbing picture of unpredictable hazards and fear, underlined with the horrors of a forgotten age when people used to kill each other without reason. They describe their memories, picturing feelings of exposure and vulnerability, and the arbitrariness and unpredictability of violent acts linking the brute force to the imagination of uncivilized and "wild" natives. Don Lorenzo, another member of the older community, analyzes the violent commotions of the past, which caused his parents like many others to flee the place, in the following way: "In those times our indigenous race was not reasonable. There was only a tiny excuse necessary to get angry and the situation escalate, and, in those times, everyone was carrying machetes." The narrative of postrevolutionary times is thereby stipulated into a fierce, raw age, where state authority was absent, and people had to fear violence, hunger and displacement. This period, in spite of its sparks of romanticized imaginaries of pureness and autochthony, can be considered a time of hardship and even a crisis in terms of social and economic stability. It was a time of insecurity and uncertainties for the population of the entire region and the newly established community of Emiliano Zapata.

When the Oil Boom hit Emiliano Zapata: The Entrance of PEMEX

The commotions of the 1940s had hardly calmed down when PEMEX entered the scene for the first time in the mid-1950s. The company found oil in a situation of economic and political instability in a community governed by indigenous peasants, without any former experience with any kind of industry or extraction. Apart from the exposure of risk due to carelessness in questions of safety and transparency by PEMEX, the inhabitants of Emiliano Zapata found themselves in a situation of powerlessness. They had very limited tools to claim their rights to property or their preferences regarding the performance of the exploration activities. Many of today's residents repeatedly call their ancestors or the ejidatarios in that time "ignorant" and poorly organized in comparison of today. Low education levels and the restricted possibilities of contestation induced a situation where the company could simply behave as it pleased without provoking serious objections. While the community members did not know about the legal framework the company should have obeyed at first, they later came to know that the company should have consulted the farmers before entering their fields and orchards. Yet, the company staff often ignored the lawful procedure.

Despite the dismissal by which the PEMEX staff claimed the territory, many people nevertheless saw how they could personally benefit from the arrival of the new powerful entity. Soon after discovering oil, the company started to build streets and bridges and secured them against robbing bands. A military sentry was built on ejido territory where soldiers could be stationed to protect the PEMEX staff and cargoes. For the community members that meant increased security, even though their own struggle with insecurity had not been the primary reason for stabilizing the region. Now they were able to use the roads and especially appreciated that the new highway and the bridge to the city centers meant they could travel without fearing for their goods or lives.

Some families, who fled the community in times of turbulence, returned to their homes to claim their rights as ejidatarios or status as rightful community members. Not all original settlers came back to Emiliano Zapata, but instead, people from other communities came looking for a place to stay. Those migrants had not been granted the title as ejidatarios, but since there was enough land in the ejido, they were allocated several plots to build new homes. Sometimes they bought the land, often in an informal way even though the land endowed as an ejido was not to be sold. Some of them settled on plots not designated for human settlement or used areas for cultivation that had been initially reserved for communal use. After the endowment of the ejido, many people had moved their homesteads to the area designated for human settlement at first. Yet, since the ejido territory remained loosely populated, in the following years some families preferred to return to their traditional settlement patterns and disseminated again over the lands originally designated for farming only. During those years, a disordered and unregulated situation of land use within the ejido consolidated, which should foster internal conflicts and complications regarding the parcellation of the ejido land later on.

While the occupation of large parts of the ejido territory was perceived as unjust and often problematic for the farmers, many reacted by seizing the opportunity to earn money working for the company instead. During the constructions of wells and installations many younger men, especially the ones without their own parcel of land, took the opportunity to work for the company as part-time laborers. While over eighty years old, Don Hernán still recalls the times he took the working opportunities the company provided when he was a young man, as many other young and able men from the community did. Yet the conditions under which the community members worked differed significantly form the secure long-term employment the staff from the cities enjoyed at that time. The work done by local residents was mainly physically challenging construction-based labor. Don Hernán remembers: "Mostly we went to the wells to lay pipelines and tubes . . . and this machine would come which was this big, and we would hook the material there and *zaz* up it went! Yes, we used to work a lot with that." Furthermore, the young men received only short-term contracts: "They usually hired people for one or two months. And when your contract was over, you would sign another one."

Don Hernán also mentioned the criteria laid down by PEMEX foremen who recruited community members when they started to build a new well, a street, or other kinds of construction work. The company preferred contracting young, strong men who could understand the tasks and instructions and therefore only offered contracts to people who spoke Spanish instead of only Totonac and hardly engaged with the older monolingual generation: "My father only spoke Totonac. Many people here were people *de calzón* in those times. Not now, those times are over. PEMEX only offered work to those who spoke at least a little Spanish." Hence, the younger generation vividly experienced the advantages of the Spanish language. They responded to the requirements of its use when working for the company by only speaking Spanish instead of their native language. In combination with the high respect PEMEX employees enjoyed due to their salary and status in the peasant community, this contributed to the establishment of Spanish as the first language in Emiliano Zapata. The described pattern applied to clothing as well. The community members had usually worn the traditional white cotton clothes of indigenous peasants in the region until then, referred to as *calzón* by Don Hernán

Figure 3.2. Construction workers in the 1970s/farmers in 2018, Papantla, Mexico, 2018 © Svenja Schöneich.

due to their fabric and color. However, the clothing was soon adapted to a more practical and mundane style. The PEMEX staff mostly wore uniforms, provided by the company but also T-shirts, or buttoned shirts and jeans as the fashion in the cities. The younger community members soon adapted this style, first to resemble the reputable PEMEX staff but also because the uniforms, made from thick fabric and did not show dirt like the white traditional clothing, were considered very practical for hard labor. Since the residents could not acquire the uniforms from the company themselves, they bought them from the staff or obtained used clothes. These remain popular until the present day for activities like farming. Don Eusebio, the agente municipal in Emiliano Zapata who collected several documents about the history of his community told me about those social changes initiated by the arrival of PEMEX during an interview: "Well, the customs changed, the way of dressing. New people began to arrive with other ideas, another way of living." He sees most of the changes that the appearance of PEMEX brought during the first boom years in the modification of the customs and points out the visible adaptation in form of the clothing style: "We started to copy them, people started to dress like oil workers because they were given the shirts, pants and shoes. To this day some people here still dress like oil workers."

A Life on Contaminated Soil: The Boom Phasing Out

I see Doña Florentina sitting on her blue plastic chair, while I walk up the road to my host family's house. She sits there every single day, in the shade of a papaya tree doing nothing more than looking at the road, squinting and trying to recognize the people passing by, since her sight is not so clear anymore. When I arrive not more than five meters in front of her, she suddenly opens her squinted eyes. "Güera,"[2] she says loudly and with a bright smile. "Come sit with me for a while, did you already have lunch? It is so hot. I don't like to eat when it's so hot. Come have some Coca-Cola; it's still cold." I do as I am told, as usual.

Since Doña Florentina is the grandmother of Doña Rositas mother-in-law and great-grandmother to the children of the house, everybody in the family got to have a quick chat with her whenever passing by her house. Sometimes we bring food for her and her husband. Many relatives live close by, even though many of their own children have moved away, like so many community members in the last decade. There were eight of them, three are still living in Zapata, four are working in other parts of the country and one son died in a fire caused by an exploding pipeline in the 1960s. She has told me about her son and how he died, but I cannot even imagine the horror of losing a child that way. The boy had gone for an errand when an oil leak up stream ignited and caused a series of explosion. When the boy crossed the bridge, he was caught by an exploding gas line. I take the glass and serve myself some Coke.

"Where did you go today?" Doña Florentina asks. "Did you go to the community kitchen?" I nod and add: "I have been conducting interviews again, you know, asking people about what they know about the oil here in Zapata and about the history with PEMEX and all the accidents that happened then."

"It was horrible," she said, "but at least we have this house now."

"Yeah, that is really good. But didn't you have the house anyway?" I did not understand what the accident might have to do with her living here.

"We had the parcel," she said, "but we only had this little hut made from straw. We did not have any belongings. My husband did not earn any money, and I had the children I had to look after while doing the chores. But after what happened to my son, they gave us a little bit of money, so we could build a house of cement like we have now." I look, puzzled, at the poor-looking hut. It is made from cement and has a ceiling of corrugated sheet like most of the houses of the community. But it only has two small rooms with very sparse furniture and no bathroom, or kitchen inside like the more modern houses of other community members.

"I did not know that you built the house with the compensation that the company gave you," I stated. "What happened back then? Did you go there and ask for the compensation?"

"No, I did not ask, I didn't know anything," she says. "They came and they gave some money to my husband. Then he built the house, but he also went to the bars and some money went away. But what could I do, I had to look after the children."

I am still a bit bewildered. Even if her husband drank some of the money away, should the amount of compensation not have been much higher considering the death of a child? Too much to drink away in a community bar? "It doesn't seem like it was much money," I say.

"No, it was not, but what should we have done, they brought us papers and they gave us some money. But we don't have the documents anymore. They have been under the bed for some time but then who knows what happened. I didn't need them, but I think we should have kept them, maybe they would have given us more if my husband would have insisted."

"But wouldn't it be possible to go there now?" I ask, even though I know that such an endeavor would be unlikely to be successful.

"We don't even have the papers anymore," she replied. "They would ask, 'how much did you get?' and we don't know anymore, and we don't have proof." She takes a sip of her Coke and then changes the subject: "You know, my other son will come visit next month; he promised—you know, the one living in Monterey. He is married to that woman and they have three children, but I don't think he'll bring them . . ." I keep listening to Doña Florentina talking about her family while drinking my Coke and looking at the little cement hut built with money that was supposed to compensate for a dead child, and I shiver a little bit despite the blazing heat this afternoon.

Risky Lives: Incidents and Accidents in Emiliano Zapata

Several smaller accidents like small gas leaks or seepages accompanied the extraction close to the community of Emiliano Zapata since the beginning. It started with minor explosions during the exploration of the oil sources, which made the local inhabitants fear for their lives and their belongings when rocks flew through the air close to their homes. After oil was found the series went on with the usual smaller accidents around the construction sites, but soon culminated in several major gas explosions, two of them causing the death of community members. The first such incident was a pipeline explosion in 1966 right under the rather new settlements, located close to the major extraction site at San Andrés. Those happened in times when the Colonia San Andrés, approx. 1.5 kilometers away from the community center of Zapata was nascent. This part of the territory was originally not meant for settling, but many of the migrants arriving with the oil boom preferred to live close to the extraction site to sell their products or services in direct proximity to their main customers—the oil workers. Therefore, many of them settled down right beside the road where many pipelines pervaded the ground.

The accident of 1966 is known in the community and beyond in the area as the *quemazón*—ten people died and eight where severely injured due to that gas line explosion. Some of the elderly inhabitants of today's San Andrés were present in the colony during the explosion, and if they did not get burned or injured themselves, they lost family members, friends or acquaintances. Doña Rita is one of them. She is over seventy years old and owns a little house where she sometimes sells snacks on a table in her entrance yard. She was born in a neighboring community in the area and came to Emiliano Zapata when she was fourteen years old and pregnant. She earned her living selling lunch to oil workers, waitressing and cleaning in a small restaurant that had just opened. When the fire of 1966 broke out, Doña Rita was in Poza Rica where she also sometimes worked part-time at another job. During an interview she told me about the day of the *quemazòn*: "San Andrés burned down. All my belongings, all that I had saved up, my radio, my clothes, my quilts . . . everything I had stored there because I went to Poza Rica. Everything burned that day." She considers herself lucky to have survived, since she herself was not present when the explosions started. She noticed the fire when a paperboy screamed outside the little lunch restaurant she worked in Poza Rica, causing her to immediately get back home. She remembered: "It was still before opening hours when the newspaper boy outside started shouting: 'San Andrés is on fire, San Andrés is on fire!' And, well, I was shocked! . . . And I started running to get back home immediately!"

When she arrived in San Andrés, she only saw burnt trees and charred ruins of houses. "Everything was burned down! Everything!" she said. "The trees . . . there had been trees there—they had burned down to ashes!" Also, the other residents who survived were in shock. Doña Rita vividly remembered her own terror and the terror of the inhabitants when she saw and heard what had happened to her neighbors and friends in the fire: "It was a cry of despair everywhere . . . I don't even want to remember it . . . When I arrived, there were many people, soldiers, policemen . . . and so many people crying and screaming, it was horrible, just horrible!"

The story of the horrors of the *quemazón* in San Andrés, understandably, is one of the key narratives among the community members in relation to accidents of the oil industry. It represents a crucial moment when the hazard induced by the pipelines and further extraction installations, which are placed within the whole community territory, became visible in a horrific way. The intensity and suddenness of the incident made the community members realize the immediacy of their exposure to potentially deadly accidents that could occur at any time right under their feet.

The inhabitants of San Andrés could not keep their old parcels and were relocated to parcels PEMEX had leased from the ejidatarios further down the highway in an act of victim compensation. The ones who took the offer and stayed, hoped for less exposure to risk due to the new (and expected) less dangerous location. Others left the community to rebuild their lives elsewhere with the company's compensation money. In the old part of the community, a few kilometers away, this danger was perceived but also justified with the illegitimate nature of the settlement of San Andrés. Through the explanation that the people there had settled right on dangerous pipelines without permission, the impression that this could not happen the same way in the community center was held up in the hope of being spared such happenings. A few years later in 1969, the case of the child who died in the explosion in today's community center proved those hopes to be too optimistic. Other accidents occurred over the next few years and the community members entered into a constant state of emergency regarding the accidents. This constant insecurity created a fearful atmosphere in the community during those years.

Another important factor contributing to the perception of uncertainty was undoubtedly the lack of communication with the company at that time. The community members barely knew what was going on under their feet, lacking technical elucidation but also detailed information about the location of the planned pipelines. Another uncertainty factor surely was the seemingly improvised evacuation process. My older informants told me that they were not familiar with security training or fire drills at that time. Most of the houses in Emiliano Zapata were still, at least partly, made from natural materials, such as straw or wood, and far from being safe in case of a fire. The custom of handling open fire for cooking or religious activities[3] increased the risk of becoming a victim of an exploding gas pipeline.

The community members of Emiliano Zapata mentioned a variety of accidents on a regular basis and the stories are well known, even from the inhabitants who migrated to the community later. But apart from the few severe cases where people died in the flames of exploding pipelines causing horror and fear, minor accidents and mishaps became part of everyday life in Emiliano Zapata. With improving extraction technology and safety measures, it was also possible to avoid accidents just as shocking as those in the 1960s, but the gas leaks and the pollution of the streams and lands continued. Emiliano Zapata remains a "contaminated community" where, apart from the damage to the environment and health due to industrial pollution (see Edelstein 2018), the immediate risks of accidents represent a factor for constant uncertainty. Affected communities must find ways of dealing with these circumstances (see e.g., Auyero and Swistun 2008; DeCesare and Auyero 2017; Kirsch 2014).

The Monetary Economy Taking Over

Before PEMEX came to the Gulf coast region, the rural, mostly indigenous communities in the area were mainly living on subsistence agriculture via the *milpa* system and practiced *trueque*[4] to sustain themselves and their families. Only surpluses and rare and expensive products like vanilla, which were sparsely cultivated were sold on the markets, allowing people to purchase the few industrial products available in the region. Those were, for example, soap or sometimes specific materials for housing, clothes, or also for medical purposes. The acquisition of such products was an exception but became the norm very quickly when the oil boom reached Emiliano Zapata.

While the agricultural practices changed with improving infrastructure, the territory occupied by the farming ejidatarios was reduced through the expropriations. The farmland was exposed to risk through pollution of the extraction industry, while selling of products and services rapidly increased with the arrival of the oil workers. Those four aspects can be considered the motor of change toward a mainly monetarily driven local economy. However, when the company entered the ejido territory for the first time, the options for commerce were quite limited for rural inhabitants. Don Umberto, one of the elder ejidatarios, remembered the economic possibility in his youth as almost nonexistent. Even though some community members earned extra money by selling vanilla, for example, there were not many options to spend that money. The shopping conditions were complicated, and the rural markets only offered basic products. "Vanilla was our main income source back then," remembers Don Umberto. "And we almost never spent any money because if you had a peso, two pesos, what are you going to spend it on? There was nothing here to buy." The money could be spent only in stores further away. "If you wanted to go buy groceries, you had to plan it in advance like a week or two." he added. "Salt, soap, oil, and rice. That is what we needed, nothing more."

When the company started the explorations the inhabitants of Emiliano Zapata were unexperienced and had no close relationship to money due to their former living conditions. Therefore, they did not know what they could or should claim as compensation from the company nor how they could enforce their demands. Therefore, many of them accepted the company's offerings without objection. This lack of involvement can surely be explained by the low level of experience with money, but another important factor was the rather weak negotiation skills and bargaining power on the part of the community members at that time. Moreover, the lack of administrative skills is a reoccurring topic during the interviews. Don Juan is one of the first inhabitants of San Andrés. He frequently mentioned the family of one of his former neighbors who fell victim to the fire of the *quemazón* during our interviews. Even when a considerable amount of money was given to the bereaved or the victims of damages, the wealth did not last for long. "This man came home one day—drunk." He starts his story. "There was a leak in one of the pipelines under his house. When he lit a match, everything exploded! His children were burned . . . he had two children, their faced were burnt but they didn't die. The company paid compensation to the man. I think they gave him . . . I don't know about 250 or 300 thousand pesos." The amount of money given to the victims was considered quite substantial at the time. But Don Juan remembers that the money did not last long anyhow: "But this . . . the man well . . . as he drank. He was always going to the bars. He had the money in his backpack, and he spent it all."

This phenomenon described by Don Juan was a common one. Instead of saving the money or investing it in farmland, people became used to receiving compensations on a regular basis and quickly spending the money. This way, the payments hardly contributed to long-term wealth, but rather created a certain dependency, which plays out as a shortcoming now in times of the oil crisis. While Colin Filer (1990) describes lacking an internal redistribution system as the main cause for a failed positive effect of compensation payments, in Emiliano Zapata, the deceptive dependency through a reliance on the oil boom impeded long-term benefit (1990: 12; see also Banks 1996: 225). The negative outcomes of dependencies developed during boom times hitting after crisis is a common phenomenon of the consequences of the temporal rhythm of oil (Willow and Wylie 2014: 225).

Emiliano Zapata rapidly transformed from a remote indigenous settlement dependent on subsistence agriculture to a place with small businesses and wage labor, even though the cash flow was never enough to emerge as a proper boomtown. Yet, the hazards of the extraction left people dead and injured and the soil, air, and water contaminated. The people of Emiliano Zapata rarely partook in any decisions of the oil company and felt extradited to this heteronomous power. The community became dependent on the industry at some point. Thus, when the oil boom started to fade, the local setting changed again according to the course of the temporal processes particular to oil extraction.

What Has Been Left for Us: The Decline

"Güera ven!" Doña Rosita calls from the living room. "Say hi to Don Aurelio!" I close my laptop and open my mosquito net to get up from my bed where I have been typing up today's fieldnotes. The sun has set and the dimmed light in the room has attracted many insects flying around. I open the curtain separating the small bedroom I share with the siblings from the living room and go over to the family gathered around the computer screen. Our house is the only one with a part-time Wi-Fi connection in Emiliano Zapata, since the parcel is located at a strategic location for an antenna and the owner of the local internet café has put such an antenna on the roof in exchange for the provision of a router for the household. Doña Rosita had gladly accepted his offer since she and her children can communicate with her husband via internet now.

I see the pixelated face of Don Aurelio smiling into the camera of his cellphone. I join the four family members to wave into the camera and also start smiling. "Hola Güera! How are you doing?" he asks when he recognizes my face behind the ones of his wife, daughters, and sons.

"I'm fine thank you!" I reply, "How was rice and beans today?" His smile turns into an agonizing grin.

"Boring," he replies, "but at least they give us plenty of food. I heard you had tamales for dinner, I'm very jealous!" Indeed, Doña Rosita had made tamales today and there were many leftovers we will eat over the next few days.

"So yummy!" I exclaim. "Isn't it time for bed yet over there?"

Don Aurelio has been working away from home and family for several years now. He had been to quite a few of the big cities in the country working in industrial construction and maintenance. Most of the time he spent in the city of Monterrey with some of his brothers and cousins from Emiliano Zapata, who all work in the construction of industrial installations. When the work for a company is done and the part-time contracts end, he and the group of friends and relatives move to the next place where they get part-time contracts in construction again. The companies usually pay board and lodging for the workers during the time of the construction while they work hard for nine to twelves hours a day. Their salary is sent home to their families. To find the job offers, they rely on a well-organized network of colleagues and acquaintances they usually know from former jobs and who recommend them to their bosses when they have found an offer. Currently Don Aurelio is in the Dominican Republic—it is his first time working abroad. He does not fancy the food the company provides for its workers this time, and he never misses an opportunity to emphasize how much he craves the food at home. "Well, you could cook some tamales over there, you just have to ask for a big pot and some firewood!" Doña Rosita says mockingly.

"They would never allow an open fire in here! And surely it wouldn't be the same as the tamales from Zapata," he responds.

Doña Rosita smiles contentedly. The last time she has seen her husband in person was four months ago when he came home for two weeks. When he does, he usually brings presents for the children and buys them new shoes or paint for their room. Last time he even brought a cellphone and also the computer screen we are looking at right now is a present from one of his rare visits. As a young man in Emiliano Zapata, he learned to weld, and PEMEX paid good money for short-term contracts for welding pipelines. When the boom subsided, many landless young men remained without their usual source of income and had to look for a place where they could earn money and maintain their families.

"When are you coming back?" I ask, as I always do when talking to him.

And he replies as always: "Soon, I hope! I hope to be there for Christmas. Only God knows!"

"They have to let you go for Christmas don't they?!" the younger daughter interrupts. "We are going to make *pierna al horno*!"

Don Aurelio smiles. "I'm sure they will princess." He surely would rather be home for Christmas but staying longer also means that the company would prolong his contract for a few more months. And being aware of the difficult economic situation he does not know when and where he could start earning money again after that. So, if the company offers him another contract, he will certainly stay and thus ensure another couple of *quincenas*[5] to send home.

After Oil: Dealing with the Downturn

With the fading boom PEMEX reduced its investments into the extraction sites of San Andrés. The activities have never stopped completely but since the late 1980s they have experienced a serious downturn, which worsened in the 1990s. In addition to falling oil prices on the world market, the sinking productivity of the sources also led to a decline in the industry in Emiliano Zapata. Don Eusebio, the agente municipal, as many of the other community members, was aware of the fact that some of the oil wells would get exhausted soon. He assumed that the company would move their activities to other more productive oil regions and supposed that the industry then focused on other more promising regions and abandoned the wells and installations on the San Andrés oilfield. "The oil activity went on to Campeche," he suspects. "Here they're only doing the necessary minimum to maintain some of the wells that already existed." By the time the company began to withdraw from the area, most community members worked partly in the agricultural sector, still vivid in Emiliano Zapata. Strictly relying on wage labor for the company was not common as job opportunities were only stable for a short time. The residents who had access to farmland cultivated crops such as maize or citrus fruits and during the harvest season, helping hands were needed throughout the region. On the territory of Emiliano Zapata itself, the possibilities of living through agriculture decreased over the years.

The lack of income was partly balanced by other work activities, but more and more people relied on regular income through compensation payments from the company if their fields were damaged. By this, people got used to the situation that receiving compensation payments from the company was sometimes more lucrative than selling their own agricultural products. This expectation, but also in part the dependency on the company's payments, intensified with the increase in pollution and with the relatively high costs of citrus production that have to be carried out hiring day laborers and organizing logistics and sales. These circumstances reached a degree to which agricultural production was only second to possible payments from the oil company and some inhabitants began to use it as an income strategy speculating for damages and expecting compensations. Doña Regina, a forty-year-old single mother of two told me about an example for such a strategy: "I have a brother-in-law who has orchards with oranges and lemons, which don't produce fruit anymore. But he doesn't want to sell it, he is even planting more orange trees," she said. "He says that if PEMEX damages them, the more trees are on the parcel, the more they will pay him . . . That is the mentality of the people here today," she alleged. "They're just waiting for PEMEX to come and drill on their parcel to receive compensation money. That's all they want."

When the company partly withdrew from the community, PEMEX also assumed less responsibility regarding compensation or community support. With decreased damages and accidents, the distribution of compensation payments became less frequent. Today many community members regret that the assumed opportunities had not been seized enough. Many of my informants mentioned other oil rich communities who were in better shape than Emiliano Zapata and a vast majority of the community members agreed that the community was in a rather bad situation because of the poor negotiation skills of their own local authorities.[6] Doña Regina sees those strategies of waiting for compensations as a cause for the downturn. She also regrets the lost opportunities through which the local authorities could have seized the situation while the boom still lasted. With respect to the oil boom that passed, she claimed: "There was more movement then, but I feel that people didn't know how to take advantage of the possibilities. Back then they could have asked for a lot more." She is mainly holding the local authorities of the past accountable for the lost opportunities: "They were the one who should have claimed more benefits for the community knowing how PEMEX profited from the oil wealth, but they never did anything." Furthermore, she condemned the lack of ambition of people who, in her opinion, are content with very little when they would have had the chance to claim more.

Soon the time of the boom became part of the collective memory as "good times" of prosperity and economic opportunities in Emiliano Zapata. Until today, many of my informants associate the oil company strongly with possibilities for work. Even though the accidents and damages are remembered as factors for constant anxiety on the one hand, the possibilities the company brought had also changed the economic strategies of the community in a way difficult to reverse for several reasons. First, the community members had become accustomed to the short-term contracts awarded in the industry for construction workers, security guards, or service providers. Many young men had been trained in construction and since the number of inhabitants increased significantly during the boom, when most people found a way of making a living in and around the industry, there were not many other possible professions. This phenomenon is widely known and has been described for other Mexican communities located in oil rich regions at the time as well (see Cancian 1994: 82). In the time of industrial development more and more people—particularly men—started working outside agriculture and a "trucking and construction generation" emerged in the 1970s and early 1980s. With the decline of the industry in their own region many saw no other option than to migrate to industrial centers (1994: 32). Also, people, especially young men, from Emiliano Zapata began to increasingly emigrate in the late 1980s. Nevertheless, this phenomenon in Emiliano Zapata is relatively weak in comparison to other communities of the country where male migration and therefore absence has shaped the local demography to an extreme degree (e.g., Gónzales de la Rocha 1993; Pauli 2000, 2007a, 2007b). In Emiliano Zapata, the presence of men is still guaranteed by many of them working in agriculture as day laborers or in other sectors in the cities.

Because of the proximity of the community to larger cities such as Poza Rica with more employment opportunities and rather well-functioning transport infrastructure, the pressure to migrate may be lower than in other, more remote communities, but it is still palpable.

Being Young in Emiliano Zapata: Generation Gap

While only a few elderly inhabitants of Emiliano Zapata remember the times before PEMEX came, the younger generation grew up in times of the oil boom. The presence of the company and the constant industrial activities around the extraction site accompanied the younger generation of the 1970s and 1980s. They were not yet born when the major deadly accidents happened, but their childhood was determined by economic growth and social patterns adapted by their parents. Now the new generation can also be considered "children of the crisis" who have not warily experienced the first emergence nor the boom times of the oil industry but rather the decline, later during their teenage years. This generation represents a crucial link concerning the awareness of oil temporalities, as it can actively shape the collective perception and molding of the current situation and the future in terms of dependency, reliance, and positioning toward the oil industry.

The generational gap in knowledge, lifestyle, and education in Emiliano Zapata is immense compared to communities in other regions, which reflects the extreme character of changing conditions in the country on a national level. However, the gap between the times of the founding fathers and mothers experiencing the violent aftermath of the Mexican Revolution in a Totonac community and the current situation embedded in a digitized world that demonstrates the global reach of the oil industry is more drastic that in many other national contexts. The infrastructure emerging around the extraction sites and the connection of the community to the rapid industrial development culminated in the current circumstances. An essential aspect of intergenerational differences is the access to the public education system. Today, the younger generation of Emiliano Zapata has the opportunity to attend two secondary schools in their community: the Telesecundaria, which opened in 1987, and the Telebachillerato in 1998. A degree from those schools allows them to apply to universities and colleges across the country, even though rural education standards oftentimes do not meet the requirements of high-ranking public universities.[7] Those possibilities distinguish them from their parents' and even more from their grandparents' generation where higher education was not an option for children of indigenous farmers.

Most parents in Emiliano Zapata appreciate these educational opportunities and encourage their children to study, expecting that this measure will someday improve their social and economic status. Since the parent generation has experienced the oil company's presence throughout its life, it is strongly influenced by the idea that economic wealth is inseparable from the oil industry. In general, PEMEX employees are still perceived as wealthy and have a prestigious status compared to farmers. Therefore, most adults in Emiliano Zapata today hope for their children to become a proper employee of the oil company instead of pursuing a kind of small-scale agriculture associated with low profit and backwardness. Also, many people perceive the work of the oil employees as less wearisome and more rewarding, which guarantees a better income and job security compared to the agricultural sector. Among survey respondents, 60 percent want their children to become employees of an oil company. This shows that the hope of improving the economic and social status of their children is linked to a job in the oil industry.[8] Therefore, it must be distinguished between construction works with short time contracts and other kinds of hard physical labor for low-skilled workers and a prestigious employment at PEMEX.

The *ingenieros* are perceived as wealthy but oftentimes less hard-working than workers or farmers. As trained staff members with permanent contracts they enjoy a number of benefits not granted to untrained workers on temporal contracts. Being part of the Sindicato de Trabajadores Petroleros de la República Mexicana (STPRM), which is particularly powerful in Poza Rica and closely linked to the dominating PRI, they usually have access to the company-provided education and health system, as well as to well-paid lifetime employment and, in some cases, even hereditary employment for their offspring. Local campesinos who work as day laborers for the company are not among the beneficiaries of the STPRM, and although they receive lower wages, they are usually hired to do the "dirty work" (see Quintal Avilés 1986, 1994). Many teenagers therefore also aim for a career in the oil sector with the idea that they will later belong to the *"petrolero* elite." Talking to Gabriel, a seventeen-year-old student of the Telebachillerato, he described the strong affinity of his classmates for a career in an oil company for a variety of reasons. When he told me about his classmates, he alleged: "They want to study petrochemical engineering. Something related to oil." He himself, however, doubted that a career in the oil industry would really bring the intended wealth now that the industry declined. Most of his classmates continue to pursue a career in oil extraction because they assume it would still be easy work with many benefits: "They practically get tricked into thinking that that's a job where you earn a lot of money and do almost nothing," Gabriel said. "They think that if you become an *ingeniero* you will be well paid, and once you retire you will receive a monthly pension, or something like that." Yet, especially since the crisis, that type of employment is hard to get. PEMEX hardly hired new employees during the course of the crisis and many members of the old staff have already lost some social and financial benefits that have been strongly associated with being a *petrolero* for several decades (see Breglia 2012: 34; Stojanovski 2012: 310). The downturn of the oil sector has led to a decrease in employment opportunities. Having received higher education does not necessarily entail better prospects in rural areas in Mexico because of the lack of job opportunities or universities, leaving young people aspiring higher education and better employment circumstances with migration as the only viable option.

For many of the families of the ejidatarios, agriculture is the supporting economic pillar. Also, during the times of the oil boom, most of the ejidatarios and their families dedicated themselves to the cultivation of citrus fruits and maize, while also working for the oil company as short-term laborers. In times of crisis the intensification or return to agricultural activities is the obvious option. But many of the inhabitants do not have access to enough land since they never were ejidatarios and did not arrange the possession of land. They came to work in and around the oil industry and are heavily affected by its decline. Therefore, they cannot bequeath land to the new generation either. Even for those who have land, maintaining agriculture is a hard way to earn one's living in today's Mexico. The smallscale agricultural sector in the country is strongly affected by the Mexican "crisis del campo" (agricultural crisis) that has weakened the national agrarian sector for several years (see Olmedo Carranza 2009). In the case of Emiliano Zapata, other hindering factors like the practice of monoculture requiring expensive fertilizers and the environmental damage left by the extraction add on to the difficulties. Large parts of the territory are not fertile enough for the self-consumption of families who have land, let alone an appealing economic alternative. This lack left many families of Emiliano Zapata in a difficult situation regarding the future of their children and many families who used to find some way to make their living with a whole set of different occupations, now have to look for other opportunities. However, not all residents of Emiliano Zapata solely blame the oil company's withdrawal for the current economic downturn. Other possible reasons mentioned include the low price for citrus fruits, the industrial damages to the soil and water, which complicate farming or the general economic crisis on a national level.

The situation of crisis and an improved system of public education in comparison to the generations before, have caused many students to leave the community after their graduation, to study and/or work in other parts of the country. Also, the less skilled younger people who may not be able to afford a private college or do not seek higher education often migrate at least for a while to one of the more industrialized regions of Mexico, such as Monterrey or Reynosa. For young single women it has become conventional to leave for the more touristic spots in Mexico, such as Cancun, where they take full-time employment as maids in the big hotel complexes of the Rivera Maya. Oftentimes they do not have an individual choice. The pressure for migration to maintain the family has become the most important factor why many of the community members wish for the oil industry to return and revive the extraction activities. Partly those hopes are met due to the restructuring of the oil sector in from of an energy reform, which promises a revival of the oil industry.

After the Monopoly: Oil's Temporalities Continued

"My son will drop you off!" Don Germán insists emphatically.

"Well, thank you very much. It's no problem to walk, it's not that far away." I try to be polite and not to strain the hospitality of my informant too much after the interview we just conducted for almost an hour and a half. But I am honestly glad he offered to organize a ride back to my house. It is already dark, the streetlights are dim, and up the hill where Doña Rosita's house is located, lamps are nonexistent. When the night falls, the street dogs become more aggressive and bark at anyone who passes, and I would feel more comfortable having some company on my way back.

"You shouldn't go alone. Doña Rosita will be angry at me if I let you go alone." He smiles. Don Germán's son Emilio has heard his father calling and comes down the stairs. "You'll drop the Güera off," Don Germán says, and Emilio does not have any objections. He grabs his car keys from a little cupboard by the doors and looks at me. I quickly put my recorder into my bag and give Don Germán a cordial goodbye before we walk to the jeep parking outside the house. It is a nice new car and the sign on the side has "Oleorey" written on it. It is recognizable in the whole community since very few people drive such a car in Emiliano Zapata. It is the only one with an oil company's name on it.

Emilio opens the door for me, we get in, and he starts the car. He slowly drives down the road and turns in at the main road. Emilio does not talk much. His father has asked me twice if I could not teach him some English since he assumes that this is what would get him promoted more easily, but Emilio himself does not show so much enthusiasm in the face of his father's ambitions.

"Thank you so much for driving me," I say to break the silence. "It has gotten dark so fast." He nods and yawns. "Are you tired already?"

"I'm *still* tired," he replies. "I have been working a lot of night shifts. In one hour, I have to get back to work."

"Where is it exactly that you work now?" I want to know. I know he works for Oleorey, one of the newer companies around that started to operate some of the oil extraction facilities in the area. It is rumored that his father got him the job as part of the deal when he was negotiating for compensation money with the firm because some of his cattle died after drinking the polluted water of the river that had been contaminated due to a spill a few months ago. The company did not want to pay at first since it was only the subcontracted entity for operation and referred to PEMEX as the company in charge. PEMEX then did not want to pay anything either because they blamed the operator. In the end, Don Germán stayed persistent and received the compensation with support of other aggrieved parties of the community. His son started his job there a few weeks later.

"I'm working in a processing plant close to Poza Rica," Emilio says.

"And you are living here with your parents?"

"At the moment I do. But I'm currently building my house," he says with pride in his voice. "Have you seen it? I'm building the second floor right now. Tomorrow more workers will come. Then a few months later the windows will be done as well."

I have seen the house under construction close to his father's parcel. It is a nice one. The general custom in Emiliano Zapata would be to move into a new house as soon as it has four standing walls and a roof, even though it remains under construction for much longer, but Emilio seems to have plans to not move in until it is done. One reason for that is that the house of his parents is large enough for him to stay there until his new home is finished. "It looks very nice already," I say appreciatively. "It seems like the company is paying well."

"It's not bad. Only the night shifts are tiring but I shouldn't complain." We already arrived at the big pothole at the foot of the hill where I live which is almost impossible to cross with a car and difficult even with a jeep. More so at night.

"I can jump off here!" I say, so he stops the car. "Thank you very much again! Have a good shift today." I open the car door.

"No problem really. Also, I've slept all day almost. I will be awake soon." He grins.

"Get home safely."

"Will do!" I reply and shut the door. I turn around and take the last ten meters up to our entrance door with long strides. The light inside the house is on, and Doña Rosita already opens the door before I can get to it. "There you are, Gürea! It's dark outside already! Did Germán's son drop you off?"

"He did!" I confirm.

"Well, that's good. Does he want to learn English yet?" Doña Rosita shuts the door behind me after I slip in.

The Fall of the Monopoly: The Beginning of a New Era?

After the decline of the national oil industry, which on the local level was accompanied by a significant withdrawal of PEMEX from Emiliano Zapata, the energy reform was supposed to revive the industrial activities. In fact, new oil companies that had been commissioned to operate the installations but could not acquire them as property yet, already entered a few years before the implementation of the energy reform due to changing regulations of sub-employment. Nevertheless, PEMEX was still the major entity performing the extraction. Recently, new firms started to take over several installations on the San Andrés oilfield and thereby started to reactivate and renovate some of the foremost abandoned infrastructure. The first company conducting activities in the San Andrés oilfield was Oleorey, a Venezuelan firm with an operating contract from PEMEX. Therefore, the main proprietor of the installations on the San Andrés oilfield continues to be PEMEX until the actual takeover of Oleorey, which was planned but not executed yet. Oleorey, therefore, not only takes over the physical installations but already holds certain responsibilities with regard to community relations. Furthermore, Oleorey also subcontracts other smaller firms for special tasks, yet the company still answers to PEMEX in every regard. The process of overtaking oilfields is therefore in process, which can create unclear structures regarding the corresponding tasks of each operating or subcontracted firm.

Don Esteban, a man in his sixties, originally comes from Emiliano Zapata. He is an ejidatario who resumed responsibility in the assembly of ejidatarios, and he is also the head of the water committee. As such he is familiar with local politics and takes an active part in community decisions. He learned about the presence of the new company when company staff members came to the assembly to inform the community members about the new operator. However the new structures and responsibilities of each firm are not always comprehensible to him; they are not comprehensible to most community members. "Well, the one that is in charge here now is Oleorey, but there is another company that is coming to work here, Oleocell, Olliver . . . who knows what they're called. They work for

Oleorey, and Oleorey cooperates with PEMEX, so many different agreements . . ." he told me, sighing. The names, tasks, and responsibilities of the new companies therefore often remain assumptions or hearsay to Don Esteban and other community members. When any problem arises, no one knows whom to contact. Therefore, this transition phase between operating companies often implies a certain degree of confusion in terms of accountability. Many now hope for an improvement of the local economy but are concerned about the agreements, which had been reached with PEMEX and were valid until now, being cancelled under the command of the new company.

Don Alberto is Don Esteban's neighbor and a fellow office holder within the ejido council. His major occupation is the cultivation of maize and oranges, and he has observed several times that PEMEX reimbursed farmers for the loss of crops because of seepages. Now that PEMEX is withdrawing and the new firms take on more responsibilities than the state-owned company did for many years before, he is worried that possible damages might not be compensated in the future, as he and others have gotten used to over the years. When I interviewed him, the company was still reacting to compensation claimed: "Well, yes, in fact one year, two years ago, they were still paying for the damages and answered some of our claims. Until recently they were still paying compensations." Yet Don Alberto worried that this might be the last time that the company would pay anything.

Even if the actual responsibilities of the new firms must become clear in the future, the notable revival of the industry made many of my informants hope for an improvement of the economic situation at the same time. Unfortunately, the hopes have not yet been fulfilled. The new firms mainly brought their own personnel and organized the accommodation and catering themselves, instead of hiring local community members. Furthermore, they did not show the engagement many had hoped for. Don Esteban therefore remains pessimistic despite increasing activities in the oilfield through the new firms. "Well, it got a little better ultimately. But since some time has passed, it's not so easy to get jobs now," he said. "Right now, it's Oleorey who's in charge, but they don't need laborers. They're just maintaining the wells that are already there. There is no employment or work for the people here."

Nevertheless, some of the changes that came with the arrival of the new firms are perceived as positive. Even if the new companies may not offer so many job opportunities, people acknowledge that at least fewer accidents have occurred since they took over. Don Ernesto is a shop owner who was born and raised in Emiliano Zapata. He has witnessed the times of the PEMEX boom, and he saw the company withdraw and the installation wither. The lack of maintenance of the installations has become a risk factor for possible accidents and damages. Now that Oleorey took over, new safety measures are in place and the risk is mitigated. Don Ernesto therefore expressed mixed feelings about the arrival of the new company, while he acknowledged the virtues of better safety measurements: "Since Oleorey started operating, things changed for better. For better because there have been no more deaths, but also for worse because there are no jobs anymore. But they are more careful with the maintenance. It's safer here now."

While the community members welcomed the revival of the extraction activities in Emiliano Zapata in general as a sign of the improving economic situation, they are skeptical of the real benefits for them. Some of their claims have already been complied by the company but most residents believe that they have done too little. Even though the new company began to contribute to the construction of public building, many people still felt that the virtues provided just had the purpose of appeasing them. Don Alberto, like many others, feels betrayed by the oil firms that offer "breadcrumbs" in his eyes rather than real recompense: "Well, yes, because they already started to give us breadcrumbs, and now they have built us a roof for the community center as well as the community kitchen, and they gave us an ambulance. But this is still too little. They just want to calm us down." The results of the questionnaire reflect this ambivalent attitude regarding the presence of the new firms. While 22 percent of the respondents agreed, that the general situation has improved since the new firms took over, 21 percent agreed that the situation worsened. However, 24 percent of the respondents feel unsure about whether it has become better or worse and agree with the statement that the situation in general did not really change.[9] The low consensus on the issue among the people of Emiliano Zapata shows their contentment and uncertainty concerning the arrival of the new companies until today.

A Look into the Future: Imagining the Time Bomb

Currently, national politics regarding the hydrocarbon sector are in a state of transition. The oil boom faded out and a crisis has induced times of economic hardship, which led to structural changes also affecting life in Emiliano Zapata. The community members that have gotten used to the presence of the oil industry had to adapt to the economic downturn and are now confronted with a new panorama. The arrival of the new firms has not yet brought the desired improvement. The economic situation in the community itself is regarded as disastrous by many residents, even more so for those without access to farmland. The current situation of upheaval has increased the perception of uncertainties in the future, while also widening the geographical gap of supporting networks through emigration. Many community members, therefore, hope for a revival of the industry despite the possible negative impacts increasing again. The predictable end of oil sources by conventional extraction is the reason for extended investment in new technologies to access sources that have been difficult to extract in the past (see Ferrari 2014: 23–24; Haarstad 2012: 1; Svampa 2015: 66). One of the technologies designed to extract formerly unreachable hydrocarbon assets is fracking (Willow and Wylie 2014: 223). Fracking therefore bears the prospect of becoming another "boom story" within the history of hydrocarbons, which is already characterized by the rhythm of booms and declines in regard to conventional means of extraction. The implementation of fracking therefore adds on to the existing uncertainties linked to this predetermined temporal process (Appel et al. 2015b: 2).

While existing conventional hydrocarbon sources are considered exhausted, the development of so far unused sites through the application of new technologies might stimulate the industry and improve the economic situation in Mexico. Nevertheless, those deliberations come with further risks. The energy reform has only brought a light revival of the activities so far, and the new companies have not satisfied the needs of the community members yet. Since the implementation of the reform and the endeavor to exploit new oil and gas resources through fracking, the issue since has also become an important topic of discussion at the national level (see Castro Alvarez et al. 2018: 1322; de la Fuente et al. 2016: Hernández Ibarzábal 2017: 364; Silva Ontiveros et al. 2018). For a layperson without any further information, the exact places where fracking has been applied are hard to distinguish from other types of fossil fuel extraction since the effects are often very similar. It is more complicated because under Mexican law, it is not mandatory to declare in what way and where fracking is applied—a fact that creates a great uncertainty among the possibly affected population (see Hernández Borbolla 2014; Silva Ontiveros et al. 2018). Veracruz and particularly the northern part of the state is the region where most fracking projects have been initiated so far according to the national media (Cruz 2018).

Also, in Emiliano Zapata the rumors of possible fracking applications have arrived in recent years. Many community members started worrying about possible increased risks of pollution and damages. These circumstances have led to a situation where many people in Emiliano Zapata express the perception that they are "living on a time bomb." Fracking is closely linked to environmental and health risks, and this risk can be understood as a practical understanding of the dangers of fracking (Cartwright 2013: 204). In Emiliano Zapata, the risk is acknowledged, but there is some uncertainty that fracking is even taking place.

Don Francisco and his family live close to one of the many installations. He has seen the company staff coming and going and he has observed their activities, but he could be never sure what the implications for his living environment actually are. When asked about the purpose of the pipelines passing under his house and leading directly to what seems to be an extraction well, he knew that they contain possibly harmful substances: "The gas comes from over there and the pipelines come from that side . . ." he said pointing at the visible lines in front of his house. "These ones are containing congenital water, dirty water, but the ones containing gas come from that other side. They all are affecting us!" and he added: "as I was saying it's . . . like a time bomb. It does affect us, but, well, I don't know what some of them are for exactly." The time bomb is a common image used by many of my informants during conversations and interviews. It implies the idea of something harmful right under one's feet that could do harm at any time. The image captures the temporalities of oil in Emiliano Zapata in a comprehensive way, connected with notions of heteronomy and unpredictable risks as well as the inevitable finiteness of abundance. The community is currently in a phase of change, where the oil boom has subsided, the crisis has left its traces and a new era of oil politics is heralded. This is accompanied by the presence of new firms and the buzzword "fracking."

The overwhelming majority of the community members I talked to had a very unclear idea of what fracking actually was or what the implications for them would ultimately be. Since no one was informed about possible fracking activities on their territory, the first time many of them came in touch with the issue was during a conference held by NGOs in 2015. Until today most local knowledge stems from information given out at that event, but not everybody attended it. Even though the conference and the local protest against fracking was captured within the regional press and the event had been diffused by various NGOs in the country (Ejatlas 2017), the interviews revealed their limited knowledge of what fracking means. Most of my informants were familiar with the term yet almost none of them could explain the technique and why it was supposed to be harmful.

Don Alberto, like many others, recall what the NGO has told the community members and expresses his doubt whether the technique is already being applied. Since he has no further knowledge about the technical details, he is unsure about the possible implications that might affect the people of the community. When he told me about the oil workers who now again revive older extraction wells, he became alert: "When they are working, we don't know if they are already using that technique. They alone know what they're doing and we don't know anything about it." What he knows about fracking is limited to rumors and suspicions: "Well, the people who claimed that they came here to inform us about fracking say, that the company is going to drill I-don't-know-how-many kilometers using certain chemicals and that there will be a lot of pollution. But that's all I know."

The community members know that fracking could include harmful outcomes, but considering the negative effects of conventional extraction techniques, are already a part of everyday life in Emiliano Zapata, the community members are unsure whether fracking has been applied or if the perceived damages are caused by conventional extraction. The uncertainty about fracking being applied or not, therefore, adds on to the concerns about possible consequences and the perception of a lasting risk from the extraction industry ultimately leading to the impression of "living on a time bomb."

The Temporalities of Oil and the Time Bomb

The temporalities of oil and its inevitable process of booms and declines are deeply intertwined with the history of Emiliano Zapata. They thereby contribute to the constitution of the space as an oilscape. The effects of the temporalities of oil play out as part of a "social time-bomb-effect," within which rapid industrial growth during the oil boom led to social change, modifying norms and social organization, which then culminated in unfulfilled expectations of long-term benefits when the boom fades and established dependencies prove non-viable leading to processes of social disintegration (see Filer 1990; Banks 1996). The process of peaks and valleys inherent to oil introduced a reordering of social patterns, while provoking anxieties due to industrial hazards, eco-risk, and an anticipated worsening of economic and social conditions. Oil extraction in Emiliano Zapata is linked to a specific perception of peaks and valleys as an analytical dimension. Yet, there are some particularities of the conditions of oil extraction in Emiliano Zapata that function as distinctive features within the analysis of the temporalities of oil and local consequences.

Founded as a settlement of indigenous farm hands on a hacienda, the community emerged under the rule of big landownership and at the time of the endowment as an ejido, it underwent the unruly and violent times of postrevolution. The arrival of the oil industry then offered safety and implemented new economic opportunities that benefited many community members. This process caused an opening to the markets and a turn toward casual labor. Accidents and damage caused by oil extraction brought new types of insecurity and concern for the lives and health of the residents. Until today, the oil industry in Emiliano Zapata is associated with economic growth and the improvement of living conditions on the one hand and damages to the environment and terrifying accidents on the other.

For several decades, the community had become accustomed to the presence of the company. When the oil crisis began and PEMEX increasingly withdrew, the community members faced new challenges in an uncertain situation. Again, they responded with an adjustment of their lifestyles, and looked for economic alternatives, for example widening the scale of family and belonging through migration. The premise of adaptation also applies in light of recent changes brought about by the partial revival of the oil industry under changed conditions such as the end of the PEMEX monopoly. The insecure economic situation, which emerged in recent years, has been met with responses such as seizing the improved education strategies for the younger generation and a diversification of occupations to earn the family income, often involving emigration of individual family members. Nevertheless, PEMEX had maintained its presence in the community and large segments of the population continued to rely partly on their economic ties to the oil industry, such as the provision of certain services and the sale of products. Job opportunities in construction or maintenance of the oil infrastructure have meanwhile mostly vanished for the people of Emiliano Zapata and many inhabitants have sought opportunities elsewhere, while sending remittances to their families. Thus, the community members expanded their support networks beyond the regional scale, as a coping mechanism during the crisis.

The detailed look at the implications of oil temporalities in Emiliano Zapata shows how the local residents respond to the uncertainties dictated by the inevitable temporal processes of oil. Nonetheless, it also shows them not only as objects to temporalities of oil, but also as active shapers of their community and lifestyles and responding to the challenges that they are presented with. Furthermore, the contemplation of the local reality under the conditions of oil in a temporal context reveals some underlying patterns, which go beyond the mere description of the industry impacts. Unpredictability and uncertainty have always accompanied the living conditions in Emiliano Zapata. Even during times of the oil boom, the community experienced more than security and growth; it found itself at the margins of the urban centers, which emerged around the oil industry in the area. Since the community had never been the preferential place for the development of a flourishing oil town in the classical sense, Emiliano Zapata fails to feature the characteristics of a typical "boomtown story"

(Gramling and Brabant 1986: 179–80). This situation caused by precarious labor conditions and a lack of benefits through development of a social infrastructure positioned the community at the margins of the national wealth generated by the oil industry (see Parry 2018).

In the community, the determination of uncertainty goes beyond the statement that the future is uncertain for all people. Here uncertainty goes further than the possibility of thwarted plans by an unforeseen event. It is linked to risk exposure through industrial pollution and possible accidents, as well as to anxiety about insecure future conditions in a post-boom era. At present, the inhabitants of Emiliano Zapata are at a turning point, which could be the possible beginning of a new crisis or a mitigation of the situation in the sense of a "boom-bust-recovery cycle" (see Brown, Dorins, and Krannich 2005) and they are looking into an uncertain future of another phase of the temporal process of oil. However, a closer look at the temporalities in Emiliano Zapata also shows how these uncertainties have always been dealt with. Despite their anxiety in the face of uncertain times, the community members have always found creative ways to cope. They have developed strategies to manage the "time bomb," which are constantly being revised and adapted, to respond to the challenges faced within the temporalities of oil.

Conceptions of time regarding resource extraction can only be understood in their plurality of cycles, durations, and velocities represented by the different levels of peaks and valleys immanent to oil (see Bear 2016; D'Angelo and Pijpers 2018). These temporal processes affect the space described as oilscape around the location of oil extraction sites, which also incorporate a particular material dimension and sociocultural particularities. These three aspects are closely intertwined and must be considered as complementary parts of a comprehensive complex. The role of material implications of oil extraction for the constitution of a "time bomb" in Emiliano Zapata, as well as the way they physically play out over time will be discussed in the following chapter.

Notes

1. *Ingeniero* technically translates as "engineer," but in Emiliano Zapata, it is a term used for any type of PEMEX staff.
2. Light-skinned persons are usually referred to as *güera* or *güero* in Mexico.
3. Altar candles are used on every house altar in almost every home in Emiliano Zapata. The syncretistic practice of having candles during every hour of the day for the household saints is still alive in the community even now, as it is in many Mexican households (see Valderrama Rouy 2005: 199).

4. A form of barter trade performed in Mexico since precolonial times among indigenous communities, not involving currency but products (see, e.g., Flagler 2007; Licona Valencia 2014).
5. In Mexico, employees usually get paid every two weeks, or after fifteen (*quince*) days. Migrants then mostly send the remittances immediately so the families in Emiliano Zapata and many other places in Mexico go to the city twice a month where they can find the cash machines of Western Union or other providers to pick up the money their family members sent.
6. "Nuestra comunidad está peor que otras porque nuestras autoridades negociaban mal con PEMEX/las empresas petroleras."
7. Mexico has several prestigious public universities. The students must pass the entrance exam and can enjoy education for a very low charge, adapted to their economic possibilities. Nevertheless, the bars for the entrance exams are high and most rural schools do not fulfill the necessary education level to prepare their students to pass the exams. Students of the UNAM, for example, are recruited mostly out of special preparation schools from which all nine located in Mexico City. Even though special scholarships for marginalized groups such as indigenous people are available after students have passed the bar, it remains almost impossible for students from rural areas with no additional tutoring to pass the entrance exams at the higher ranked universities of the country. This has been criticized for a long time but remains the norm until the present day (Reina 2016; Seco 2013).
8. "Yo quisiera que mis hijos reciban un trabajo en PEMEX/las empresas petroleras un día."
9. "Desde que las nuevas empresas petroleras (como Oleorey) entraron se ha empeorado la situación general" / "Desde que las nuevas empresas petroleras (como Oleorey) entraron la situación general no ha cambiado" / "Desde que las nuevas empresas petroleras (como Oleorey) entraron se ha mejorado la situación general."

CHAPTER 4

From an Ejido to an Extraction Site
Materialities of Oil in Emiliano Zapata

> If you want to build a well, you can't because pipelines pass underground. Or you want to pave your yard, and you can't because of the pipelines. And you start thinking: Well, oh my God, there are so many pipelines, if one of them bursts, we won't even have time to run away anymore.
>
> —Doña Anita

The material modifications and moldings of the community and the landscape induced by the oil industry have inevitably become the foundation for everyday life and consequently inscribed onto the lives of the people over time. Right at the beginning of my first stay in Emiliano Zapata, I was confronted with the dominant narrative of the constant fear of accidents in relation to industrial installations on one hand, and the unknown, possibly toxic implications of the extraction activities on the other. The perception that the territory of Emiliano Zapata was being undermined by pipelines was very strong, since those installations represent something hidden and invisible, which is unpredictable and therefore, potentially dangerous. The negative experiences with such facilities in the past contribute to ongoing uncertainty, as is evident from the initial statement of Doña Anita, a middle-aged wife, who owns a shop in Emiliano Zapata together with her husband. They attempted to expand their shop, however, this was made impossible by the large number of pipelines under their parcel, preventing any attempt to dig for construction purposes. During this process, she became increasingly aware of the material risks that the industry posed and was worried about potential accidents that might occur at any time. The residents of Emiliano Zapata today perceive their community and its surroundings as a dangerous place, where the material forms of oil extraction represent a constant hazard. The infrastructural installations, processing plants, wellheads, and several other inscriptions of the oil industry in Emiliano Zapata thus became the material manifestation of the time bomb.

The materialities of oil are also deeply intertwined with its temporal dimension and therefore, the two aspects of the resource are often difficult to disentangle (Richardson and Weszkalnys 2014: 6). This chapter will focus on unraveling the material dimensions of oil extraction in Emiliano Zapata and their implications for community life, without disregarding temporal matters. To do so, the oil materialities will be introduced in the sense of their physical representation, experienced through the human senses. Anthropologists have engaged with the senses in a particular manner since the 1990s, when the ethnographies of the senses recognized the importance of the acts of seeing, listening, and feeling for the perception and embodiment of the world and particular culturally shaped contexts (e.g., Geurts 2002; Press and Minta 2000; Stoller 1989). The central argument of the anthropology of the senses articulated by Rubert Cox in his overview on anthropology of the senses is therefore "that our senses are specific to their historical conditions and subject to change" (2018: 1), which shows the historical and cultural dimensions of sensory experience. Furthermore, sensorial experiences also vary for individual actors in different situations, as well as across sociocultural contexts, while constantly being transformed (Beer 2014: 153; Howes 2005: 11).

Entering the ejido of Emiliano Zapata, the materialities of the oil industry can be immediately experienced at various sensory levels. The environment around the community is pervaded by infrastructure facilities of the extractions such as roads for transport and pipelines, which are visible everywhere even though only a small fraction of the pipes are installed above ground. Within the community and its surroundings, processing plants exude sharp exhalations, colorful warning signs call for caution with regard to the pipelines lying close to homesteads and fields, and gas flares produce a disturbing noise at all times through the week. The broad road that leads directly through the community is frequented by trucks transporting material and staff, in addition to the agricultural products of the local fields and several public buildings. The ones that are sponsored by oil firms are marked with the respective company logo. Thus, for the inhabitants of Emiliano Zapata, the presence of the oil industry has had a significant impact on their immediate living environment. This inscription of oil infrastructure and facilities implies a constant disturbance of the senses and a latent perception of the extraction activities prevailing around them. To cope with these disturbing stimuli at the same time, a certain level of "anaesthetics"—a term that Susan Buck-Morss (1992) describes as a selective numbing of the senses in order to deal with the invasive stimulations of the modern environment—takes place, which helps the residents to deal with the strong excitations of their environment (see Cox 2018: 1). At the same time, the facilitation of infrastructure has also been perceived as beneficial for community members. The material manifestation of oil and its extraction is an important component of the sociocultural transformations that have taken place over time in Emiliano Zapata, and therefore an integral component of the oilscape. Furthermore, it represents a decisive element for the comprehension of the "time bomb" in the local context.

Sensing the Oilscape: Material Inscriptions of Oil

"It looks like there have been people here again," Don Gonzalo says. Don Germán nods. We are standing at the shore of the small river called Los Tejones that represents one of the main sources of water for the community members of Emiliano Zapata. The turbid water was blocked with several hoses at a point where it looked particularly dark. Somebody has dug up some pipelines that now lie around in parts. Also left is a seemingly homeless red fire extinguisher next to the now blocked stream. Is the fire extinguisher meant to put out the river? Unfortunately, it is not as paradoxical as it seems. Several pipelines of different girths are protruding from the little hill slope beside the river and spots of potentially inflammable crude oil are visible at several heights on the shore, completing the picture. I approach them curiously. This is the first time I can see the crude oil with my own eyes—the substance that determines everything! It is thick and black and looks a little bit like fresh tar that I have seen coming out of machines, meant for road building. Is that really crude oil? I guess it is, but I am not an expert and here in Emiliano Zapata, I have come across all different kinds of substances related to the oil industry. Nevertheless, I have not had the chance to look at the oil itself so far. Gas and most fluids used for processing are usually transparent or are transported underground by pipelines that make them invisible in an everyday setting, but they have distinct, sometimes sharp smells that one can perceive. Close to the processing plants that are distributed among several places on the ejido and close to human settlements, the air is filled with industrial odors and whirring and pumping sounds that resound day and night. Extraction penetrated the senses everywhere in Emiliano Zapata one way or another.

I step back and join Don Germán and Don Gonzalo, who allowed me to accompany them when they go to inspect the seepage. They are standing a few steps upstream and from this vantage point, I see what Don Gonzalo meant: I also spot some tools lying around, a bucket, and some unidentified cans. Did somebody try to fix the seepage? The arrangement does not look too professional though and I doubt its success. "We have to call the *ingeniero* again." Don Germán says. "They have to do something soon or people will get anxious because of the water shortage." The seepage has been there for quite some time now. I was first alerted when community members saw several dead fish further down the stream, and some said that they had smelled gas. This time the water committee and the farmers reacted quickly and did not use the water of the stream for watering their fields or animals, and more importantly, they also prevented the pumping of the water into the pipes meant for human use. The company had promised to fix the leak as soon as they were informed, but until now, it looks like only provisional measures had been put into place. Pollution via leaks and seepage is a very common problem in Emiliano Zapata, almost so much that many residents deal with it rather grudgingly.

"Have any fields been contaminated so far?" I ask my companions, who did me the favor of letting me tag along with them when they decided to inspect the leak again before the upcoming ejido assembly.

"No, not yet. Several people complained though because the plants won't grow as fast as usual, and they suspect the seepage has something to do with it." Don Gonzalo answers.

"And do you think they're right?" I want to know.

"No, because they haven't used the water from the river. They want compensations, but the company won't give any to them. The soil hasn't been fertile here for some time already."

"And why do you think is that?"

"Many reasons, I think. The heat in the summer has gotten very strong in the last few years. Many people have gotten sick from the contamination. In addition, they keep draining the petroleum from the earth for so long now. No wonder the fields aren't fertile anymore."

I am not sure what to make of his answer. "But what do you think the extraction has to do with the decreasing fertility?"

"Well, I think the oil is like blood extracted from the earth. If they continue to exsanguinate the earth, then it's only logical that it can't grow new crops." Don Gonzalo turns around and follows Don Germán who is already walking toward our pickup truck. I do likewise and while we drive off passing row after row of orange trees besides the road, I keep thinking about this perspective on what oil could mean. In the distance, the roaming flame of the gas flare, visible from almost every spot within the community, accompanies us, almost as if standing sentinel over Emiliano Zapata.

"Conspicuous at First Sight": Visible and Tactile Materialities

In Emiliano Zapata, the material traces of hydrocarbon extraction are immediately perceptible to the senses, with the most striking probably being the visible ones. The first thing that attracts attention when entering

Figure 4.1. A month-old seepage within the river, which awaits repairs, Papantla, Mexico, 2017 © Svenja Schöneich.

the community is undoubtedly the insistent presence of gas flares, which cannot be overlooked. In particular, the one closest to the settlement area, overseeing the main road and the community center with an illuminant flame, has been the topic of public and internal discussions and the cause for sleepless nights.

There are three gas flares around Emiliano Zapata, which are so close by that they are visible from the community. One of them is in immediate proximity to the settlement and commonly referred to as the *quemador* when it features in conversation. It has been the cause of distress for the community members since its inception in 1979–80. Even though many community members have become accustomed to its presence to a certain degree, most residents still perceive it as a constant disturbance, particularly due to its fluctuating intensity. Sometimes, the flame burns brighter than on other days and even at night, a flare several meters high lights up large parts of the community. Hence, it can be comprehended that outsiders, who are not used to its impressive appearance, are often bewildered when they first encounter a gas flare so close to the settlement. The community members who had moved to Emiliano Zapata after the installation of the gas flare, described their concerns especially with reference to the beginning when they were unfamiliar with its function and possible effects.

Figure 4.2. Burning flame of one of three gas flares located in immediate proximity to human settlement, illuminating the main road during the daytime in Emiliano Zapata, Papantla, Mexico 2018 © Svenja Schöneich.

One of them is Doña Luisa, a woman of about thirty. She came to the community eighteen years ago to marry and is now living on a small hill with a view of the gas flare with her two children, while her husband works in Monterrey. Sitting in front of her home in the shade of a banana tree, she recalled her impressions of the first few weeks in the new home after she married an Emiliano Zapata resident: "Well, when I got here, I was still surprised by the effects of the gas flare. It was so bright, and it lit up almost the whole community even in the middle of the night. But my biggest concern always was the smell of gas in the air. Sometimes the smell would get more intense than on other days and I was very afraid of an explosion."

Besides worrying about the contamination of the air, the pollution of the water and soil are constanty discussed topics. There are pipelines protruding at various spots, some of them very close to the creek. The first signs of a leak are often dead fish floating on the surface of the water, because the seepage is not always due to crude oil, but could be transparent chemicals. Then the community stays without water, sometimes for weeks. Since Doña Luisa's arrival, the river has been polluted multiple times and the community members do not drink the water anymore but buy water for human consumption from retailers. Fortunately, people are rarely harmed in contrast to animals and fields, as Doña Luisa vividly

From an Ejido to an Extraction Site | 113

Figure 4.3. Decaying industrial installations—a pipeline and an unreadable sign—amid corn crops and orange trees, Papantla, Mexico, 2016 © Svenja Schöneich.

described: "The plants simply dry out; they rot from all the pollution." She explained about the contaminated fields. "Also, the creeks get contaminated. There are no shrimp anymore. There were plenty of shrimp here before; you could see them in the clear water. But now all the shrimp and fish died."

The presence of the potential source of contamination is often directly visible and palpable. Wellheads or deposits of fluids and pipelines are usually located within areas used for crop cultivation and somehow, they have even become part of the visual identity of the fields. Sometimes, the respective installation is separated from the farming spots by a fence and has signs with technical explanations. Those installations may not be touched directly. The gas flare, which is enclosed, is only to be approached by company staff. However, the installations mostly fit seamlessly into their surroundings. The few description signs are often in bad shape, as are the installations themselves at times. In this way, the pipelines aboveground, the wellheads, the valve plugs, and the description signs and all other types of installations become part of the environment, blending with their surroundings to form a visible and touchable embodiment of extraction. They thereby set the boundaries for the oilscape in this case, which is formed as a multilayered space on the ejido territory intermingled with the extraction site.

The knowledge about potential risk without exact information about operating modes is imminent within many contaminated communities (Auyero and Swistun 2008: 374; Edelstein [1988] 2018: 9). Most of the installations in Emiliano Zapata emanate a certain discomfort about possible damages due to their alienated appearance and unknown functioning, the gas flare in particular. Its sensory disturbance is so obvious that many community members have expressed their concern to the staff working at the processing plants. Among them is Alejandro, a PEMEX worker I had the chance to talk to during his shift. He lives in Poza Rica like most of his colleagues and has a house and family there. He only comes to Emiliano Zapata when his shift at the processing plants starts and otherwise has little contact with the community members. However, he talks to them now and then, for example, on his way back home, when he grabs a few tacos at one of the stands. A certain frustration is palpable when he talks about the gas flare. He has tried to calm the residents when they agitatedly asked him about the flame. "Well, the flame is normal." He explained. "When we reach a certain pressure, we have to burn that extra gas. We wouldn't want to realease the gas into the air just like that, right?" However, the suspicion remained, despite his attempts at providing infromation: "But the people, they just see the flame and they think that the village will catch fire, because they don't know any better." The local complaints, caused by what he interprets as a lack of information, bothers him. He pointed out the fact that the oil company also brings benefits to the community. And in fact, the infrastructure development that PEMEX fosters is also visible in many parts of Emiliano Zapata. The presence of PEMEX is evident, for example, in roads built by the oil firm and in buildings like schools or workshops, constructed with company money. They bear witness to the social involvement of the company. Alejandro listed all the support elements that the community has already recieved: "PEMEX says to them: "You know what? I'm not going to give you the money directly, but I'll help you to, let's say, to build a school." And the company has given them many many things over the years." Therefore, he is convinced that the people of Emiliano Zapata have also benefited more from the oil industry than they would have suffered negative consequences.

In fact, today almost every public building in Emiliano Zapata sports the company brand, and this makes the presence of the oil companies even more visible. The communal kitchen was established as part of a program that benefits the communities affected by the extraction, initiated by PEMEX in 2013. In recent years, schools have been built or expanded on the same site. Even the community ambulance sports the company brand, since it was financially supported by the company. Moreover, subcontracting companies as Oleorey have contributed to these facilities too. In this way, the oil industry has visibly inscribed itself into the appearance of the community and its surroundings at different levels and in diverse ways. In this way, the oil industry contributes both actively and passively to the architectural appearance of the buildings and therefore, also to the materially manifested visibility of oil extraction.

"What Keeps Us Awake at Night": Audible and Olfactory Materialities

In Emiliano Zapata, both hearing and smell play an important role for the sensual perception of the oil industry. The aforementioned gas flare, for example, is not only visible, but also audible, since its wavering light produces a whirring noise day and night. The people in the community talk regularly about the permanent disturbance of the noise from the gas flare. Many of them still perceive it as a constraint in their everyday lives, even though they have reached a certain degree of habituation. The disturbance of the gas flare is augmented through the fact that the intensity of its flame is somewhat unpredictable. The extraction process produces a certain amount of gas that must be burned to prevent its unfiltered release as harmful emissions. Intensified oil extraction also means an increase in disposal of gas, which is reflected in the height of the flames and increased sound. This unpredictability increases the feeling of exposure and concern, believes Doña Maria, who is living in a house at a small crossway. "The worst thing is that they don't warn us. They just suddenly open the gas valve to burn the gas so that the pipelines would not explode, and the noise gets really loud and scary. It hurts the ears." She emphasized on the intensity fluctuations of the gas flare and the irregular periods of its functioning as factors that increase anxiety: "You can't sleep in peace at night because you always expect them to turn it on any minute. Also, during the day, it could happen any time really."

But it is not only the gas flare that generates disturbing sounds in different intensities. Within the community, there are more noise releasing installations, for example, the processing plants that are connected to the gas flares and are called *turbinas* by the residents. During processing, the turbines also generate dull humming sounds that are distressing to the community members, especially to those who own homes close to the installation. One of them is Doña Amalia, who lives down the road. She was born and raised in Emiliano Zapata and is married to an *ejidatario*, who also grew up in the community. Throughout her life, she has become accustomed to the audible effects of the oil industry around her and therefore, she takes it as something normal—as a part of her daily life. But as someone who has witnessed many accidents, she also knows about the unpredictable hazards induced by the extraction. Hence, she is aware of the harmful potential of the sounds generated by the installations, while being familiar with their functioning—at least from a non-oil expert's perspective. Therefore, she expressed a different view on the risk of noise disturbance. She has become so accustomed to the sounds of the processing plant close to her house, that a disruption of the activity frightens her even more than its permanent continuation. "Other people say, we have gotten used to the noise and we actually really have, I think. We notice it more when it changes," she told me. The community members have adapted a certain level of "anaesthetics" (Buck-Morss 1992 in Cox 2018: 1), which means that they have managed to suppress certain strong stimuli to shield themselves from constant exposure to heavy excitations of their environment. Yet, the stimuli now function the other way round, and the community members become alarmed the moment the stimuli are interrupted, because this could have a possibly dangerous cause. "There are times when you have gotten so used to the sound that you don't even notice it until it suddenly it becomes silent. Then you become worried and ask yourself: 'What happened, why did it stop?'" affirmed Doña Amalia. "You start to worry that now it is going to explode or something. The same, when the volume turns up. Then you also start to worry."

The extraction of hydrocarbons not only produces noise but can also be perceived by a distinct smell. The installations release various types of industrial odors, for example, from injection wells, leaking pipelines, and again gas flares. For the community members, these odors are not only a nuisance in varying degrees, but also present constant exposure to potentially toxic fumes. The industrial malodors are often the subject of conversations and have been mentioned to me in many interviews. Moreover, due to past experiences with gas explosions that have caused deaths and injuries, the community members are sensitized to the smell of gas that could possibly stem from leaks. They know the various smells well enough to distinguish harmless ones from potentially dangerous ones. However, due to a lack of thorough knowledge about the chemical releases, a strange industrial smell always causes uncertainty. Many people therefore are constantly worried about possible gas explosions, especially if they have witnessed the accidents that have occurred in the community's past. One of them is Doña Elena, a widow in her sixties who has lived in Emiliano Zapata all her life. In our interview, she tells me about her anxieties with regard to the odors emanating from the pipelines close to her house. The leaking pipelines should have already been fixed probably, but Doña Elena is still worried because she notices some smell coming out. She lived in Emiliano Zapata when the major deadly accident known as *quemazón* occurred in the 1960s and is still distressed by the memories of youth when she and her family had to leave the house in a hurry several times when somebody smelled gas and warned the neighbors. She still cannot give up on the idea of a leak that could cause an explosion right under her feet, especially when she smells industrial fumes close to her house. "Everywhere I step is a gas pipeline. Right now, the ground we sit on is pervaded by pipelines." She told me while we are sitting in front of her house. She pointed to the spot right next to us: "There is one over here just a few meters away, which had a leak once. The smell was horrible. We had to call the *ingenieros,* and they had to come and fix it and they did. Now it doesn't smell but I'm afraid it could start again." Having seen the accidents that can occur when a pipeline explodes, Doña Elena gets restless when she smells gas. The fear of explosions has become a constant concern for her: "If one of the many that pervade my yard explodes . . . there will not even be ashes left of us."

Even though many residents of Emiliano Zapata feel disturbed by the noises and smells of the industry, which affect their daily lives and cause fears of accidents, they have also become accustomed to them to some extent. Most community members know the different sounds and smells, which could come from a leak and can thus predict an accident. The experience of the people in Emiliano Zapata, however, shows that the residents do not completely ignore the negative stimuli around them, but select the noteworthy, potentially harmful ones, which differ from the ones they experience every day. Doña Juanita, an elderly resident living in the community since she was born, told me about the industrial smell in the community and how she has adjusted to its existence. Nevertheless, she also mentioned a certain odor that she detected one morning that differed from the ones she was used to: "Suddenly I noticed this different smell and went out to see where it was coming from. I notice when something is different, and it concerns me." The recognition of industrial materialities is much more pronounced, given the increased risk perception. The residents such as Doña Juanita have learned to distinguish between the different kinds of stimuli, thus ignoring the ones that signal normalcy, while paying attention to those that point to potential risk. I myself cannot remember noticing a special smell on the morning that Doña Juanita mentioned. To an outsider, the industrial smells are all more or less alike and equally perturbing, but Doña Juanita, as many others of the Emiliano Zapata residents, is able to distinguish between them.

"Hidden in the Subterranean": The Presence of Concealed Materialities

The material presence of the oil industry in the community can be seen at various levels. Some of them are directly perceptible to the human senses, others only indirectly through their presence. This applies first of all to the equipment that goes underground and with which the hydrocarbons are extracted, such as the drilling material, and for the substances that are extracted or used for the extraction process. These kinds of installations are never visible to the residents of Emiliano Zapata except in cases of seepages or leaks, when they might pollute the rivers or the soil. Since crude oil and natural gas are the target resources, these substances are the most important assets in the industry. At the same time, however, the substances remain hidden because they are transported in probably the most common materiality—a dense network of underground pipelines. Due to its proximity to the many extraction wells and processing plants, the entire community of Emiliano Zapata is pervaded with pipelines. Some of them protrude in parts of the community and are therefore visible, but most of them run underground and can only be adumbrated.

Even though the pipelines are not always visible and cannot be touched, the people of Emiliano Zapata are quite aware of their existence.

Figure 4.4. Pipelines protruding in a field in Emiliano Zapata, Papantla, Mexico, 2017 © Svenja Schöneich.

This manifests for example, in the restriction on building wells, as Doña Anita complained in her statement at the beginning of this chapter. The course of the underground pipelines also translates into a limitation for sewage system installation and the construction of roads. Furthermore, the installation and maintenance of the pipelines require the opening of the earth's surface, which confines agricultural activities and can cause inconvenience for the residents, when taking place on housing parcels.

Don Francisco is one of the younger residents of Emiliano Zapata, who is a permanent member of the community. He has several jobs for which he regularly commutes from his home via the main road to Poza Rica. His house is situated next to an extraction system in which the flows of liquids that come from several pipelines are regulated. His father inherited this house and when he moved there about a decade ago, the plant was already built, but was not yet operational, probably due to the decline in industry activities at the time. Four years ago, the plant resumed operations, thanks to a new company. Don Francisco knows about the pipelines that run directly under his house and lead to the processing plant. For him, they represent more of a problem than the plant itself. Their installation and maintenance require access to his parcel, where plants and trees get damaged. He also worries about the health of his family, as toxins flow through the ground beneath their feet. "Everything here in Zapata is pervaded by pipelines! Everywhere people are affected by it . . . you can ask almost everyone here. Everyone is affected by the pipelines from PEMEX!" he exclaimed. The pipelines and their transmitted substances are perceived as part of the sensory experience of the materialities of oil in Emiliano Zapata. Since the conscious perception of the material presence of the oil industry and its effects is primarily related to its risks, the correlation of pipelines as a material part of the oil industry, is most likely to be seen as a risk factor. Despite their presence during interviews and talks, for most community members, the exact course of the pipelines and their content remains unknown. This way, the pipelines become the material representation of an obscure hazard lurking underground, even more vividly resembling the the image of a time bomb.

Material Effects on Environment and Agriculture

The truck that drives down the highway behind me seems to be too fast for the questionable road conditions. As he comes closer, I take an extra step aside to let him pass. The sound of the engine is deafening, and the road seems to shake as the truck rushes by. It releases an exhaust cloud around me, which increases the heat for a few seconds—if that is even possible. As the truck roars off, some oranges tumble down and roll to the side of the road. I pick them up and check them for edibility. Two out of the three pass the visual test and are stored in my small backpack as provisions for the day. Like most trucks driving on the main road at this time of the year, this one was loaded with oranges that were not secured on the loading area. The loss of a few fruits makes no difference for the driver, as their price is low, and the delivery is not calculated per piece but per tonnage. Lately, oranges began to dominate the landscape of the ejido in an almost aggressive way.

The orchards on both sides of the road stand as green espaliers, baked as always in the heat of the afternoon sun. These days, however, it has become busy because the harvest season has reached its peak. Throughout the day massive trucks dominate the roads with their loading areas full of fruits. I am on my way back from the house of Don Enrique, who is one of the oldest members of the community, after conducting an interview with him. He told me about the times when the ejido was founded and people relied mainly on subsistence *milpa* agriculture. I can imagine that the landscape is very different from what I witness today. Emiliano Zapata was relatively remote at that time and the area was characterized by dense vegetation in which vanilla plants grew slightly as tendrils on the tree trunks. Corn and beans were cultivated by slash-and-burn agriculture on the slopes of the hills that run through the ejido. On this hot day, about six decades later, the picture looks very different. The main road I am walking down crosses precise rows of orange trees on both sides, all about the same size with spaces to walk in between and almost no weeds on the ground that could disturb the orderly impression. "When PEMEX came and built this road, we finally got to the markets," Don Enrique told me. "Then everybody started to plant oranges because they fetched much better prices than normal corn." His words echo in my head when another truck passes by. The heat has become very intense during the last hour and caused the harvest activities to halt for today.

At the old gas station to my left, about fifteen young men have gathered and stand in the small shade of its roof. The station itself has not been in use for several years, but during harvest season it turns into one of many collecting points for workers and products. The men are chatting and drinking beer, while waiting for the trucks to pick them up with their day's work. I do not recognize any of them, since they are not regular residents of Emiliano Zapata—they are only here to work and populate the otherwise deserted orchards for a few weeks in the spring and now again in the fall. They are farm hands, *jornaleros*, who are scouring the orchards for mature fruits, which they put in large baskets on their backs. They carry them with the strength of their necks as the baskets are fixed around their foreheads. During harvest season, anyone who owns an orchard needs help and young men from the area, who have no farmland, take the opportunity to earn some money in other people's orchards. The golden fruits are then transported to collecting points and loaded onto the large trucks. Thousands and thousands of fruits are loaded up each day building orange mountains, which travel by truck many kilometers down the roads. The price for oranges is calculated in tons—and tons of them are leaving Emiliano Zapata each day, going to the cities of Poza Rica and Martínez de la Torre where they are processed. The work is hard and the pay is often low, as are the opportunities to find work in the rural areas of northern Veracruz.

Curious glances follow me as I point my steps to the left at the small intersection that leads to the community center. The asphalt of the road stops abruptly, where I turn left and I leave the route that was once built by and for the oil industry and that now also forms the basis for the agricultural economy of Emiliano Zapata.

From *Milpa* to Monoculture: From Monoculture to Oilscape

In many parts of the Totonacapan coastal areas, oil sources were discovered and were already being commercially exploited in the first half of the twentieth century. During the advancing industrialization related to the oil industry in the coastal areas of Totonacapan, the commercialization of agriculture started its triumphant advance relying largely on the infrastructure facilitated by PEMEX as an indirect effect of the proceeding oil industry (see Gonzáles Jácome 2007: 69; Popke and Torres 2013: 216). As one of the communities where the industrial exploitation of oil sources did not commence before the 1950s, the more recent history of Emiliano Zapata is strongly linked to the *milpa* system as the main economic basis with its specific social and cultural implications. When asked about the living conditions in the community before the entrance of PEMEX, the older residents of Emiliano Zapata almost always mentioned the variety of foods they cultivated through the milpa agriculture, which is perceived as the most incisive differences in today's agriculture. One of them is Don Adolfo, a man in his seventies who grew up in Emiliano Zapata. Today, all his children have migrated to the more industrialized cities of northern Mexico such as Monterrey and Reynosa, while in contrast, he spent his youth in the community living off his *milpa*. He enjoys recalling the old days when he was a young man. Even though the work was hard, he remembered the times as pleasant, since there was always enough and even more varied food: "The *milpa* was beautiful; I had corn, beans, squash . . . everything. If we wanted something, we just went there and got it. It was a time of abundance back then."

Although the cultivation patterns have changed since the times described by Don Adolfo, many community members rely on agriculture in one way or another and the soil still has an important function for the provision of food. The campesino identity remains strong in Emiliano Zapata, although nowadays the conditions have changed and the main products are usually citrus fruits. When asked if the orchards of oranges that dominate the picture today existed at that time, his answer was clear: "No, because there was no road. You could not get to the city so easily." When PEMEX built the paved road that enabled transportation and safer traveling, people and goods could now travel to the cities of Papantla or Poza Rica with more ease. Suddenly, the community members found themselves in a situation wherein they could transport their agricultural products not only safely, but also efficiently to the urban marketplaces and subsequently sell them. The main road connecting the San Andrés oilfield and subsequently Emiliano Zapata to the cities of Papantla and Poza Rica, became the manifestation of the increased connectedness of the formerly remote community with the urban centers of the global market economy and has thus changed the local economic strategies (see Dalakoglou and Harvey 2012: 459; Harvey and Knox 2012: 523). Faced with these new possibilities, many farmers took the opportunity to change their production to citrus fruits. While vanilla was still a sought-after product, new crops like Serrano chilis, bananas, or papaya entered the market. Moreover, coffee, tobacco, and sugarcane soon became important economic factors for the area. After the prices for bananas and vanilla dropped by the end of the 1960s and 1970s, large-scale citrus orchards became increasingly dominant in the area and continue to be so until today (Popke and Torres 2013: 215–16).

The shift to monoculture not only implied promising revenues, but also transformed the organization of labor and even the environmental conditions. Besides improving transport modalities, the road also facilitated the influx of labor and migrants. The citrus fruits that most residents started to cultivate, are always harvested around the same time and require support from day laborers, who need to be mobilized. Its organization shifted to a higher professionality of labor division and the emergence of a large group of day laborers (see Benquet 2003: 131; Popke and Torres 2013: 216). Before, the fieldwork was mainly done by the families themselves, relying on a system of reciprocity that banked upon the efforts of neighbors, relatives, and compadres. Thus, the shift from *milpa* to commercial agriculture and wage labor, initiated changes in the social fabric too. Don

Antonio, the store owner who remembers the times before PEMEX, began to modify the territory and compared the commonly used *milpa* system to the new farming patterns. He recalled the times before the cultivation of oranges started, when the area was widely covered by native forests referred to as *monte*. Within this area, the farmers used to set up their *milpas* with slash-and-burn agriculture and gathered wild fruits and sometimes hunted animals. The industrialization of the Gulf coast was accompanied by increased deforestation and the opportunities for hunting and gathering wild crops were diminished in the whole area of Totonacapan. The changes in the land use implied a dominant orientation toward cash commercialized agriculture (e.g., Chenaut 2010: 57; Velázquez Hernández 1995: 175). In Emiliano Zapata, cattle also play a role, albeit a minor one, within ejidos such as Emiliano Zapata. Today the cultivation of crops such as oranges predominates pasture, as it is space consuming and thus mostly practiced by large landowners.

The decline of the *monte* and the areas dedicated to *milpa* changed the appearance of the landscape around Emiliano Zapata significantly in the course of only about thirty-five years. When the farmers started to increasingly cultivate cash crops, the landscape tilted toward monoculture and new materials such as fertilizers and pesticides entered the agricultural cycle. Don Emilio has been a farmer since his early youth, as his father before him. Now he is in his seventies and still recalls the years when farming patterns changed in Emiliano Zapata. During the 1950s and 1960s, he, like the other community members, used to the *milpa* products and wild fruits to supplement the daily bumper food supply. In the 1970s, he started to cultivate oranges for the first time. Compared to the present day, products appear more labor-intensive to him and require several additional products, such as fertilizers and pesticides that need to be purchased: "This type of orange that we have now, you have to pamper a lot. You have to fertilize it and spray pesticides and whatnot," he complained to me. The expenses for fertilizers and pesticides used to improve the yield or the decrease in prices for agricultural products on a national level, deminished the gain from citrus fruit cultivation over time. Moreover, the sheer quantity of citrus fruit production in the area nowadays fosters fierce competition between individual producers, but the alternatives to a more profitable form of land use have become scarce. Many community members, therefore, additionally engaged in part-time wage labor activities and thus developed "semiprolitarian" working patterns—a concept relating part-time rural laborers to urban capitalist development (see Cancian 1994: 77). Financial income enabled the acquisition of new materials for housing and thus changed the physical appearance of the community from dispersed huts made from natural materials to houses built with more enduring materials such as concrete and corrugated metal. The changing architecture, therefore, also forms part of the material formation of the oilscape, as does the frequent pollution and contamination induced by the extraction activities.

Doña Anita was born in the nearby city of Tecolutla and came to Emiliano Zapata in her twenties when she married her husband. In general, she considers life in a rural environment healthier compared to the cities, as she claims. But her experiences in Emiliano Zapata were not as expected. Confronted with several cases of diseases in the community, she began to worry about the industry's negative impact on people's health: "Apart from the smell, sometimes I think that here in Zapata there are many diabetics. I think that the smell might be affecting us. Young people in their twenties with diabetes. I wonder because usually you would assume the food in the countryside to be healthy." Doña Anita's thoughts reflect a common concern for health issues in the community. The effects described by her may be due to the agricultural patterns as well as the extraction activities. Since most community members lack information about the substances that are there or could be exposed to, many feel insecure and fear intoxications or accidents. The types of diseases for which the oil industry is blamed, varies from diabetes to heart and lung diseases, and to a type of rash, which is very common in Emiliano Zapata during the most intense summer heat. However, the exact cause for the increased intensity of the perceived disease in the community is often not very clear. Most people associate them with the contamination of the living environment, and therefore, the air they breathe as well as the food and water they consume. Doña Anita gives an explanation for the cases of disease that she mentioned, and I heard from most community members, who have listed diseases as effects of the oil industry: "The soil is contaminated, the oranges are contaminated, the air we breathe is contaminated. Sometimes at night I look out the window and see the gas flare, and I wonder: Why are we even here?"

Most of the campesinos in the community have experienced several instances of damage to their cultivations over the years, either through the use of territory for the construction of installations and pipelines, or through seepages affecting their fields. Such accidents are quite common—in my one-year field research alone, there were three instances of seepages in the river—and in the questionnaire, 82 percent of the respondents affirmed that they themselves, an acquaintance, or a relative from the community had suffered damages caused by the oil industry.[1] Through several leaks, chemicals and sometimes crude oil seeped into the ground and caused the crops to wither. The damages are paid by the company, but the farmers claim that the pollution has a lasting effect that is not compensated for since it did not occur directly due to the industrial activities in that particular moment, rather representing a long-term effect.

The decreasing fertility of the soil, climate change and the emergence of certain diseases are also associated with the oil industry at a secondary and an indirect level. As a secondary effect, the frequent contamination of the soil through the oil industry causes diseases and decreases the yields of agriculture. Deforestation causing the perceived temperatures to increase and the biodiversity to diminish further, is a consequence of the expansion of the extraction infrastructure. Indirectly, the effects of monoculture, the increased usage of agricultural chemicals and the ongoing deforestation for the expansion of commercial husbandry are also associated with the oil industry, since the cultivation of cash crops had started with the development of the industrial infrastructure. Thus, the cause and effect of diseases and the quality of the soil are difficult to distinguish for the community members, but equally interpreted as effects of the oil industry that contributed to the establishment of the manifestation of the oilscape. Doña Juanita put across this doubt that many community members harbor, in the following words: "Everything here became lost when PEMEX came, but sometimes one can't explain exactly why. Whether it's pollution or deforestation, or if we're causing it ourselves? We do not know; however, we see that there is something wrong."

Material Modifications of the Oilscape during Crisis

Ultimately, the industrial activities in Emiliano Zapata have declined with the fading oil boom, a fact that had severe consequences for the materialities of oil for the community too. The activities at the extraction wells and the processing plants have decreased during the last decade, less staff is transported to the site and the opportunities for day laboring in the oil industry have also decreased. However, with the fading boom and less extraction activity, the material construction of infrastructure and their inscription in the territory of Emiliano Zapata led to a changing set of circumstances for the community members, which call for new strategies of adaptation and dealing. Many residents and campesinos, who were concerned about the frequency of accidents and the high level of pollution, might hope for a betterment of this situation, but then, the processual withdrawal of the companies also implied further consequences that manifested in the physical appearance of the now decaying materialities and introduced novel hazards.

The issue of safety in terms of possible accidents is a recurring topic for most of the community members who became accustomed to frequent incidents and accidental pollution over the years. In the first years of the presence of PEMEX in Emiliano Zapata, safety measurements were a minor issue, but the provisions changed in the wake of the first major accidents. When the industry began to develop during the first few years, the oil workers had to adhere to very few regulations and handled their tasks in a rather unconfined manner. Don Emilio recalled the times when the people of the community went to the extraction sites to sell food and alcoholic drinks to the oil workers there, without having to pass any examination with regard to industrial safety: "My business was great back then! Everybody made a lot of money who went and sold drinks or food to the petroleum workers. We sold beer, some even sold ice—I have no idea where they got the ice from, but somehow they did, and they took it all up to the platforms and sold it to the workers who drank a lot." But soon the situation changed after a few incidents had occurred and more stringent safety measures were introduced: "But when the first accidents happened, they start to forbid that. We weren't allowed to sell alcohol anymore it was forbidden to drink." Hence, these regulations increased the safety in the industry, but at the same time, it became harder for the inhabitants to sell their products, since they were not allowed to enter the extraction sites and installations any longer. During the boom times, many community members still profited from the opportunity to sell food or supplies to the oil workers through the opening of stores and restaurants, or they were sometimes even hired on a part-time basis at the company canteens. But over time, the provision of the company staff became even more professionalized, and the local residents had fewer opportunities to do business with them. During the times of the fading boom, from the second half of the 1980s, fewer workers came to the sites and business opportunities were consequently curtailed.

At the same time, the increased safety measures and the diminishing of extraction activities in general, led to a decrease in incidents and the number and frequency of accidents and damages was reduced. This was perceived as at least partly a relief for some of the community members. When new companies were subcontracted by PEMEX in the last ten years, they brought their own staff and were also stricter in terms of safety. Don Ernesto is in his sixties and is a store owner in Emiliano Zapata. He was born and raised in the community. He remembers several accidents in his lifetime, and he also had experience as a laborer for the oil company at times. He told me about the time of the boom, when he was working as a short-term contractor for PEMEX, placing pipelines and repairing leaks: "When I was working with the company, I had to repair several oil leaks. Any time day or night. When there was a leak, we would rush there and repair it, at any time." At the time, he and his colleagues were very busy,

Figure 4.5. Abandoned processing plant at the cuartel in Emiliano Zapata where various decaying industrial installations and provision facilities for company staff are located, Papantla, Mexico, 2016 © Svenja Schöneich.

and frequently had to even work night shifts: "Sometimes they would call you at four or five in the morning: 'We've got another one over here' and you had to hurry to get there as fast as you could."

During that time, he witnessed several incidents, but his last memory of a lethal accident dates back many years, and he claims that fewer accidents occur today due to higher safety measures and less activity. When asked how he would assess the situation, his opinion was twofold: "It changed for the better—for the better because there have been no more deaths. And for bad. Because there are no jobs." The diminished activity also means fewer accidents and less contamination at first sight, but even though no deadly incidents have occurred in the last decade, pollution and contamination remain an issue. The old pipelines continue to leak, and Emiliano has witnessed several cases of seepages. In particular, the pollution of the river that serves as the water supply has upset the community members.

With the withdrawal of PEMEX, the infrastructure, especially the net of pipelines pervading the whole community, now started to lack maintenance. During the peak of activity, the company staff was always around and took care of the installations and pipelines. Community members who were hired like Don Ernesto, were basically living on-site to repair damages as soon as they occurred. Now money and staff are short, and with time, the old industrial infrastructure has started to deteriorate. PEMEX abandoned several of their installations when the oil boom faded out, which are now left to decay. Among them is a whole area called the *cuartel* where various processing plants, accommodation, and provision facilities for company staff is located. Moreover, many of the pipelines that still transport industrial fluids are now disregarded in terms of maintenance.

Don Aurelio, the husband of my host family and a man in his early forties, was born in Emiliano Zapata and grew up during the boom time. Since his father had many sons and only one ejidatario title to hand down, Aurelio started to work as a day laborer in construction and maintenance for the oil industry. During the fading boom, there were no job opportunities anymore, and he and several of his brothers and acquaintances from the area started looking for work in the industry elsewhere. He now works in the cities of northern Mexico and ultimately has started to work for transnational firms that even sent him and some colleagues to neighboring Latin American countries for several weeks. The contract terms in construction usually last only a few months. Then the assignment is accomplished, and the workers have to start looking for work elsewhere again. His family in Emiliano Zapata depends on the remittances he sends and awaits him when he gets home after a contract ends. I interviewed him when he was at home for a visit, when the contract he had been working on ended, and he had to look for the next opportunity. Since he is familiar with the technical implications of industrial installations, he is well acquainted with the tasks in construction and maintenance. When asked why he does not look for work in Emiliano Zapata or at least the area, rather than in other states, he replied: "At the moment there are not many opportunities. The drilling is done, and the re-dilling as well. There won't be much more." But the infrastructure must also be maintained and PEMEX has reduced their efforts due to a lack of personnel and monetary capacities.

Don Aurelio is concerned about the consequences that the lack of maintenance has triggered and might continue to have in the near future: "Well, the pipleines have to be maintained. There are a lot of pipelines here which are thirty to forty years old that are not working anymore, and lately they were a lot of leaks. Last year there were a lot more leaks here than usual." In order to retard the decay, PEMEX started to contract new companies for the task as soon as foreign companies were allowed lawfully to take over PEMEX installations. The new companies were supposed to conduct the necessary renewal on several kilometers of pipelines, but due to discordances concerning the payment, the maintenance task was delayed and unfinished.

Don Aurelio heard about this contention via acquaintances he knows from his activities as a construction worker and is concerned about the development since they mean a potential risk for the people exposed to the pipelines: "They now hired a Venezuelan company that won a thirty-year contract to provide maintenance to PEMEX installations. But PEMEX hasn't paid them yet," his former co-workers told him. And he continued sharing more insightful knowledge: "There is a one-year contract to renew thirteen to fourteen kilometers of pipelines. But in fact, they just renewed like maybe seven, six kilometers in total and then left work unfinished. That is dangerous because when they reactivate the lines again, they're probably going to crack."

Although the inscriptions of the materialities such as the dense net of pipelines have caused quite some damages and preoccupied the community members, they have now become a material part of the living environment, which must be properly maintained in order to prevent further hazards. A simple withdrawal of the oil industry from the community is therefore not a satisfying option for the residents of Emiliano Zapata, even though it has caused nuisances and anxiety with regard to its negative consequences for life and the environment of the community.

The diminished extraction activities often leave the people in the community bereft of the income sources and the—even though sometimes deficient—safety provisions that they are used to. The abandonment of the installations and the toning down of the maintenance now presents them with further challenges. Many of the residents therefore hope for a revival of the industry, which would also allow for securing the infrastructure, in addition to an improvement of the economic situation. Don Adolfo is, as many others, convinced that PEMEX has to return to Emiliano Zapata to prevent further damages to their infrastructure. When asked what he thinks about a possible return of the company, he even claimed that there is no other option for Emiliano Zapata than to come back and continue their work on the industrial infrastructure: "They have to come back. For one simple reason: There are pipelines here that are more than fifty years old that are about to burst." And he leaves no doubt about the consequences of a lack of mantainance on the community. According to his assessment: "Ten more years, and there would be many, many people dying. Ten more years, and that's it. Because there is a pipeline there where we took a water sample that already burst once and contaminated the river. PEMEX took care of it but that was just this one time. Ten more years, and goodbye."

The material installations of the industry have started to deteriorate as a consequence of the oil crisis, and the oilscape enters into new processes of restructuring. Even though many residents would prefer a life without the oil industry in their community, my interviewees could not think of alternate options for different lifestyles that would not include the oil industry in one way or another. The people have gotten used to the inscription of the materiality of oil and to a certain degree, become accustomed to disturbance and contaminations as inevitable consequences. When Doña Juanita thinks of possibilities for the future in Emiliano Zapata, she, as many others, envisions a comparable model to the life during the oil boom, but with improved conditions: "For me, it would be better if more companies came here, but they offer jobs. To improve the community. But they shouldn't continue to pollute, which is difficult to do. Maybe that would be too much to ask," she said. For her, the negative consequences of oil extraction have already integrated irreversibly into life in Emiliano Zapata. As a child, she has witnessed the lives of her family being based on small-scale agriculture and the *milpa*, but she perceives the modifications that the environment underwent since then as unalterable, which prevents a return to that lifestyle: "Well, the whole area would have to be cleaned up, so that there would be no pollution no contamination anymore. But that's the question, how to clean it up? I guess that would be impossible," she said with a certain resignation.

Transforming Materialities: Dealing with Physical Manifestations of Oil Extraction

"Do you want milk in your coffee?" Doña Chavelita appears behind the curtain separating her kitchen from the living room. She holds two coffee mugs in one hand and milk in the other. The rain patters heavily against the windows. It had started to rain last night and continues until this afternoon, but the temperature only fell about three degrees, which now creates tropical conditions with a humidity that condenses on the inside of the windows and makes them blurry.

"Yes, please," I answer. I take a piece of the sweet white bread with sugar on top and dip it into my sweetened coffee. When it rains outside, everyone in the community has coffee and sweet bread in the afternoon, and I have also become accustomed to it. Coffee in the mornings, on the contrary, is rather uncommon.

Doña Chavelita takes a seat on the other side of the table. "Look at your shoes!" she exclaims, and I look at my wet feet covered in mud. "Why did you come down here? This weather is terrible." When it rains, the streets, except the paved main road, become rivers of mud and most people avoid going outside. Work in the fields is impossible in this weather anyway and the community members usually stay at home. "I wanted to talk to you today. I assumed you would be home," I say.

Doña Chavelita strokes her hair back and pulls it into a ponytail with deft hands. She had come to the community with her husband about thirty years ago. Her father was originally from Honduras, and he and his wife settled in the area after he came to Mexico to look for work. He and Doña Chavelita's husband worked as day laborers in construction for the industry, but when the boom faded, her husband went on to look for opportunities elsewhere and left her with their two children. She kept the house by the main road and installed a little vending spot outside her house under the roof of the small porch where she sells sweets and snacks to passersby. Her father and mother passed away years ago. "Well, what do you want to talk about?" She asks. "You want to know about PEMEX right?"

"Yes, exactly." I answer. "I want to know about your experiences with the oil industry and the extraction here in Zapata."

She sighs. "Look Güera, the times when there were opportunities here have passed. Now, only contamination is left." She takes a sip of her coffee. "PEMEX had left the community dry. There is not much left for us now."

"I saw that they recently started to renovate the school." I counter. "Aren't those people from PEMEX?"

"Sure, that's right." She nods. "But that is very little in comparison to what they earn with all the oil they have extracted here. Yes, they have done a few things, they have given us the *comedor*, the roof over the central meeting place, and they have renovated the school buildings. But we need more teachers, for instance. And the *comedor* already has cracks."

Indeed, I have seen the cracks in the building. A week previously, two PEMEX workers had come here to inspect them, but they said that this was normal and was no reason to worry. "And the sewing workshop, right? People here have earned money working for them."

"Yes, they have, but that was a while back. Even this house"—she points to the roof and the floor—"is built with what my husband earned and my father before him. But it is small, and it is old; it needs fixing in several places. But I don't have the money. I have to struggle a lot and there are very few people passing by lately, so business is not good. Most of the people who stop are truck drivers during the harvest season and sometimes the *jornaleros*." She takes another sip of her coffee. "And the sewing workshop," she adds, "did you notice that nobody is using it?"

"Yes, I have" I reply. "But why is that? Aren't people interested in sewing? Maybe they could sell some clothes or mend something here for the community members."

"In theory, yes," She says. "But that would require us to invest additional time, time we would need for doing chores. Moreover, the workshop was given to the *ejidatarios*, since they are the ones who suffered most damages given that it is their territory. And you know what happened next? They handed over a certain amount of material for sewing, but that material disappeared rapidly. Maybe some have sewed something with it. Maybe some have taken some drapery for themselves. And now? With what should we sew?"

"The people would have to invest first," I admit. She is right.

"Exactly. And where should we get the money from? Maybe the *ejidatarios* will take some money out of the supply and buy new material, but then it's only for them."

"So, you think the programs that PEMEX introduced have not benefited you much?"

"Not much. Yes, they have done some works. That's true, but my point of view is that they could do more. Now their own installations are rotting and they don't do much there either."

I stare out the window while my now lukewarm coffee gets colder. Many of the houses here have been built with material bought with money that was earned one way or the other via the industry. However, many people struggle to get by, especially since the opportunities for work have diminished.

"Aren't you hungry? I'm hungry!" Doña Chavelita suddenly exclaims. "Come eat with me, I'll make us some *huevos a la Mexicana*!"

"I won't say no to that," I smile.

She gets up and goes over to the stove. "It has gotten so dark already," she said and turns on the lights on her way. Looking at the naked light bulb on the ceiling, I can see that it is made of corrugated sheet iron as in most houses around. I can also see that it is attached to old pipelines as shoring, as is quite common with the houses in Emiliano Zapata.

Failing Materialities: Damages and Compensations

Not all infrastructural facilities the community is provisioned with today were constructed by PEMEX but the presence of the company indeed had a big influence on infrastructure development, especially in the 1950s and 1960s when the area was of a rural character and many local communities were quite remote (see Chenaut 2010: 57; Popke and Torres 2013: 215). While the road and the bridge are perceived as beneficial to the community, that was not their original goal. In actuality, they were built to facilitate extraction logistics. In contrast, the oil company also participated in other installments designed to fulfill the purpose of benefiting the community as part of a set of sustainable development goals or corporate social responsibility (CSR) matters, and they paid compensation to the affected community members in lieu of the damages caused to the environment. These measurements were designed to compensate disadvantages and damages caused by the industry to the population.

During the first decades of PEMEX's operation in the San Andrés oilfield, benefits for local communities affected by extraction activities, like Emiliano Zapata, have been a very minor issue for the company (García-Chiang 2018: 2). When the oil company arrived in Emiliano Zapata, arrangements with the residents were mostly conducted in an unofficial and not so transparent manner. At the outset, the company often claimed plots and marked them within the territory without the authorization of the farmers. Don Umberto, one of the oldest community members and part of the ejido council, remembered how during the first years, the practice of compensations depended on the individual decisions of the leading foremen if damaged crops and terrain was compensated for: "One day one of the petroleum workers told me: 'You have to claim the damage now that the foreman comes.' I didn't even know that was possible and I was surprised. 'And then I get paid for it?' I asked. 'Yes,' he said." Nowadays, Don Umberto, like his fellow farmers, know that damage must be compensated by the company, but during the first few years, the farmers did not know their rights and even less about how to go about claiming them. Therefore, many of them were never compensated for the loss of territory of crops during the first few years.

PEMEX did not make their practices transparent to the residents in the first years and during the 1960s and 1970s, this practice changed only a little. Nevertheless, the community members engaged in negotiations with the staff and achieved several informal agreements regarding compensations for their losses over time. As the industrial activities increased in the area, PEMEX also contributed to the progress of buildings and facilitated access to the water supply they installed in the community. Unfortunately, this supply crashed after a severe flood in 1999 and was not reestablished afterward. Furthermore, the company offered several benefits for the community, and continued it in the 1980s and 1990s, when they contributed to the construction of buildings for official use like the schools and the agencia municipal. Furthermore, the official policy of the company toward the establishment of stricter safety regulations and the furthering of development contributions for affected communities had undergone changes. The payment for damages was also regulated and today follows a catalog of fixed prices depending on the damaged good. In 1996, PEMEX implemented security and environmental protection practices into their company guidelines and thus created the Corporate Industrial Safety and Environmental Protection Division. The division aimed to carry out safer and more environmentally friendly operations (García-Chiang 2018: 2). Many community members perceive the increased safety mechanisms and in particular, the services, to be a valuable contribution to the development of Emiliano Zapata and associate these benefits directly to the establishment of the company. Don Esteban, like many others, is convinced that the material development in Emiliano Zapata would look very different without the contributions the company facilitated. Asked about how he would imagine the community today if PEMEX would not have come to Emiliano Zapata, he emphasized the importance of the road built by the company for the present state of the community: "The company built the highway and that was very important. We didn't even have a road, nor the secondary school and not even the primary school. Maybe we could have built them without the company's money but only with great sacrifices." While the creating of benefits and compensations for affected communities has only been a very marginal issue for PEMEX for many years, ultimately, the implementation of measurements of benefits for affected communities has increasingly become part of the company principles.

In 2006, PEMEX integrated a new model for sustainable development into their corporate strategy, which among other things, was supposed to further environmental protection and beneficial works and actions in affected communities (García-Chiang 2018: 2; García-Chiang and Rodríguez 2008: 26). The trend to further incorporate responsibility toward the public and with it, the population affected by its activities, has then spread internationally. A global CSR movement further institutionalized social responsibility mechanisms into the economy in the 2000s (Dolan and Rajak 2016: 1–2). As a national player of international economic importance, the company PEMEX has introduced CSR into their 2010–2025 Business Plan, as one of the four lines of action in 2010. Thereby, PEMEX seeks to implement CSR mechanisms to "improve the relationship with various stakeholders and incorporate sustainable development in business decisions"[2] but also implements sustainable development measures for affected communities and promotes social development via mutually beneficial works and donations among others. A program called Programa de Apoyo a la Comunidad y Medio Ambiente (PACMA) was launched in 2013 as a support program for communities and environments that are part of the PEMEX operating areas. It officially promotes social development through investment based on shared responsibility between the public and private sectors. The program is funded to around 2 percent through contracts signed between PEMEX and its suppliers or subsidiaries. In the past, there were some questions about the transparency of the PACMAs, but recently the Inter-American Development Bank has named the model for a best practice example in its Extractive Sector and Civil Society report 2018 (Milano and Irazábal Briceño 2018: 80–82; PEMEX 2018; Redacción Proceso 2017). Emiliano Zapata has profited from this program so far through the

From an Ejido to an Extraction Site | 135

Figure 4.6. Signboard by PEMEX at the fence of Emiliano Zapata's *telebachillerato*, which is renovated with money from the PACMA program, stating the exact sum spent and the number of beneficiaries, Papantla, Mexico, 2018 © Svenja Schöneich.

construction of a sewing workshop and the community kitchen, in addition to the renovation of schools.

Hence, the benefits for the community are mainly of a material nature and are manifested in the form of buildings or roads that require mainly a onetime investment rather than long-term projects. Before a new project is implemented, the company usually contacts the local authorities who then discuss the matter with the inhabitants and report back their priorities to the company. This enables the community to take part in the decision-making process in the context of new installments. Nonetheless, their actual options for participating in determining the support programs are limited to a minimal level. During my interviews, the programs and accomplished works of the oil companies were frequently mentioned, but most people saw them as low threshold and perceived the community as being entitled to more benefits due to the severe effects that the oil industry had wreaked on their territory and lives.

Most community members today, therefore, appear rather unsatisfied with what they have received from the oil company. Don Alberto is a sixty-year-old ejidatario. He has witnessed the beginnings and the boom of the company and lived through the decline of the industry. When asked about the benefits that he thinks Emiliano Zapata enjoys because of the oil industry, he admitted that there are certain positive effects, but he is also convinced that the benefits do not outweigh the negative effects: "If we talk about benefits—yes, there are some. The highway for example, so we can transport our products, but in fact our community suffered a lot of accidents and damages. More than other communities. It was more damages than benefits. Let alone the pollution." Benefits facilitated by the oil company thus form part of the "resource effect," where the benefits of the oil industry are rather short-term measurements that do not offer real alternatives or lasting changes for the betterment of the community members (Weszkalnys 2016: 132–33). But even though the material compensations from the company have often caused discontent to the residents regarding their deficiency, they have contributed to the provision of a variety of facilities in Emiliano Zapata. They, therefore, present a way in which physical manifestations of compensations within the community become an extension of the materialities of oil, inscribed into the ejido and communal territory of Emiliano Zapata.

From Peril to Virtue: Repurposing Oil Materialities

During their long history with the oil industry in their territory, the community members of Emiliano Zapata have become beneficiaries of a material endowment with infrastructure and the provision of buildings. Nonetheless, those measurements were taken mainly as an initiative by the company as part of their CSR or sustainable development agenda and the community members themselves had little room for participation in the decisions. In the meantime, the residents of Emiliano Zapata have developed further strategies for dealing with the material implications of oil on their own agenda, which allow for a higher degree of self-determination. Thereby, the material elements of the oil industry are taken out of their initial context and new meanings and purposes are assigned to them. The frequent usage of roads and bridges built by PEMEX for the transportation of agricultural products may already count as an example of such a reinterpretation of industrial infrastructure. However, even if they were not built with that original purpose, their utility did not exclude use by community members. In other cases, the residents of Emiliano Zapata also use infrastructure that was determined for a completely different purpose and reinterpreted it. This is, for example, the case for decommissioned[3] pipelines as described in the vignette at the beginning. Many people have built their homes with money that they have earned from the industry.

Elderly community members told me about the composition of wooden posts or bamboo with roofs of palm branches, now most residents own homes made from concrete. With the boom of the oil industry, several work opportunities and options for participating in the local economy exceeding the limits of the community, found their way into Emiliano Zapata. With their rejuvenated income situation, the lifestyle also changed, including housing patterns. Material for house building is costly and particularly after the boom had faded and the economic upswing turned down for the community members too, several people resorted to improving their houses by borrowing material from their surroundings. The most obvious and practical option for the purpose is pipelines since they are durable but relatively lightweight, available in all sizes and spread all over the community. Pipelines, therefore, became a common material used in home improvement, as buttresses or the support framework for roofs.

Decommissioned pipelines can also serve as fences or can be bundled together to function as little bridges over streams of water. Sometimes, they even become improvised playgrounds or benches. In this way, old pipelines have become part of the physical experience of the living environment in Emiliano Zapata. Here, they not only fulfill their purpose as transport infrastructure for industrial fluids, but also serve as a contributor to the material composition of private spaces such as houses and backyards or public spaces such as bridges and recreational areas.

However, it is not only pipelines that are repurposed by the community members. Abandoned installations are partly used for novel purposes

Figure 4.7. Decommissioned pipelines used as ceiling joists of a house in Emiliano Zapata, Papantla, Mexico, 2018 © Svenja Schöneich.

Figure 4.8. A large, decommissioned pipeline used as a bench on a playground in the colony of San Andrés in Emiliano Zapata, Papantla, Mexico, 2018 © Svenja Schöneich.

that differ from their original intent. During my research, I participated in meetings that took me to the old sentry, abandoned by PEMEX. Now that PEMEX has left the space, the ejido council repeatedly tried to reclaim the area, but the term of contract prevents the usage of farmland for other activities. Usually, the community members avoid this area, since its secluded location and the critical safety situation in the region causes them to be apprehensive of interrupting illegal activities. In special cases and with the approval of the company, those spaces become partly re-inhabited for short periods of time. In this case, an association of an anti-drugs movement had rented out the facilities, led by Don Raymundo, a local member who lives in San Andrés. The sentry was then used for a two-day venue, where people of different ages with problems related to drugs and alcohol, came together to receive assistance and strengthen togetherness. Most participants came from the local area, but some even arrived from faraway places like Mexico City, since the organization is part of a nationwide network. Don Raymundo, a man in his forties who was once an alcoholic, organizes local meetings on a regular basis and facilitated the contacts that allow for such camps to be conducted in this particular space. Since it is difficult to find proper locations for carrying out such undertakings, the idle installations represent a useful opportunity.

As many of the spots within the ejido territory cannot be used by the community members anymore since they are still officially occupied by PEMEX, even though they are not in operation, several farmers have started to illegitimately use the areas anyway, mostly for crop cultivation, but sometimes even for housing. In the ejido council, the risk regarding constructions and cultivations in a certain proximity to PEMEX installations are frequently discussed. On the one hand, the risk of loss is higher within the range of the installations, even if they are not functional. On the other hand, farmland has become scarce and the extension of the utilized territory might imply higher yields and additional income. Therefore, people frequently pass the minimum distance to the installations to expand their farmland, risking their crops and even their health or lives. Sometimes, these kinds of risks are calculated and can be comprehended as part of a strategy for reinterpreting material risks factors for personal benefit.

Doña Regina is in her late thirties and lived all her life in Emiliano Zapata. While she has separated from her husband after the couple had some troubles, both her sisters are married and live in the community, one to an ejidatario. Doña Regina is very active in the community, participating in several of the community committees, and therefore, is quite familiar with many people and the community. She is always well informed about what is going on in Emiliano Zapata, more so because of her customers, who often stay and chat when visiting the sewing workshop where she offers services to community members. She participates in all community assemblies and has a critical stance on questions regarding benefits from the oil industry, which is why she engaged in activities to make claims from the company in cases of damages in public spaces and supporting other community members to present their case to PEMEX staff when they have been affected by damages or disturbances. Therefore, she is often frustrated when other community members do not participate in the same way. When I asked her why she thinks that in Emiliano Zapata, very few people engage in protests against the oil company even though they frequently suffer damages, she responded: "They don't want to, because of the money. Because they are waiting for PEMEX to come and find oil under their plot. They want the money, that's why they don't want to sell the land either." Being a small-scale farmer does not bring much income anymore and even the cash crop products often do not sell well and furthermore, underscore a fierce competition in the market. Agriculture mainly only pays off when a rather big area is available to be farmed. In some parts, where the soil does not serve well for cultivation, or many pipelines or installations complicate agricultural activities, the farmers continued to sow crops and hope for compensation money, in case damages arise. Doña

Regina explained: "I have a brother-in-law who has an orchard close to one of the installations, that he didn't want to sell because he's awaiting a leak or damage. The orchard is not even fertile anymore, but he would wait for something to happen so he would get compensation money."

However, not only does her brother-in-law passively await damage on his unused land to come through, but he actively engages in activities that would raise the value of the affected land and consequently, the respective compensations. "He planted some orange trees there because he says that the more damaged trees there are, the more money they will get." Said Doña Regina, and with a certain frustration she added: "That's how he thinks, and many others do too. It became a business for many farmers, and they don't care if their plants dry out or become polluted." Through this and other strategies, the community members have found a way of turning risk into virtue. While the material modifications of their territory by the industry have led to increased jeopardy for their surroundings, people adapted by developing mechanisms to deal with that risk, to work around it and seize the materialities of oil in their own way. They thereby even managed to partly transform perils from oil materialities into potential benefit. The oilscape in Emiliano Zapata, therefore, is not only imposed by the material terms of the oil industry, but actively negotiated and shaped by the community members and their practices of adaptation and repurposing oil extraction materials too.

The Materialities of Oil as Inscriptions of the (Time) Bomb

In Emiliano Zapata, the presence and the material implications of the oil industry have left visible, audible, and palpable traces everywhere in the community. They are detected by the community members, who partly negotiate their intensity through selective perception on the one hand, and on the other hand, have developed adaptation and coping strategies that allow them to act on and to interact with their living environment despite the challenges posed by the temporal process of oil. The effects of the extractive oil industry have inscribed themselves into the local environment to a degree, to which they have become integrated into the material appearance of the community Emiliano Zapata. This process of transforming Emiliano Zapata into an extraction site includes also the integration of risk as well as benefits of the oil industry into the living environment and have called for manifold short-term coping mechanisms as well as long-term adaptation of local sociocultural patterns on the part of the community members (see Oliver-Smith 2013: 277). Hence, they themselves are actively taking part in the constant reshaping of the oilscape.

While the infrastructure patterns of the area have been significantly determined by the oil industry, the landscape around the extraction sites progressively adapted to the constructions and newly created routes of transportation. At the same time, the community support programs have benefited the residents as a consequence of industrial development. First, the modifications within the economic basis, namely subsistence agriculture, then led to a new set of changes including the connection to local markets and the subsequent adaptation of consumption patterns. The community members were exposed to new types of food, but at the same time, the variety of agricultural products for autoconsumption declined. The incoming flow of money, job opportunities and goods altered the housing patterns as well as the options for work outside of agriculture. Yet, the difference in this case compared to others is the establishment of the extraction site not only in the wider region, but directly on the community territory, which came with a set of particularities of the situation.

There are monetary benefits and the provision of buildings as part of the company CSR measurements, both of which are perceived by many as positive contributions to community life. Therefore, the material impact of the oil industry on the residents of Emiliano Zapata becomes a double-edged issue. While their lives are inevitably tied to its implicit benefits, they also live with the constant fear of installation failures that would mean toxic or explosive accidents for humans and animals or at least serious damage to the fields and water sources. Nevertheless, the community members found ways to deal with the uncertainties via selective perception of warning signs, for example, the awareness of the distinct scent of particular toxic fumes or the recognition of certain noises that indicate failing facilities. Through processual habituation and overlooking some inevitable risks as a consequence of the lack of information, the community members managed to adapt to the uncertain situation despite being constantly exposed to health threats (see Auyero and Switsun 2008: 374; Salas Landa 2016: 730–31).

After the fading of the oil boom, the oil crisis has presented the community members with new challenges. While a number of accidents happened during the first decades of the San Andrés oilfield, the now abandoned facilities and decaying infrastructure present novel risks to their environment and increase the feelings of insecurity. The community members cope with the risky implications of polluting or failing installations by claiming compensation payments and benefits for damages. Nonetheless, most inhabitants of Emiliano Zapata today are unsatisfied with the benefits they receive from the oil company and consider them only short-term and insufficient in light of the negative outcomes. The benefits provided by the industry have thus caused a "resource affect"

(Weszkalnys 2016: 132–33), where short-term benefits do not offer a viable solution for the creation of livable futures in the long term and are therefore perceived to be deficient.

Apart from claiming certain benefits from the oil company, the community members of Emiliano Zapata also developed strategies for direct appropriation of the oil materialities. The process of appropriation and repurposing of oil installations manifests, for example, in the way in which the community members make use of oil pipelines and integrate them into their housing patterns and public places. Especially in times of crisis when material for house building is difficult to obtain and pipelines are poorly maintained by the oil companies, this practice has become a valuable coping strategy for crises and has also become a prudent way of dealing with decaying infrastructure. Another way of transforming the material implications of oil and assigning beneficial properties to them are, for example, the reinterpretation of risk and mitigation. Community members use the promising compensation payments for damaged crops, cultivating plants close to the extraction facilities, where there is an increased probability of them being affected by seepage, thus enhancing the probabilities of being granted compensations. The community members engage in these actions as strategies of dealing with the uncertainties surrounding them, utilizing the materiality of oil itself.

Notes

1. "Yo he sufrido daños o conozco personas de aquí que han sufrido daños por PEMEX/las empresas petroleras."
2. "PEMEX (homepage)." Retrieved 5 April 2022 from pemex.com.
3. The illegal excavation of pipelines is a recurrent issue in Emiliano Zapata and has been a pressing issue for the oil companies that are reliant on an intact net of pipelines and the unauthorized removal can provoke severe accidents and seepages of toxic fluids. During my research, I have encountered two cases of unauthorized removal via narrations that had taken place only shortly before, but I have not witnessed the actual act of extraction. As people know well about the illegal character of this endeavor, it is difficult to document it with conventional ethnographic methods and since the issue only plays a minor part in the overall analysis, I did not pursue the matter explicitly.

CHAPTER 5

Dealing with the Dragon
Social Dynamics and Ambiguity in Emiliano Zapata

> You see, PEMEX is like a dragon. And what are we? Nothing! Because the dragon is very powerful, and it is burns us. We're nothing against PEMEX.
>
> —Doña Maria

Hydrocarbon extraction, its temporal consequences, and its material implications determine many aspects of the local lifeworld of the community members in Emiliano Zapata. Oil extraction is accompanied by certain social dynamics that exceed the influence of tangible and temporal aspects, as mainly in the context of company-community relations, and specific social settings determined by the circumstances surrounding extraction (see, e.g., Cochrane 2017; Silva Ontiveros et al. 2018). The oil extraction in Emiliano Zapata has an impact on the social dynamics within the community and contributes to the set of different uncertainties. The oilscape of Emiliano Zapata is a multidimensionally constituted space, which is formed in a processual manner by constant renegotiations and reconfigurations through the dynamics of its social actors. The creation of such a space is often a conflict-riddled process over economic and ideological resources and understanding these tensions can contribute to an understanding of major issues (Low 2014: 35). In order to understand these dynamics, this chapter will complement the previous analysis, focusing particularly on the involved actors and the interactions and practices through which they create and negotiate the oilscape. The circumstances that shaped local relationships and ways of interactions between actors are changing and, in this way, create new challenges.

In its long history with the oil industry, Emiliano Zapata has built a multilayered relationship with the oil companies as acting entities characterized by inherent power structures. Its status as a state-owned company has given PEMEX the dominant authority for extraction and processing activities in the country as well as in the community. Hence, PEMEX has become synonymous with the oil industry in general for many of the community members and continues to be so. Therefore, for many, PEMEX has become a ubiquitous entity in the local context, which is perceived as a kind of "monster" at times, while the local residents are condemned to its destructive powers. The image of such a powerful and even dangerous monster has been captured impressively by Doña Maria during an interview, when she denominated PEMEX as a "dragon"—a metaphor she used for the oil company to describe the relationship between the community and the company from her point of view. This metaphor symbolizes the unequal power relations between the company and community, which dominated the territory for many decades. PEMEX as a powerful player, had a significant impact on the area's regulations, modified the material surroundings, damaged the soil, and polluted the water, but also created new income prospects and lifestyles and introduced compensation guidelines. For many, the company thus also became a symbol of wealth and economic opportunities. The local perception of the oil company is thus highly ambivalent among the community members and depends on individual trajectories, social and economic statuses as well as personally established relationships.

The oilscape of Emiliano Zapata has been the stage for several land conflicts between community and company and also between different community groups, all of which are influenced by issues of presence and interests of the oil industry. The company as a dragon is perceived partly as destructive, partly as a patron, but always as a powerful entity. The metaphor of the dragon reflects the ambivalent perception of community-company relationships that determine the social dynamics through the interaction between oil company actors and local residents. The particularities of the social dynamics determined by the conditions of oil extraction contribute to the set of uncertainties emerging within the oilscape and call for new strategies by the community members in response to them. In this way, these uncertainties directly reflect back on the composition of the social texture.

The Dragon among Us: PEMEX in Emiliano Zapata

"Come in," Doña Clara says and then examines me from head to toe as I enter the room. Then suddenly she recognizes me and all the little wrinkles on her face seem to disappear when she opens her mouth to a wide smile. "Güera!" she exclaims, immediately getting up to pull out a chair for me and sit down with her.

I hurry to forestall her, but she moves with surprisingly quick, small, and stiff steps, and I have to take the chair from her firm, calloused hands after she has already grabbed one from the pile of plastic chairs in the corner of the room. I know Doña Clara is still surprisingly agile, but her nimble movements sometimes surprise me anyway. The gray-haired woman in the simple white-and-brown patterned dress and worn flip-flops in front of me sits down, looks at me excitedly, and pushes a glass and the two-liter bottle of Coke toward me over the table.

Doña Clara was born and raised in Emiliano Zapata. She is one of the very few women to hold the title of an ejidatario, which she received from her husband, who died a couple of years ago with no son in the community who wanted to inherit it. "But I'm thinking of dividing up the land and giving it to my children in equal parts so they won't fight over it later," she told me last time I visited her. But that would also mean that she would have to convert it to single property—an issue at the center of a simmering conflict within the community, where members constantly fight over tenure and the exact measurement of parcels. The territory Doña Clara has for disposal is not vast but is just enough to plant some orange trees for the market and a little corn for home consumption. The modest one-room house where six people currently live has no floor slab, and the bathroom is an outhouse in the backyard, shielded by black plastic tarp.

Doña Clara lives here—with her daughter-in-law and one of her sons. Her husband, by whom she has seven children, left her years ago, and she is happy about that fact since their relationship was marked by constant domestic violence. Today, all her children except one son have left the community to look for work elsewhere. She gets a grim expression on her face and a reproachful tone in her voice when she talks about them. "They don't send me any money. They are a bunch of drunks and gamblers!" Just one of her many sons stayed. But according to her, he is the worst of all drunks and does not take care of his wife and kids because he spends the money at the cantina. I am a little uncomfortable with her telling me this in the presence of her daughter-in-law. She makes breakfast for me, even though I had just eaten and explicitly said "no" when asked if I wanted anything to eat. But I should have known that this was not a real question for Doña Clara, so my response was not a real answer either. While I am eating my enchiladas like a good girl, I enjoy it when she tells me more about her life.

Doña Clara was one of the few people already living here when PEMEX came for the first time to do the exploration. "They came and started to put some dynamite right here in the backyard," she remembers. "I was just a little kid, and I was so scared when the explosions began! Also, it was really dangerous, because suddenly big rocks and smaller stones flew through the air and could hit your house! So, every time they screamed 'Cohete,' we all ran as fast as we could." She and the other children were frightened by the explosions, but also very curious about the strange men coming into the community. Usually they were nice to the children and sometimes brought gifts. Doña Clara remembers that at first, she was afraid of the oil workers, but then got used to them being friendly visitors or customers for her parents and neighbors when they sold them food or offered minor services. She soon began to regularly go to the installations at noontime to sell lunch. When her children were born, she brought them with her. Selling lunch was a nice way for her and her family to earn some extra money. However, neither she nor her relatives ever established personal relations with the *petroleros*. They remained visitors passing through or customers for services and goods, but she herself did not engage with them more than this. As one of the few ejidatarias, she has reported damages to her orchards when they became polluted over the years, and she got compensated. "It's not a lot they're paying," she says. And the humble home silently confirms that statement.

After our conversation, we sit in silence at the table for a while, listening to the TV hanging on the wall. The sauce burns in my mouth, and I have to drink some more glasses of Coke until I manage to quench it on my tongue and palate. I am sure she will not let me go without giving me some of her homegrown, dried chilies, which are so hot that it is impossible to have more than three of the pea-sized red fruits in a quart of enchilada sauce. I will certainly leave her house with stomach almost bursting, on the verge of a sugar rush and at the same time amazed by Doña Clara's stories. The curiosity for more will certainly drive me back to her house again soon.

Developing the Community

In Mexico, as in many parts of the world, companies in the extractive industry have taken on important social tasks in the affected areas. During the first major upswing of PEMEX in the 1950s and 1960s, the idea of the company at the time was to provide certain social services to employees and local residents. In this way, PEMEX delivered what was at that time a national consensus on "development" for many rural areas. I had the opportunity to talk to a rather high-ranking PEMEX official from the general directory, who told me about how he interprets the the role of the company within the national economy. "In fact, this is something I always emphasize," he said. "In many areas of the country the first civilizing entity that brought development was PEMEX looking for options to explore new oil sources." For him, this implied the role of the company as a generator of wealth, as well as the provider of jobs and services for the population:

> That is why PEMEX has many employees. Because PEMEX also incorporates a medical service, and a series of different other sections like "communication." I for example went to a school especially for children of oil workers . . . they gave us everything, that we needed. The books, the notebooks, the pencils, everything. In fact, they even produced our notebooks in the PEMEX workshops.

Due to its status as a state-owned company, it was assumed that PEMEX had a general social interest in benefiting the entire nation and therefore every Mexican citizen, through its oil profits. The company soon established an impressive internal infrastructure for its workers, who enjoyed the benefits of an internal PEMEX social and welfare system (Czarnecki and Vargas Chanes 2018: 76). The industry was established as a representative unit of the hydrocarbon industry and as a pillar for national development. This also implied a prioritization over other sectors or forms of land use as in the case of ejidos. Even though ejido land was technically inalienable, Article 27 of the 1917 Constitution encompassed the possibility of expropriating strategic resources for "the common good" for guaranteed indemnifications (del Palacio Langer 2015: 22). This rule has been applied specifically to the interests of PEMEX as an important entity for national economic development. After the nationalization of the hydrocarbon sector in 1936, PEMEX expropriated large parts of the national ejido territories for extraction, as was the case in Emiliano Zapata. The ejidos were indemnified accordingly—though this process was often contentious. Adherence to this law was accompanied by aggravating circumstances, as the nationalization of hydrocarbon resources and the status of PEMEX as a state-owned company also meant that an explicit implementation of CSR measurements was not considered necessary in the company's Code of Conduct. PEMEX was supposed to work for the benefit of the entire population (2015: 138).

The oil explorations in the respective regions have resulted in several urban areas where the local economy relied almost entirely on the extraction and processing of hydrocarbons, as was the case for the city of Poza Rica (see Salas Landa 2016; Quintal Avilés 1994). However, this was not the case in all oil-rich areas. Especially in regions with a strong presence of agriculture based indigenous communities, the idea of industrial development has often clashed with rural realities. The national vision of a complete integration of the indigenous population as Mexican citizens often failed because there was a lack of mechanisms to recognize and foster diversity (Rincón Gallardo 2004). The PEMEX-led oil industry has been assigned a "development contract" for rural areas, while severely lacking in sensitive implementation guidelines. My interview partner reflected on this era, acknowledging that the integration of indigenous people into a homogeneous society of Mexican citizens through industrial development failed. "The intention or the underlying will of the Mexican state was . . . to integrate them as proper citizens," my interview partner conceded, talking about the indigenous people of Mexico. He explained: "Here in Mexico it would be unthinkable to just see them as 'indigenous.' That would go against everything that we wanted or believed in, because it is a nation of citizens."

Emiliano Zapata was one of the rural indigenous communities he referred to by the time PEMEX conducted the first explorations. In this context, it was partly integrated into the oil industry, not on a voluntary basis but because of its location. With the expropriations of large parts of the ejido territory, the company's presence in the community became even stronger and the industry continued to spread. This process caused tensions to prevail between the community and company, and also between different groups within the community. Land conflicts, which arose through the industrial development, remain an issue in Emiliano Zapata until today and have thus affected the social dynamics as well as the appearance of the oilscape in a particular way. The company's presence in Emiliano Zapata is not only evident from equipment, installations, and pipelines, but also by the presence of its staff. Since the beginning of the extraction in 1956, the oil workers have interacted on a daily basis with the residents, and for many community members over the years, the staff thus personified the company. When PEMEX entered the community, it was welcomed as a guarantor of security and economic stability by several of the inhabitants, and its workers were perceived as patrons who would facilitate protection and benefits. At the same time, many community members expressed discontent with the disrespectful way the company's employees claimed the territory, but they also acknowledged the company's power to do so. PEMEX established itself as kind of an almost almighty entity that punishes and sometimes rewards, or at least compensates, as impressively illustrated by the comparison of PEMEX with a dragon in the quote at the beginning of this chapter. The dragon is able burn whoever stands in its way, constantly threatening the community and forcing it to obey its will. On the other hand, it also benefits the community by constructing infrastructure and offering certain goods and services during the years of its operation.

One of the first factors through which the presence of the oil industry became tangible for the community members was PEMEX staff commuting from the city to the extraction sites, entering and crossing the community. The oil company expanded its activities rapidly and needed an increasing amount of territory to extend the extraction, which is why about 250 hectares of Emiliano Zapata were expropriated for extraction purposes during the boom. Having the extraction taking place so close to their homes created several contact opportunities with the PEMEX staff for the residents, including new income strategies. Many of them started to sell food or goods to the PEMEX workers and the workers themselves mostly strove for good relations with the community members, among them many women, who did not have the opportunity to earn an income before. However, the close contact between community and company personnel led to a variety of changes within the social structure of the community.

Gender, Traditions, and Social Norms in Times of the Oil Boom

During the oil boom, the numbers of inhabitants increased, because many people from all over the region, looking for security and a source of income, recognized the opportunities offered by PEMEX. Some of migrants who came to profit from the economic upswing came from the area of Totonacapan and spoke Totonac as well, but the majority had to rely on Spanish to enable the communication with the original population of Emiliano Zapata. The former social structure of the community started to shift from the traditional Totonac household organization, being patrilocal with strictly divided gendered labor tasks and agriculture for subsistence toward a model that included merchants, single men and women without close family ties, and other differing lifestyles.

Adaptations concerning Spanish as the main language already started with the establishment of the first school in Emiliano Zapata in the 1940s, but it was enforced even more for the practical reasons of communication with inhabitants from other places and the PEMEX staff. Doña Ana, the sixty-year-old daughter of such an already-deceased dancer told me: "Look, back then the community, it didn't look like it does now. Now PEMEX is already established here. But before it did, our parents, for example my father, he was very indigenous." Elderly people with a traditional way of life and cultural practices from pre-colonial times, such as the ceremonial dance of the *voladores*,[1] were rather reluctant toward the appearance of the oil company," she told me. "But after they died, PEMEX was allowed in after all." Apart from old traditions vanishing, which were associated with an antique and less desirable lifestyle, new forms of everyday life performances became popular. Novel moral and social norms were brought in by the oil workers, who until today belong to a mainly male dominated professional category (see Mottura 2017; Palermo 2017).

Soon the PEMEX staff introduced new forms of possible gender roles to the community. Some of the oil workers started to engage with young resident women, stressing the dominant social norms. Even though the moral standards have been modified during the last decades, the role of women from the community engaging with oil workers is still considered sensitive, where oftentimes conflicting ideas of morality apply. Many families sought to prevent the contact between their daughters and the oil workers, because they feared immoral behavior, leading to illegitimate pregnancy in the worst case. Again, others, however, even encouraged their daughters to get in contact with the PEMEX staff because they enjoyed a high social status in combination with wealth and high education standards. Furthermore, they were the main customers at many stores and in the restaurants and the owners strove for friendly engagement with their customers.

Doña Imelda, a woman in her fifties is the daughter of a shop owner from Emiliano Zapata. She has several daughters from different fathers, none of them living in the community, but all providing her with the necessary money to support her children. She is grandmother of three and her daughters are unmarried as well as herself. The fathers come to visit them sometimes, but mostly they are not part of the life of their illegitimate children. Doña Imelda told me about the time her father, a native resident of the community, had opened his shop. Her family still spoke Totonac at home at first, but she says that she hardly remembered anything today since her parents did not continue to talk to her in their language. Their store was mainly frequented by oil workers and teachers who were the main customers and who spoke Spanish and the parents also started speaking Spanish with the customers and also within their own family: "I didn't learn how to speak Totonac. My older sister still did, but at that time in 1956, my mother said, they had a shop where teachers and oil workers came to buy things and drink beer, and I was raised speaking Spanish." Doña Imelda remembered that her father was very friendly with the oil workers who were his customers and started drinking alcohol with them: "There were many oil workers coming to the store. We had a jukebox playing music and everyone was in a good mood and my father used to drink with them. My father had many friends among the oil workers. He got along with them really well!" Doña Imelda's father did not only engage in a very friendly manner with his customers but encouraged her to do the same. Especially when the oil workers came regularly to have parties and bought beer at his shop, he encouraged her to dance with the oil workers: "I was going to the dances. I still very much like to dance! And my father would tell me to dance with him, and I did. I was young back then. And when an oil worker would come to us he would tell me to dance with him as well, and I did."

This behavior was not welcomed by all of Doña Imelda's neighbors, not even by all her relatives. But she claimed that she liked that lifestyle, appearing attractive and mundane to her at this time: "I like to make conversation, I like to laugh, and my family criticized me for it. They said I looked like a *chichí*—'little bitch' in Totonaco. But I thought, 'Let them talk, that's how I am. I like to dance and make friends.'" Yet the intentions of the oil workers were often of a sexual nature, which were often even furthered by her father. "My father tried to hook me up with older oil workers and I danced with them." The idea of engaging with the oil workers from the city seemed pleasurable for many young women, and they enjoyed going to public dance events, learning dance styles from the cities. The oil workers mostly did not bow to social pressure concerning possible marriage with the women in the community and in most cases did not attempt to engage in serious relationships. For the women, this created pressure and in the case of Doña Imelda, despite of enjoying the dances and the attention of the oil workers, she also had some negative experiences with men she was involved with. She suffered unwanted pregnancies and an abortion after she started a romantic affair with one of the oil workers, who was already committed to another woman in the city. She quickly realized when she got pregnant and told him. He then asked her to abort, and she did. "I packed my things, and I wanted to run away to see him, but before I could, I was told that he had a girlfriend," she said. "He said I should take the tea. And I did. I was not even two months pregnant, like one month and fifteen days." What Doña Imelda described applied to many young women in the community when the relationships with people from other parts, mainly from urban areas intensified during times of boom. On the one hand, they were attracted by new opportunities and a pleasant lifestyle but along with them came novel expectations concerning their roles and behaviors, for men as well as for women. Women for the first time now had the opportunity to gain an income on their own, for example, by selling food and therefore reaching a certain independence from the traditional family model. But this also meant a modification of expectations toward them and sometimes pressure to move toward an "urban way of life." The latter included wealth and independence but also alcohol and an increased risk of possible sexual abuse or the complications of unwanted pregnancies. The stores, the bars, and also the brothels came with the oil workers to the community, as has been documented all over the world in cases in which a big company accessed a rural area (see, e.g., Cancian 1994; Davidson and Davis 2012; Harma 2009). With them came money, goods, and shifting ideas of lifestyle and role models for both genders.

PEMEX Personnel and Community Members

Until today, oil company personnel still are the customer target group of many community businesses, but only few contacts have become personal acquaintances, and even fewer have transformed into enduring relationships. Most community members perceive the PEMEX staff as "the others" even now and in contrast to cities like Poza Rica, the element of identification with the company is rather low, despite its long-term presence. Pablo, a PEMEX staff member from Poza Rica, who worked on the San Andrés oilfield for many years, described his view of how the community members of Emiliano Zapata perceived PEMEX employees like him: "Well, at the booths, where we go for lunch sometimes, they treat us well. But many people who pass by, they look at us and make a face. They see us as the bad guys." He, like most of the others, keeps his distance from the community. These limited interactions between the community and the company's staff are certainly one of the main reasons for the lack of identification with PEMEX in Emiliano Zapata. Moreover, the low-paid part-time contracts that the residents could mostly manage to get, limit the ability and willingness of the community members to associate themselves with PEMEX. Hence, PEMEX did not become an integrative entity, but remained an external force to negotiate with in order to gain benefits and minimize damages.

During the 1950s until the 1980s, the official PEMEX guidelines for company-community relations were rather unconstrained and allowed the executive team a great deal of individual interpretation and guidance. The way PEMEX was perceived by the community members, therefore, often depended on the individual relationship with the oil workers. This partly changed in the 1980s and 1990s, when some internal guidelines were introduced, but a modification of the official Code of Conduct was first conducted in the 2000s, when CSR measurements were officially incorporated into company policies in 2006 (García-Chiang 2018: 2). When damages or seepages occur, the community members report their claims directly to the company, which then responds to them. Unfortunately, the official way of reporting damages often takes some bureaucratic effort and the company often takes a long time to initiate the repair. Several of the seepages in one of the two small community rivers were fixed during my field research stay of many months, and the community members complained about this and other delays PEMEX caused in repairing damages by not responding promptly to claims. The people whose plots were affected by pollution, or a possibly cracked pipeline, had to endure the uncertainty of waiting for an indeterminate time for the company to inspect or fix the problem. Many community members, therefore, found ways to work around the official reporting structure by establishing personal contacts with individual company staff members.

Don Francisco is a middle-aged man who lives with his family next to an extraction well close to the main road. He inherited the house from his father and is, therefore, used to the industrial activities since his early childhood. When I interviewed him, he complained about the lack of commitment from PEMEX, when pipelines under his house got damaged. I asked him how he normally reported damage to the company, and he told me that usually one would go to the main office in Poza Rica or call an official hotline to the headquarters. Since it takes a long time before somebody reacts through official channels, he calls the personal phone number of one of the PEMEX *ingenieros*. Don Francisco pulled out his mobile phone and showed me the number among his contacts on the screen that belongs to one of the *ingenieros*. The *ingeniero* gave his number to Don Francisco during an inspection of damage after Don Francisco complained about the long delay in response to his notification. Now he can simply call a leading staff member directly and the issue gets attended to a lot faster.

While many inhabitants like Don Francisco have established contacts with staff members, the connections are strictly professional. Most inhabitants do not identify themselves with the company or maintain personal relationships and most of them see an unbridgeable gap between themselves as community members and the oil company and its staff. This is also due to the limited options for proper employment for the residents. When talking about employment opportunities at PEMEX, I often asked if my interview partner ever worked for the company. Most interviewees denied it at first during the interview, but it turned out that the person worked in construction, service, or elsewhere at some point. Doña Maria has several male relatives who worked in construction and as day laborers for the company over the years. On being asked if she knew people working for PEMEX, she answered: "No, here we don't know anyone working for PEMEX. They're all from the city. We don't know them." When asked again later whether PEMEX sometimes offers jobs to community members, she reaffirmed her statement: "No, we're all campesinos. Because there are no jobs for us to work for the company." Later during the same interview, I wanted to know if her husband or her sons worked in construction for the company and then she conceded: "Yes as *obreros*.[2] They went to the excavations and they helped to maintain the pipelines." This kind of work is not seen by locals as "working for PEMEX." Instead, a strict line is drawn between the "real" PEMEX staff and low-wage workers, that is, people who only receive short-term contracts. This is in line with the company policy, as PEMEX has not been looking for local employees to integrate into the staff since the beginning of its activities in the community. Therefore, the residents of Emiliano Zapata see a big difference between *trabajar en PEMEX* and a proper *petrolero* or *ingeniero*. Technically, *obreros* also have the possibility of joining the Sindicato de Trabajadores Petroleros de la República Mexicana (STPRM), but in Emiliano Zapata none of the marginal and short-term workers in construction or maintenance became members of the union. Most consider themselves campesinos and never strived to unionize, while the STPRM has never explicitly advocated the inclusion of rural day laborers, whose agenda was perceived as too different from the claims and goals of the oil workers in oil towns like Poza Rica (see Quintal Avilés 1994). Paradoxically, the unionized PEMEX staff is perceived as a group of the "urban elite," in contrast to the rural farmers who, occasionally work as day laborers.[3] PEMEX employees maintain a physical distance from the community and restrict direct interactions with the villagers to official business relationships, such as purchasing services or goods. No one in the community ever worked as a permanent PEMEX employee. They come to work every day from the cities of Papantla or Poza Rica. When I asked if Doña Maria knew about company staff living in Emiliano Zapata, Doña Maria said: "Well, I actually don't. They usually arrive in their company vans together and stick to themselves. They sometimes come to buy something, but most of the time they just pass by and go directly to the pipeline they are sent to check on or whatever they are sent to do and then get back."

Nevertheless, a handful of PEMEX employees who worked in the San Andrés oilfield for a long time stayed in the community after retirement. Yet, they see themselves as simple workers and not as leading personnel referred to as *ingenieros*. Don Aturo is one who worked for PEMEX for many years. He was born in the area around Poza Rica and started working at the lower end of the corporate hierarchy. During his time working for the oil company, Don Aturo became familiar with the company system. He explained why he and most of his colleagues had little contact with the residents from Emiliano Zapata when working on the San Andrés oilfield, although they were in charge of the leaks and seepages the residents often complained about: "Well, there were an infinite number of leaks, but that was no longer our responsibility as workers. We only were to look where the leak was coming from and to isolate it, not to repair it. Isolate it and that's it," he told me. Yet, the actual repairing, as well as the negotiation for compensation for affected community members corresponds to PEMEX employees. During that time, Don Aturo and his colleagues, who worked every day near Emiliano Zapata, never directly witnessed compensation payments or the negotiations about damages with the community members, only higher-level employees dealt with the local residents directly, especially in case of damages or reparation claims. In this way, the internal organization of PEMEX contributed to a certain distance between company personnel and community members, a common approach for companies in the extractive sector (see, e.g., Appel 2012b; Auyero and Swistun 2008; Cross 2011). Therefore, PEMEX continues to be perceived as a powerful external entity rather than a factor amenable to integration and even less for self-identification.

Conflicts and Corruption: PEMEX Expropriating the Ejido

PEMEX started in 1956 to build industrial infrastructure in Emiliano Zapata but made the first official request for expropriation about eight years later on 24 September 1964. Until then, the construction of installations had already caused damage and limited the use of several areas within the ejido. The inconvenience was compensated by individual payments before the official indemnifications were paid to the ejidatarios. At that time, compensations were only paid for damaged soil, plants, and other goods. When the expropriation was finally implemented eight years later, PEMEX initially claimed 106.3474 hectares of land from the ejido. But before the expropriation was executed, the company again revised the measurement and decided to claim double—an additional 106 hectares—266.3474 hectares in total. The ejido council objected to that claim, which for many seemed too much territory and after a new series of measurements and negotiations with the ejido assembly, they reached a consensus with the company on a total of 185.42 hectares in 1976. The expropriation of $3,671,331.84 was paid that should be divided equally among the affected ejidatarios (Reporte Proyecto IICA-RAN 2012). However, not all of them were satisfied with the agreement. And indeed, new measurements carried out by the ejidatarios showed that PEMEX was in fact, occupying the 266.3474 hectares they originally wanted to expropriate, while they only paid for the contracted 185.42. At that time, the majority of the ejidatarios had already agreed to the payments and signed the documents, so that regress claims could not be asserted. The ejido was governed collectively as a communal landholding and each ejidatario used a part of the communal land according to the agreements made in the assembly, without exact documentation about who cultivated what on which parcel. In the realm of the agrarian counter reform of 1992, this principle was changed when the farming parcels were supposed to be exactly measured and officially assigned to individuals. The program, PROCEDE, was initiated with the purpose of surveying and certifying the individual parcels and respective land rights of each ejidatario. After the designation process, each ejidatario received a certificate that enabled the successor to apply for an actual property title (see Smith et al. 2009).

In Emiliano Zapata, the ejidatarios were not eager to certify land parcels in the beginning because they had become accustomed to their distinct way of distributing the territory among themselves. Yet, the legalization also promised benefits, like the possibility to sell the land later, which was not yet allowed. Don Esteban, a native of Emiliano Zapata and an ejidatario, has served in the ejido representation several times in different positions. He inherited this title from his father, and now he is in favor of the new regularization, as he told me: "With the certificate, you would be able to deal with any individual matter. But now we can't do that just because we don't have a document. Also, at the moment we can't prove that there were irregularities when PEMEX paid the indemnity." Hence, for the ejidatarios the regularization would have two main beneficial effects. First, they would have the possibility to make individual decisions about the parcels without having to get permission from the assembly for every legal question, and second, without regularization some claims against PEMEX cannot be made without official titles. In 2002, the ejidatarios decided to make an initial attempt at regularization. In 2004–5, a second attempt followed, since they could not agree upon the parcel sizes, followed by a third in 2007 via the government program PROCEDE. Apart from the personal disagreements between individuals, a major problem in finalizing the process was the expansion of the area occupied by PEMEX. During this process and the corresponding inspection of old documents, some inconsistencies were discovered. The ejidatarios recognized that the territory occupied by PEMEX was larger than the 185.42 hectares that the company had officially expropriated. In addition, it turned out that the indemnification payments were distributed unequally between the ejidatarios. These discoveries soon led to internal conflicts between the ejidatarios.

Don Simón, a farmer and ejidatario in his forties, inherited the title from his father recently. He became a secretary of the comisariado ejidal in 2016 and along with the comisario, he started to regulate the disorderly paperwork of the ejido. They resolved the vexing issues and hoped that the fourth attempt at official regularization, which took place in 2016–17, would be successful. In 2016, he told me about the conflict smoldering in the ejido assembly at that time, concerning the unsettled payments for hectares that PEMEX had occupied but not expropriated, and traced them back to a corruption case in the 1970s. By revising old documents, he revealed that some of the ejidatarios received more money than others, even though the amounts should have been evenly distributed. Meanwhile, PEMEX paid for fewer hectares than were actually occupied, as

Don Simón explicated: "Now it turned out that the that PEMEX paid less indemnification money to the ejido, than they were obliged to. Only a few ejidatarios knew and they accepted the payment. They never distributed the money equally between all of them."

By studying the old endowment papers, Don Simón discovered that PEMEX had paid indemnifications for a group of only thirty-one ejidatarios representing fifty-eight in total. By the time the agreement was settled, the ejido was not yet officially divided into individual parcels, while the payments were granted individually, but not to all. It is suspected that a group of ejidatarios had accepted individual payments from PEMEX in return for agreeing to the expropriation of the smaller area. Yet in Don Simón interpretation the indemnification was not rightfully conducted for the simple reason that the ejido was not divided into individual parcels back then, but the decree individually lists the names and the amounts of money. In a decree from 1976, the thirty-one ejidatarios who were individually paid by PEMEX are named, the first official expropriation then was decreed on 10 November 1978. After the document about the payment of 1976 had been dug up in the context of the regularization process, the ejidatario assembly started to retrospectively reclaim the irregularity of the process with the company by presenting a list of the missing twenty-seven ejidatarios who had not received the payment. The claims against PEMEX have not been successful so far, as the company holds the official paperwork with the endowment of the expropriated territory. As Don Simón remarked: "PEMEX claims to have already indemnified the 185 hectars. And many of the ejidatarios who were paid back then are already deceased." Therefore, the ejidatarios did not receive any payments from PEMEX retrospectively. Attempts by the assembly to resolve the problem by claiming money for the areas, which are considered to be affected by PEMEX installations but have not been properly indemnified, were unsuccessful as well. These claims can only be asserted when the people of Emiliano Zapata manage to agree on the regularization of each parcel.

Complications within the Regularization Process

During the attempt at regularization, which was initiated this time under the new program of FANAR, which subsidized PROCEDE[4] in 2007, a map was constituted showing the areas affected by PEMEX. However, the *ejidatarios* did not agree on the cartographic boundaries of their parcels. The map shows serious effects on the human settlement for which the community members have not yet been compensated either. Again, this can only be asserted once the regularization process is legally completed.

158 | *Living on a Time Bomb*

Map 5.1. The surface of the ejido Emiliano Zapata 2007, highlighting Plots and Parcels occupied, or affected by PEMEX Installations. Courtesy of the Comisariado Ejidal of Emiliano Zapata.

This includes a larger area, which was not part of the indemnified surface of 1976. PEMEX built turbines and the gas flare here in 1980, but instead of claiming an additional expropriation, it paid a *pago de ocupación superficial*. This allows the company to operate on the area for a certain number of years, as opposed to the expropriation, which is unlimited by time.

Since the company has abandoned several of these installations, the community can legally reclaim these areas. Don Simón reported from his meeting with the government agency Procaruría Agraria, which suggested that the ejidatarios should agree on the boundaries of the human settlement area, also called *fundo legal*: "We went to the agrarian procurator's office and they told us: 'it is important that you constitute the *fundo legal* in your community first, because PEMEX is affecting the nucleus of the human settlement.'" With the titles that the ejidatario and each community member would get with the regularization of their parcels, they could then make their claims against PEMEX in case their parcel is affected, or they could reclaim the territory that the company no longer uses. Therefore, Don Simón, like many others, is in favor of a quick regularization process. But not all the ejidatarios agree with him. Many of the elder assembly members have received the indemnification payments and do not see the necessity of a parcel regularization, because their corresponding area is not affected or has been properly paid already. Instead, they fear the potential consequences, such as increasing fees after the endowment of the parcels. Don Simón acknowledges these concerns, but he still insists that it would be worthwhile considering what the titles could enable: "They say that the only reason for the government to grant us the certificates is that they want to charge more taxes. And in fact: If we get the titles, we actually will pay more taxes. But also, the land would be worth more money or, in other words, what we call capital gain."

Many ejidatarios are still reluctant to conduct the regularization process, also because many of them have already sold parts of the parcels they were assigned internally by the assembly. Technically this is not allowed under ejido law, but nevertheless, many ejidatarios already started to sell or rent more and more of their corresponding territory, often to close family members. Since this practice is not legal and therefore also not officially documented, the ejidatarios are free to negotiate the price and the conditions. The practice of illegitimately selling and renting ejido land has been established for many years in Emiliano Zapata. Now, many ejidatarios fear that a regularization would also regulate the prices and conditions of the sale. Don Simón admitted: "The ejidatarios don't want to report their profits from the sales. They don't want to make it transparent. Technically, they are not even allowed to sell, but sales are already taking place." He sees a possibility to resolve the problem with support from the propietarios—community members who live and work on building plots or parcels without being granted the ejidatario title.

Over the years, the community has grown steadily and many people who came here were never interested in becoming an ejidatario. They would much rather settle down to work in the service or construction sector. Hence, the number of community members who are not ejidatarios has grown steadily, while the number of ejidatarios has remained the same since the 1960s. The regularization of the housing area must be conducted by also integrating the community members living there without being ejidatarios. They also have a particular interest in conducting the legalization of their plots, since they are affected by PEMEX installations for which they could then theoretically claim compensation payments or devolution of the territory. One particular problem that hinders many propietarios from acting is the same reason why many ejidatarios are not in favor of regularization—they sometimes received documents for the plots and parcels they bought from the ejidatarios, which are not lawfully valid, due to the prohibition of the ejidatarios to sell the land in the first place. Now, many are worried that their titles, therefore, would not be officially validated retrospectively, and they would lose their properties. Others are more optimistic, since they have the titles from the ejido assembly and assume that the complications would fall back on the ejidatarios in a worst-case scenario. Unfortunately, the ejido assembly has the final say regarding the regularization, as Don Simón lamented: "There are a lot more propietarios than ejidatarios. So, the majority is in favor, but the ejidatarios do not agree. The law determines that the assembly of ejidatarios has to reach an agreement to constitute the *fondu legal*, so only they can ultimately make the decision."

In 2016, a fresh attempt at regularization was initiated. The process failed a year later, after internal conflicts led to Don Simón and his companions being charged and replaced by a new comisariado. The new leaders are not generally opposed to a regularization under the government program, but they have argued against several legitimation attempts by their precursors. They particularly objected to a possible retroactive reimbursement to the ejidatarios or their families, who were not indemnified by PEMEX in 1976, and the prevention of further illegitimate land sales. Many of the ejidatarios are against the final regularization, not only because of the higher taxes they would probably have to pay, but also because they would certainly lose some of their sovereignty. As long as the ejido parcels are not individually assigned, they are free to decide how the territory is governed. If the assembly agrees on an issue, the ejidatarios can distribute the land as they please, and although they are not officially allowed to sell or rent parts of the land to non-ejidatarios, this had been practiced for many years. A regularization would, therefore, restrict its governing power and give the propietarios certain rights and competences.

In some ways, however, it would serve the interest of the ejidatarios to regulate the land. First, they would obtain official ownership of their parcels and selling of parts of the land would be legal and safe. In addition, they would also have the possibility to claim damages and return occupied land from PEMEX, which is not possible in the current situation. The energy reform has an aggravating effect in this decision-making process, as a potential takeover of the PEMEX installations by a new company would ultimately reduce the possibility of claiming incomplete indemnification in retrospect. Emiliano Zapata comprises only fifty-eight rightful ejidatarios, but this minority is entitled to make all decisions about the land within the realm of the ejido. This imbalance is stronger than in other ejidos, as its history included income opportunities in the service and construction sectors by the oil industry. Therefore, many immigrants did not see the need to apply for an ejidatario title here. Unlike Emiliano Zapata, there is not a single ejidatario living in San Andrés, as this colony was founded at the time of the oilfield development and populated by people who earn their income in the infrastructure facilitated by PEMEX, such as in restaurants, stores, barber shops, or in construction.

San Andrés: A Settlement between Oilfield and Ejido

The settlement of San Andrés represents a part of Emiliano Zapata, where the developments induced by the oil industry became exemplarily visible to the entire community. The *colonia* was founded in the early 1960s, when some people from the neighborhood of the settled in the immediate vicinity of PEMEX installations. They prepared meals for the passing oil workers and offered goods and services in improvised stores and snack bars, or they went to the extraction site every day to seek opportunities for casual work. By then, the community of Emiliano Zapata comprised only about five hundred residents and the ejido territory was large enough to provide land for more inhabitants. These people also settled so close to the PEMEX installations, they actually lived on land that the company was occupying anyway. Having a location so close to the extraction site brought the benefit of being close to the target customers, but with the disadvantage of living on a ground that was strongly pervaded by pipelines and not meant for settlement. After ten people died in the gas explosion of 1966 known as *quemazón*, PEMEX financially compensated the settlers and leased part of the ejido territory, about 1.5 km from the community center, to relocate the San Andrés settlement to a less dangerous area in the same year.

Today, there are very few people in San Andrés who personally witnessed the accident. Some of the older residents vaguely remember the times when the settlement was located closer to the installations and recall when PEMEX reimbursed the victims and acquired part of the ejido territory for them to settle on. Don Amado is one of the older residents of the colony. As many of the first settlers of San Andrés, he is from the rural parts of Puebla and grew up under very difficult circumstances. His father left the family very early, and his mother died a few years later, so his older siblings raised him and his younger siblings. His family owned very little property, and he inherited no land to work on, so as a youth, he had to leave and look for work. He shares the difficult childhood and his upbringing in poverty with most older settlers of San Andrés who were drawn by the boom of the oil industry that offered an alternative income to a group of poor rural but landless sons and daughters of peasants. Don Amado learned to cut hair, but without seed capital, he did not find a

Map 5.2. OpenStreetMap of Emiliano Zapata highlighting the Colonia San Andrés © OpenStreetMap-Mitwirkende (www.openstreetmap.org/copyright).

place where he could settle down to open a salon. In an interview, he recalled how he came to San Andrés in the first place: "I wanted to work in Poza Rica, but I couldn't. In every hair salon I went to, they asked me for a person that would recommend me. Well, nobody knew me there, who was going to recommend me? I returned and took the bus to Martinez, but I didn't arrive there, I passed by this place, and I stayed here ever since."

Most inhabitants of San Andrés have similar stories to tell in which they did not originally intend to go to Emiliano Zapata and settle down close to the oil installations, but rather passed by on the way to a larger city in the area. They saw opportunities to work or to sell services and goods, and they stayed there in improvised small huts. In the beginning, the ejidatario assembly under its former comisariado, was rather open-minded about the new settlers. Since PEMEX had paid for the plots they occupied, and the new settlers did not even show any interest in setting up farming parcels or applying for titles as ejidatarios, they posed no real competition. The ejidatarios even allowed more people to settle in the area when new migrants arrived after the relocation in the 1960s. A few years later, however, the ejidatarios not only tightened their policies with the election of new representatives, but even demanded the land back and wanted the settlers to leave, as Don Amado recalled: "Later another man came into office. And that's when the conflict began. The started to claim that we should leave this place. The conflict is now more than twenty-five years old and still remains." The ejidatarios went to the municipal authorities and filed a complaint against illegitimate occupation of the ejido territory in the early 1970s, but Don Amado and some of his neighbors from San Andrés were able to defend their right to stay on their parcels by showing the documents they had received from the comisariado and PEMEX when they were relocated. Afterward, several of the ejidatarios still tried to convince the settlers to leave the territory, but they had no legal basis to act upon anymore.

The land conflict with the ejidatarios, the distance to the community center, as also the shared identification as migrant merchants rather than farmers rooted to the land, led to the development of a strengthening identity as "residents from San Andrés" rather than as community members of Emiliano Zapata. The inhabitants of San Andrés acknowledge their administrational assignment to Emiliano Zapata, developed family ties and friendships and some of them even hold offices in community politics. Nevertheless, many inhabitants of San Andrés foster their own feelings of cohesion. They identify themselves with their settlement as merchants who emerged through the business opportunities facilitated by PEMEX rather than with the ejido and campesino community as they perceive Emiliano Zapata. As PEMEX had assigned them the territory they are occupying until this day, the company furthermore, serves as a legal patron to them. Doña Minerva is the daughter of residents from Emiliano Zapata, but she moved to San Andrés about a decade ago to live with her husband from San Andrés. During a focus group interview with the inhabitants of San Andrés, she explained why she as many others, perceive San Andrés as an extended part of the oil industry, with PEMEX being the patron of the colony:

> We were so to say, an "extension of PEMEX," that belonged to the company. Back then there was an economic boom, there were jobs, everything we could ask for. People came from all kinds of different places and settled here, sometimes within the boundaries of the ejido. Then PEMEX relocated them, to this area to take them out of the ejido. Technically this piece of land where we live now belongs to PEMEX.

She pointed out the different economic basis that San Andrés has in contrast to Emiliano Zapata, which forms a different kind of shared identity: "People come to do their business here. Here we are businesspeople, so to say. Everybody here has a small business—a store, a booth or a cantina. Over there it's different. Maybe it's the economy over there, right? People work their fields and orchards, and they live from day to day. Here we have more economic activity."

The relationship with Emiliano Zapata is still difficult due to the land conflicts in the past, and several residents of San Andrés favor the liberty to establish their own community with its own legal status. So far, there have been no serious attempts to legally process independence, and such an endeavor would be difficult since the colony is still located within the limits of the endowed ejido territory. Yet, San Andrés started to establish its own institutions and already has a church, a small primary school, and even a kindergarten at its disposal. Furthermore, the Instituto Nacional de Estadística y Geografía (INEGI) started to count San Andrés as an independent community in their last census from 2010, which is seen by many inhabitants of San Andrés as a further argument for San Andrés being independent from the ejido. Since 2014, the inhabitants of San Andrés also started to hold their own *fiesta patronal*, an annual celebration of the patron of each community (usually the titular saint). In the case of Emiliano Zapata, the *fiesta patronal* is on 12 December, as the day of the Virgen de Guadalaupe, the patron saint of Mexico. San Andrés would have been part of this celebration as part of the community but started to organize its own celebration on 29 November, the day of Saint Andrew, their titular saint, and therewith, demonstrated a certain self-adscription as an independent community. Doña Minerva emphasized the success San Andrés already had in establishing new public services for themselves, while the inhabitants of the center of Emiliano Zapata are perceived as quarrelsome: "Emiliano Zapata doesn't like progress. They don't want new things in the community. They fight a lot; they always have conflicts among themselves. Here we don't. People in San Andrés are very united."

When PEMEX started to withdraw from the area and abandoned many of the installations, the economic situation for many residents from San Andrés became increasingly difficult. Most of them relied in one way or the other on the flow of oil workers and goods for their small businesses. However, many of them can still sell enough to sustain their families due to the customers that pass by during the time of the orange harvest season, or they look for other opportunities to earn income. When PEMEX abandoned many of their installations during the crisis, many ejidatarios from Emiliano Zapata saw that as a possibility to claim back the hitherto occupied territory. That also included the parcels that PEMEX had leased for the San Andrés colony after the accident in 1966. Since they still did not have the legal basis for reclaiming the land officially, the authorities from Emiliano Zapata did not try to relocate the colony but wanted to sell them possession titles for their homes, even though the territory still counted officially as part of the indemnified territory from PEMEX. However, since PEMEX was no longer present on the scene on a regular basis, the inhabitants of San Andrés feel abandoned by their patron company. Yet, the

Figure 5.1. The colony San Andrés beside the main road, Papantla, Mexico, 2018 © Svenja Schöneich.

ejidatarios could not get legal approval to reclaim the occupied areas from PEMEX until now and, therefore, the colony remained and persists till this day, belonging to Emiliano Zapata on an administrative level. In case the regularization of the ejido under the government program FANAR is to be conducted in the future, the ejidatarios could then try to reclaim some of the territory occupied by PEMEX, possibly also the parcels occupied by San Andrés, exposing the residents of the colony legally to the decisions taken in Emiliano Zapata. Recently the relationship between Emiliano Zapata and San Andrés was challenged through novel land distribution schemes, which might be soon established via the regularization of the ejido.

Changing Social Dynamics after the Energy Reform

Despite the rather early hour, the sun is burning mercilessly from the cloudless sky and even though the assembly room the casa del campesino at the main square in the community center provides shade and the windows are wide open, the heat is already crawling into the room. The meeting should have started at 10 o'clock, like Don Alberto, the comisario ejidal, told us the day before, but when I arrived on time at the *auditorio*,[5] there are only very few people present. Now, almost fifteen minutes later we are all together, not more than eighteen individuals sitting on the rows of wooden benches in the assembly room. Two vehicles finally arrive a few minutes later and park directly in front of the *auditorio*. The first one is showing the PEMEX logo and a second one displays the lettering from the company Oleorey. Three people are getting out of the first car, two men and a woman, while two men get out the other car. All of them are wearing company overalls except the older man from Oleorey who is wearing jeans and a blue shirt also portraying his company logo. All five greet the comisario ejidal who was waiting for them standing by the door.

While two of the visitors wait in the background, three men stand up behind the small desk. They look oddly small in front of the big painting of revolutionary and peasant leader Emiliano Zapata at the back wall, which now seems like a relic from another era. The tallest one standing on the right starts to talk. He is wearing glasses and has a PEMEX badge on his overalls and presents himself as a PEMEX staff member. As he speaks, the two visitors in the back start to hand out two different attendance lists to the people on the bench, one for each company. "So, like we already told your comisariado ejidal who called in this meeting, we want to announce an increased activity of the gas flare within the coming four weeks," the speaker reveals his reason for coming here. He continues with a talk about technical matters and details on why this measurement is necessary—mainly because a large quantity of surplus gas has to be burned that accumulated during the recent extraction activities. The other two men in the front add some detailed information here and there and all of them assure the group that everything will be done to properly control the burning—a fact they emphasize a lot. Then they offer to answer questions if the people of Zapata should have some. Many hands immediately go up: People do have questions!

Most of them are worried about accidents that might occur or the noise disturbance caused by the increased gas flare activity. Some get angry mentioning former spills and accidents that have not been resolved. Others complain that this meeting was scheduled at very short notice, so there was no time to mobilize more people to attend today. The agente municipal is furious, which may also be due to the fact that the company seemingly ignored the protocol to contact him first to call the meeting but informed the comisario instead. He points out that one of the recent seepages has still not been resolved. When he called the PEMEX people, they referred him to Oleorey, who then said that PEMEX was responsible. In this way, the seepage continued for weeks. Other community members nod in agreement, the unresolved questions of responsibility between the companies are at their expense. The company representatives remain friendly but distant while facing the accusations. They say that other people from the company have been responsible for what happened in the past and relegate responsibility—they are only responsible for informing the community, stating that they do not know much about the problems of the past. Some community members do not believe them and get up angrily and leave, but a few remain seated and demonstrate interest in what the representatives have to say. The comisario raises his hand and proposes that the companies could do something to compensate the disturbances. The visitors listen and nod but before one of the company affiliates responds, the first speaker calls up the next person who raised his hand to speak and the issue remains unresolved for now. Once again.

The Entrance of a New Company: Oleorey takes Over

After seventy-six years of PEMEX's monopoly, new companies and thus new players are entering the scene. The San Andrés oilfield is not yet assigned to a foreign company, but the Venezuelan firm Oleorey is already in place as a subcontractor and is probably going to take over the installations in the following years (García-Chiang 2018: 4–5). The residents of Emiliano Zapata became accustomed to the influence of PEMEX over the years and today, the people who remember a time when the company was not present in the community are significantly outnumbered. PEMEX had subcontracted other national firms for basic construction works in the area since it started operating, which then used local labor forces, long before the energy reform. Yet, the state-owned oil company always represented the responsible entity in charge (see García-Chiang 2018). PEMEX staff assigned the work to be done, contracted the conducting staff, and oversaw the construction work. Since the oil company owned the hydrocarbon sources and managed the extraction sites and the territory expropriated from the ejido, PEMEX had been the major counterpart in question of indemnification and compensation payments. When the new Venezuelan company, Oleorey, started to take over several installations on the San Andrés oilfield after 2012, it was difficult for the community members to get accustomed to a new entity being in charge aside from PEMEX. To date, PEMEX is still perceived as the equivalent for any extraction related entity and most of my informants still tend to equate it with the term "oil company," even though they know about the position of the new firms as operating entities. Don Clemente, an ejidatario and native of Emiliano Zapata, has lived through more than six decades of PEMEX reign. As one of the elder residents, he is used to calling everything related to the oil company "PEMEX." He explained to me: "Now it's actually no longer PEMEX, there is another company in charge now. They call it Oleorey, it's a foreign company. That is the one that controls all the wells now, and not

PEMEX anymore. People still call it PEMEX, because, you know, we are used to that."

The new company, Oleorey, follows guidelines different from PEMEX with regard to hiring local workers and many community members of Emiliano Zapata lament the fact that they rarely contract laborers from the community. The first thing Don Clemente, as many of the community members told me about the new operating company, told me was the difference regarding job opportunities between Oleorey and PEMEX: "Now there are practically no jobs anymore, they abandoned everything. People no longer have the opportunity to work around here. At least when PEMEX was in charge there were jobs." But it is not only the lack of jobs that was perceived as more complicated with the new company as compared to PEMEX. In particular, the protocol of accountability in cases of damages and claiming the corresponding compensations became more difficult. This situation in Emiliano Zapata is no exception. Foreign firms often follow different rules when it comes to accountability, which creates a challenging situation for local residents (see Hernandez Cervantes and Zalik 2018). When damage occurred, the residents of Emiliano Zapata often relied on the contacts they had established with individual PEMEX staff members with whom they had already negotiated a procedure of how to treat issues like seepages and disturbances. In that way, the question of accountability had entered a personal level, which had created at least some trust within an often hardly reliable system of compensation management. In more severe cases, the community members had even gone directly to the PEMEX headquarters in Poza Rica to report the damage. Now that foreign firms are taking over, people feel unsettled and wonder how those issues will be dealt with in the future.

Many community members are used to contacting company staff directly in case of a complaint, but since Oleorey took over, the changing conditions in terms of contacting the company had led to discontent among many affected farmers. Don Esteban, an ejidatario with a lot of experience in enforcing compensation claims against PEMEX told me: "This new company . . . I don't know where the headquarters of Oleorey is, and where to get our compensation." He shrugged while looking at me. "None of us really knows. Me and the others we have struggled to report damages to them and get our compensations, because we don't know where to go. With PEMEX this was different. Everybody knows where the PEMEX offices are and where you had to go." The established protocol in case of emergencies or complaints have been disrupted because of the lack of availability of company staff from Oleorey in contrast to PEMEX in the past. Whether this issue is a long-term matter due to the transition phase during the processual establishment of a new company or rather a permanent problem due to the company's different approach is not certain yet.

The presence of the company represents an inconvenience on several levels not only for the community members from Emiliano Zapata, but also for the PEMEX staff that had been stationed at the San Andrés oilfield for many years. New workers are taking over jobs that corresponded to PEMEX team members before and the processual privatization causes tensions within the working environment for PEMEX.[6] Therefore, many of the staff members also consider the (albeit fragile) equilibrium, established between company and community, to be in danger. For example, local PEMEX workers complain about the inexperience their new colleagues demonstrated when they started working on the San Andrés oilfield, which could cause further accidents and complications. Alejandro is one of the PEMEX workers who had been laboring at the installations close to Emiliano Zapata for many years. He criticizes not only the lack of experience from the workers of Oleorey when they entered the area, but also their bad behavior in the community, claiming that it would cause the general image of oil workers to deteriorate. "What happens is that here there is a company called Oleorey," he started our conversation about the situation for him and his co-workers after the new company started operating in the area. "Those guys have to start from zero, because they don't know anything. They start from scratch. Besides, they walk around and make all the girls falling in love, sometimes also the wives." He took a sip from his Coke and continued: "We're talking about people who are already married. The locals they don't like that and that way our [oil workers'] image is seriously damaged."

In the meantime, most community residents in Emiliano Zapata do not seem to have a particularly bad image of the Oleorey staff members. Despite the complications regarding accountability for damages, the new firm is often perceived as more complaisant in terms of the implementation of community support programs and CSR. Oleorey participated in several of the recent installations such as the community kitchen or the sewing workshop, or the renovation of the school in collaboration with PEMEX. Don Esteban told me that the Oleorey staff has recently approached the ejido council and other local authorities to establish contacts with them and asked the authorities for priorities regarding support programs. The company then financially supported the construction of several public buildings: "Recently, Oleorey approached the comisariado. They presented themselves to him and said that they also wanted to support the community and asked what we would want them to do for us," he said. And indeed, the community authorities seized the opportunity and asked Oleorey for a new school building, which the company then

Figure 5.2. Entrance of the primary school renovated by PEMEX and Oleorey in Emiliano Zapata, Papantla, Mexico, 2016 © Svenja Schöneich.

started financing. However, many community members, remain skeptical about the benefits in the long term, but they acknowledge the increased effort of the new firm to grant certain benefits as part of their CSR measures.

Oleorey itself assures commitment to the needs of the affected communities close to its operations, but also refers to its position as an operator under PEMEX. As part of their obligations in this capacity, they formally acknowledge their duties toward the communities. Valeria is one of the few Mexican employees of the company based in Poza Rica and is in charge of the company-community relationship. I had the opportunity to interview her. We met one afternoon in a cozy café in Poza Rica over a coffee and some snacks. She made a friendly and committed impression to me when she talked about her work and how she always tried to fulfill the needs of the community members. Yet, when talking about the community relations guidelines for the company, she pointed to PEMEX as the contractor: "In the end, we are under contract with PEMEX. We have an obligation to support the communities where we are working, which is called a *licencia social*." Valeria also emphasized the commitment the firm has with PEMEX as the contracting entity in the first place. PEMEX required them to follow certain guidelines including the dedication of a certain percentage of their annual income to community support programs. She, furthermore, acknowledged the difficulties that the company recently had with the people from Emiliano Zapata, but also pointed to the limitations of resolving the tensions under the conditions that PEMEX imposes on them. "Unfortunately, we had some misunderstandings with Emiliano Zapata." She said, sounding regretful. "There are times, when the community asks us . . . I don't know, to build roads for them . . . and we are not authorized to do that, and people get angry because they think we just don't want to. But if it's not approved, the company loses money." Valeria was understanding regarding the community members needs and regretted to not be able to meet their expectations but referred to the strict requirements for CSR measures, which limit her actions. Her company acts under a contract with PEMEX, allowing for certain rights, but still treating the company as an operator of PEMEX property. This constellation fosters room for misunderstandings and unclear responsibility distribution, causing new tensions between the community and the company.

Resisting New Uncertainties

With the modifications in preparation of the energy reform, Oleorey took over the operation of several former PEMEX installations, among them the gas flare. Since the new operators were not familiar with established protocols between company and community, which hitherto were fragilely balanced, they kept the gas flare running constantly day and night and with increased intensity. While PEMEX operated the gas flare, the community members already felt disturbed by its visible and audible presence, but at least its intensity was reduced on a regular basis allowing for a pause in the disturbance. Its intensity sometimes began to rise even all night long without prior notification and many community members felt severely hampered and disturbed in their everyday lives. Afterward, the intensity decreased for some time, but then was frequently increased again in an unpredictable manner. So, when the situation did not improve after an intervention by the agente municipal, some community members did not see any option other than to engage in open protest by 2014–15.

The last time open protests had occurred was in 2003, when community members from Emiliano Zapata joined peasants from fifty-six communities from the area the city of Poza Rica against PEMEX. The protesters took umbrage at the unfulfilled promises on the part of the company to pave and maintain the main roads in the area when instead the roads were further damaged with heavy machinery. The protest was initiated by several communities in the whole region, not by the residents of Emiliano Zapata alone, a fact by which the protesters ensured a stronger stance against the company. PEMEX promised more benefits for the communities, but the inhabitants of Emiliano Zapata claim to have hardly noticed an improvement. This time the community members engaged in protest again mainly because they did not see any other option to see their claim answered.

Don Fernando's orchards are close to several PEMEX installations. When I interviewed him, he remembered the time when the light and sound of the gas flare was unbearable: "Well, now, you cannot hear anything. It's quiet now. But if you had been here when the loud noise started last year . . . No, no, no, you would not have understood a word from me standing right next to you." He told me. So, the community asked the agente municipal to intervene, and he did so by contacting the company and asking them to tone down the activity at least at night. Don Fernando continued: "Then the agente municipal went to ask them about the noise, and they said they would be extracting more oil—I don't know how much—so they were asked to turn it down. A lot of elderly people like us, some were almost going deaf." Unfortunately, the outreach remained unanswered for about two weeks and the disturbance continued. Neither PEMEX nor Oleorey assumed the responsibility, and the community members could no longer rely on their past established personal contacts, as no staff member would assume responsibility. The community then saw no other way than to engage in open protest: "But it lasted about fifteen days, day and night, and the flame of the gas flare was lighting up the community every night as well. So, we started protesting." The protest in Emiliano Zapata was organized and joined by a few other local leaders in the region. They decided to block the bridge over the Remolino River, and consequently, the main passage for the oil companies to access the San Andrés oilfield.

Unfortunately, the movement was not as successful as many community members had hoped it would be. The police intervened and two leaders of the protesters were arrested. The arrested community members were supported by NGO lawyers, who managed to avoid a trial, but the fellow protesters were nevertheless scared and halted their actions. However, many community members were disappointed by the minuscule achievement gained through the manifestations and expressed a feeling of impotence against the powerful companies and the government protecting it. Don Alberto, who has been dealing with the impacts of the oil industry for most of his life, has also been part of the protests, as was his brother. He felt that Oleorey was not open to negotiations as PEMEX had been in the past. To end the protests, the company intervened with the support of the police and two leaders of the protesters were arrested, one of whom was Don Alberto's brother. The two leaders could then defend themselves with the support of an NGO lawyer. Despite the relatively unscathed outcome for the leaders, the fellow protesters were frightened, fearing the powerful firms, and they stopped their actions. Don Alberto remembers being scared after the arrest and thus resigned from the protest and pointed out the power of the oil company that the community is unable to withstand: "They only wanted to scare us. And the truth is that you know that they have all the power. And the one who has the power wins in the end."

Even though the protests were stopped, and many community members were disappointed by how little was achieved, at least some of the claims were answered after the these events. Even when local media reported and journalists made the claims public, the oil company did not respond as the community members who participated in the protests had hoped. The loud noise of the gas flare was toned down, and the community members were promised to be alerted to an increase in the activity of the gas flare in the future. The recently organized protests and the increased willingness to again participate in such openly articulated resistance is a new factor within the set of mechanisms for responding to uncertainties. They are a result of the changing circumstances of shifting power relations and an altering composition of the social dynamics within the oilscape of Emiliano Zapata in the aftermath of the energy reform.

New Technologies and New Actors: The Anti-Fracking Movement

The protests in Emiliano Zapata that had taken place in 2014–15 drew the attention of local environmental organizations and activists. Since the implementation of the energy reform, protest movements against major extraction projects and neoliberalization of the energy sector had emerged. The issue of fracking had specifically caused agitation due to the great uncertainty of the technique with regard to environmental and health risks (see Bradshaw and Waite 2017; Smartt Gullion 2015; Williams et al. 2017). Since the fracking sites had not been marked implicitly as such in the region, many potentially affected communities had become concerned that fracking might be taking place close to their homes without their knowledge (de la Fuente et al. 2016: 64; Hernández Ibarzábal 2017: 367–69; Silva Ontiveros et al. 2018: 482). Thus, a joint movement of activists and communities against the implementation of fracking arose with a critical discussion of the issue on a national level (see Ánimas Vargas 2015; de la Fuente et al. 2016; Silva Ontiveros et al. 2018).

In Emiliano Zapata, the topic was publicly discussed in 2015. The press had just released data of fracking showing that Veracruz was the state with the highest number of operational fracking wells by far and inhabitants in different places of the state were concerned about its future implications (Chenaut 2017; Cruz 2018). The then agente municpal Don Eusebio heard about the implementation of fracking in the area and like many others, he was concerned if that also indicated a possible health and environmental threat for Emiliano Zapata. When I interviewed him in 2016, he told me how he became aware of the possibility that fracking would soon be applied in Emiliano Zapata too: "Well, we heard in 2014 that here in the region fracking was going to be implemented. But this was supposed to happen already in 2015," he said. The municipal authorities then denied any fracking, but Don Eusebio, like many others, remained suspicious. "I think that it's because of the falling oil price. That's why they stopped the activity. But it's not off the table yet! That doesn't mean that it's not going to happen later." He then started to read and hear more about fracking in the media, which increased his concerns. He worries that more damage on the territory will occur and the risks will intensify as soon as the company would start fracking. When he was approached by a group of local activists belonging to the AMCF, he agreed to hold a conference in Emiliano Zapata, where various communities of the region were invited to participate in informative talks and activities to engage in protests against fracking. The event, "Encuentro Regional Norte-Golfo por la Defensa del Agua y el Territorio Frente a los Proyectos de Muerte," was held on June 20 and 21 in 2015: and provoked a national, and partly international media response (e.g., Administrador Regeneración 2015b; Ejatlas 2017; Lastiri 2015).

Many, but not all, community members of Emiliano Zapata participated. During the event, groups of urban artists from Mexico City offered to decorate the houses of community members willing to participate with street art graffiti depicting statements against fracking. The graffiti are still visible and send a message of strong disapproval and engagement of protest of the community members of Emiliano Zapata. The activists asked the participating community members as to who would be interested in having their houses painted and presented a set of graffiti motifs the people could choose from. Several community members agreed and today their houses or stores display different graffiti against fracking.

Yet, many community members still cannot imagine what fracking exactly is. Most of the local knowledge about the topic in Emiliano Zapata stems from information given out at this event, which was not attended by the entire community. The term, fracking is familiar to the community members, but what it implied remained unclear. Due to allegations con-

Figure 5.3. Anti-fracking graffiti in Emiliano Zapata, Papantla, Mexico, 2016/2017 © Svenja Schöneich.

cerning its harmfulness, the community members perceived it as a new threat, but on the other hand they were already used to many types of risks with regard to oil extraction. From this perspective the application of the new technique confirms or even intensified the existing social patterns of environmental injustice as it has been shown for similar cases (see, e.g., Cotton 2016; Delgado 2018; Malin et al. 2018). Furthermore, fracking as a part of the energy reform, was a possible factor for a successful revival of the economy after the crisis. Moreover, it remained unclear if fracking had been implemented in the community. Don Eusebio requested information from the oil company and the municipal authorities but could not get a satisfactory answer to the question: "The officials did not tell us anything. They even said they wouldn't know what fracking is, that that they wouldn't know of any fracking pit nearby." When he referred to the event held by the nationally recognized NGO, the authorities reacted reluctantly and accused the NGO of spreading false information. While a strong mistrust about the integrity of government authorities and PEMEX, which is prevalent in Emiliano Zapata, the group of activists who started to approach the community emerged as a group of new potential allies.

During my interviews, many community members expressed their support for the NGO, who also had lawyers within their ranks who had already supported the residents of Emiliano Zapata during the arrests after the protests against the gas flare in 2014–15. During the event that lasted a few days, an assembly of the community was also held with the purpose of claiming the territory officially as "free from fracking," which would serve as a publicly signed statement of resistance against the technique. Initially, the community could not agree on whether to sign it or not, since several of the ejidatarios were against it. The ejidatarios were not the only ones who remained skeptical about the act of signing the statement and the general intentions of the activists. Some of the other residents did too. Don Alberto from the ejido council doubts the good intentions of the NGO for the community and pointed out during our interview that the organization could be working for the government and/ or seeking to enrich itself via its seeming support for the community: "Some *compañeros* wanted to sign this act, but we didn't know if they are really on our side or if it's just a way for them to get money from the government." He himself prefers to be cautious with the organizations as he suspects a possible withdrawal from their side without complying with the agreements taken with the community beforehand: "Many times they told us that they would stand with us but when the government comes and tells them to back off, they do as they're told. They just say that they couldn't do anything for us, and that's it." After the anti-fracking event, some community members lamented the diminishing NGO engagement with the community. For the community members of Emiliano Zapata, the meaning of the presence and role of actors like NGOs is not yet determined. Some see them as possible allies, while others remain skeptical about their motives.

With the organization of the event, the media interest in Emiliano Zapata increased significantly in contrast to past years, as fracking represented a late breaking topic on a national level. Local newspapers published reports about the event and the situation of Emiliano Zapata contesting PEMEX and the oil industry in general. Due to the topicality of fracking in Mexico, national and international researchers such as myself started to explore the topic. Recently, some papers about fracking in the area and also about Emiliano Zapata, focusing particularly on oil extraction, have already been published (e.g., Checa-Artasu and Aguilar León 2013; Chenaut 2017; Aguilar León 2018). Anthropological and archaeological interest, particularly in Totonac ruins or Totonac cultural practices, is not uncommon for the area, but as Emiliano Zapata is not perceived to be an indigenous community nor are there any anthropological sites close by, the community had hardly been the focus of research interest. For the community members, this interest represented a new experience of visibility that transcended the local horizon. Suddenly, they were questioned by outsiders who wanted to know about the oil industry and, of course, about fracking in their community on a regular basis. Some community members welcomed the opportunity to talk about their concerns because they hoped for even greater visibility in the media and national discourse and wanted to make their case. But not all community members are eager to constantly share their opinion and knowledge on the issue with outsiders, especially since most of the journalists and students repeatedly asked the same questions.

During my second research stay one year later, the public interest in fracking in general and in Emiliano Zapata in particular had already declined. The representatives of the press continued to report about claims against the oil company in cases of major seepages, as had occurred in 2017 on a minor scale, but the general interest was declining. The NGOs were no longer active in the community, even though some activists continued to keep personal friendly contacts with individual community members. Marta Conde and Philippe Le Billon claim that "alliances" do not have only an enabling effect on communities engaging in resistance but can also have a hindering effect (2017: 692). This also holds true for Emiliano Zapata, where the new allies supported the resisting community members on the one hand, but left them partly disappointed on the other, after the public interest in fracking as a "hot issue" decreased. It could not be clarified with certainty if fracking occurred close to the community and/or on the ejido territory or not, nor if it will be applied in the near future. In the meantime, it was revealed that the possibility of fracking being applied further to the southwest region of the area is much higher due to the particularities of the local geological formations (see AMCF 2019; CartoCrítica 2019).

The interest in current changes on the local level induced by the energy reform, and particularly a possible application of fracking had created a type of hype that attracted new actors, who then withdrew again after the hype had subsided. Some community members were disappointed by the reduced attention and more so by the relatively scarce practical achievements in context of their claims for more benefits and community support programs. Yet, these new actors had also started to play a role in the community life and influenced the relationships between actors and thus caused several alterations within the oilscape. The NGOs had provided the community members with new resources, such as legal support and public surveillance regarding the possible ways of contestation, and the journalists and researchers increased the visibility of the community's interest within public discourse. They had, therefore, also influenced the disposition of the community members to find new ways of articulating protest. Yet many residents of Emiliano Zapata were skeptical regarding the intentions of the outsiders. They were disappointed by the declining interest in their community after the hype and perceived the situation as even more uncertain than before. Either way, the social dimension of the oilscape in Emiliano Zapata was reconfigured through the entrance of new actor groups with the implementation of the energy reform and the possibility of fracking being applied.

Ending the Age of the Dragon: The Energy Reform as a Turning Point for Social Dynamics in Emiliano Zapata?

The rise of the oil industry and the extensive oil extractions on its territory has shaped Emiliano Zapata and its surroundings as a space that I refer to as an oilscape. It underlies constant transformations through modifications of the material environment over time, and also through human practices and interactions and thereby the dimension of social dynamics contributes to the constant reshaping of the oilscape (Low 2014: 35). Since the beginning of the industrial activities, PEMEX has established itself as a major player within this oilscape. The company changed the living conditions and was soon perceived as a dominant institution, exposing the community members to life hazards and health risks. As a powerful company, PEMEX was compared to a "dragon," who sometimes acts ruthlessly and does not assume its responsibilities and thereby, endangers the residents, but who can also bring in wealth and opportunities. This ambivalence created uncertainties, to which the community members responded by using mechanisms of adaptation. They do so by targeting the company staff as customers of products and services, establishing personal contacts with PEMEX personnel in order to skip lengthy processes of officially enforcing claims, or engaging in negotiations over jobs and compensation with the company. However, their bargaining power is rather limited, and many community members feel that they are essentially at the mercy of PEMEX.

The interactions between the community and the company and its staff have played a key role in demarcating territory space and thus in defining ownership and access rights to land. In this way, the ejido was challenged by both the company's interest and the internal interactions of the community members who split into "ejidatarios" and "propietarios." The murky and corruption-laden process of indemnification for the territory expropriated by PEMEX, caused internal conflicts, which were revived as the ejidatarios started the regularization process for individual parcels as a part of the agrarian (counter) reform of 1992. On one hand, the regularization may be the only way to assert claims for compensation retroactively, while on the other hand, it challenges established patterns of government and sovereignty.

In the course of the energy reform 2013/14, new companies and its employees have recently entered the social space and expanded the spectrum of actors, thus changing the social dynamics of the oilscape. Oleorey acts as a subcontractor of PEMEX and slowly takes over the operation of several oil installations, as well as more and more responsibilities toward the community. This poses new challenges for the community members, such as the foreseeable but indistinct deadline for settling land disputes, as it will be impossible to reclaim payments or land from PEMEX after the activities have been taken over by a new company. On the other hand, the energy reform also introduces new opportunities. As the new companies started to revive some of the formerly abandoned installations, many community members saw options for an improvement of the economic situation. Another element of the energy reform was the implementation of CSR measurements in the energy sector and PEMEX has introduced several strategies to do this in close cooperation with new firms entering the market. Some community members, therefore, reported positive experiences with the engagement of the new company and also hope for improved maintenance of the old oil infrastructure, which caused many concerns in the community during the oil crisis. At the same time, non-transparent structures have led to confusion and to a lack of accountability in several cases of damages or accidents, generating a new set of uncertainties the community members faced by taking new measures with support of new allies such as the engagement in open protests.

While the introduction of fracking as a new extraction technique did not just confirm existing patterns of social and environmental injustice (see Cotton 2016; Malin et al. 2018), the public attention regarding the issue had also another effect: the breaking with the binary relationship between the community and one powerful oil company. Through the shifting power relations different forms of articulating protests also emerged. Aside from the new firms, other new actors, such as representatives of the media, activists, or researchers suddenly entered the oilscape and rearranged the old-established relationship setting. The energy reform therefore represents a new turning point in the course of oil extraction over time, through which the oilscape enters a further process of change. While old uncertainties remain to some extent, new ones emerge and the strategies to deal with them are readjusted again.

Notes

1. The dancers of the ritual dance of the *voladores de Papantla* is a popular ritual, as well as a tourist attraction in the area (see Bertels 1993; Schöneich 2014)
2. Simple workers, in Zapata usually understood as day laborers.
3. Around 63 percent of the survey respondents have worked on such a contract or know somebody close to them who had over the years: "Yo he trabajado por ejemplo como contratistas para compañías o empresas petroleras o conozco a alguien cercano que ha trabajado así."
4. The government PROCEDE was cancelled in 2006 and subsidized by the new program FANAR. Both programs serve the same goal of regularizing ejdio and communal land to individuals aiming for a processual transformation into private property.
5. An *auditorio* is a roofed square and meeting point where most assemblies take place and represents the center of most of the communities in the area. In Emiliano Zapata, the *auditorio* is located next to a building gallery with several rooms for public administrational tasks.
6. Newly introduced conditions regarding tensions about the energy reform and the privatization of the hydrocarbon sector among PEMEX staff, present worthwhile topics for further research. The reform has been discussed mainly in terms of political and economic factors, but not yet following an actor centered approach regarding the oil company staff (see, e.g., Alvarez and Valencia 2015; Vidal Cano 2016).

Conclusion

The community and ejido Emiliano Zapata is inseparably entangled with the national and global history and consequences of oil and gas extraction. The accompanying circumstances of oil extraction have contributed to the constitution of a space, which is shaped by temporal and material properties of oil, as well as by a specific social environment defined by it. Thus, I have proposed the concept of the oilscape as an analytical tool to comprehensively assess this space and show how its three main dimensions play out in the case of Emiliano Zapata. Thereby, each of these dimensions provokes a set of different uncertainties community members have expressed with the metaphor of "living on a time bomb." Today, the residents of Emiliano Zapata found ways to deal with these uncertainties by using different mechanisms of short-term coping and long-term adaptation and thus developed the capability to continue their lives on the time bomb despite the ever-changing challenges. In this conclusion, I will briefly summarize the key findings of the preceding analysis and discuss them in relation to the literature on oil extraction and uncertainties. Thereby, I will also address the open questions, which arose through the analysis process. In the epilogue, I will provide an outlook on recent changes in Mexico's national oil policy and place the new processes into the wider context of oil extraction uncertainties.

I chose to look at the community and ejido of Emiliano Zapata as a space defined by oil extraction, drawing on the "scapes" approach by Arjun Appadurai (1990) as a concept for analyzing different dimension of flows. It stems from the term "landscapes," which bears the idea of a geographical location, but offers a novel take on spaces by emphasizing the perspectival nature and multiplicity of shapes in certain areas (1990: 33). Oil and its extraction are usually linked to a specific location, which is geographically limited (Rogers 2015a: 371). These spaces, however, encompass more dimensions than the concept of spatiality, but rather are constructed through a process of constant transformation via their material and temporal properties, as well as through a particular social dynamic through which the actors passively and actively shape the space (see Low 2009: 22; Löw 2008: 25). The "oilscape" is based on the concept of the "minescape" by Melina Ey and Meg Sherval (2015), which was developed as an analytical approach to extraction site research. It considers the particularities of resource extraction and takes the constructive forces of conflicting ideas and processes into account, which are entangled in a complex spin of politics, human action, and physical outcome. It thereby emphasizes the sociocultural significance of the terrain (Ey and Sherval 2015: 177). As the name suggests, the concept of the minescape was developed primarily for mineral extraction sites, and although mineral extraction is in many ways comparable to oil extraction, it falls short when taking into account the specific material and temporal properties of oil. While the concept of minescape focuses on "resource extraction as a dynamic, contested terrain with complex sociocultural, material and discursive dimensions" (2015: 177), I have adapted the concept for an analysis of oil extraction sites by also understanding them as a processual consequence of entangled material sociocultural dimensions associated with extraction. With this, I have emphasized the temporal particularities of oil as the third main aspect. In doing so, the concept considers the circumstances of extensive long-term oil extraction, which follows the temporal characteristics of a resource with economic booms and busts (see Ferry and Limbert 2008: 3; Reyna and Behrends 2011: 5; Rogers 2015a: 367). An oilscape is thus understood as a space where industrial oil extraction has inscribed itself over time in the material manifestation of landscape, housing, fields, and infrastructure, as well as the social texture and behavior of the local residents.

The oilscape is characterized by a set of uncertainties that are reflected in various aspects of the lives of community members in Emiliano Zapata and are linked to the particularities of each dimension of the oilscape. The associated uncertainties become an integral part of the local living conditions (see Pijpers 2018: 29) expressed in Emiliano Zapata through the metaphor of a "time bomb." This happens through the constant perception of health, life, and environmental risks from industrial pollution and accidents (see, e.g., Auyero and Swistun 2008; Cartwright 2013; Vásquez 2014), but also through the uncertain temporal progression associated with crisis-ridden economic processes (see, e.g., Limbert 2008; Weszkalnys 2016), precarious working conditions and status (see, e.g., Han 2018; Parry 2018). The latter results from the uncertainties inherent in a weak position within a larger framework of national and global power hierarchies (see Calkins 2016; Han 2018; Parry 2018), which are particularly evident when it comes to resource extraction and wealth distribution (see Kirsch 2014; Parry 2018; Pijpers 2018). By exploring how people act and react in such situations, a more comprehensive understanding of their strategies can be gained. It can also be shown how these uncertainties reflect back on the sociocultural patterns in the long term. In order to analyze how uncertainties in Emiliano Zapata's case arise, how they are interconnected, and how community members respond to them, I systematically approached each dimension: the temporalities as certain temporal processes of economic boom and bust, and the materialities in the way the extraction and production of oil materially shapes the surroundings (see Rogers 2015a: 366).

As discussed above, oil is particularly bound to a specific temporal process of peaks, that generate wealth and economic growth associated with industrial pollution and the expectation of an inevitable end of the economic boom, when the well is exhausted, or the oil price drops. This is followed by an eventual recovery of economic conditions or stabilization of alternatives, that allow the affected population to persist until the next decline. This temporal dimension of a certain ending of the boom, even at peak times, is particularly strongly linked to oil as a resource (e.g., Cepek 2012; Dyer 2002; Kaposy 2017; Limbert 2008). By following the temporality of oil in Emiliano Zapata as one dimension of the oilscape, I first showed how the oil extraction has intertwined with the history of the community over more than six decades. PEMEX appeared in Emiliano Zapata in times of political unrest and thus encountered an uncertain situation before the oil extraction began. Since then, many conditions in the ejido territory have changed for the community.

However, the uncertainty remained and manifested itself in other, new aspects of community life—the extraction caused damage and accidents that endangered the health of people and the environment. The residents of Emiliano Zapata responded by adapting their behavior to more easily access the benefits of the oil boom, such as creating jobs, speaking Spanish instead of Totonac, reorganizing their income strategies and social norms, and claiming compensations for territorial damage. When the boom faded and the crisis began, the uncertainty increased again as established economic opportunities began to dwindle. The community members then increasingly took advantage of an improved education system established during the boom and coped by emigrating and continuing to send remittances back. This strategy is not long-term, but may evolve into one if the need for remittances persists. The implementation of the energy reform has brought new challenges with it, but it also opened up new opportunities through the expected revival of the oil sector. The temporal processes of oil extraction thus shaped the living conditions of the community members of Emiliano Zapata, but by reacting to the uncertainties inherent in these processes, they also became actors of the temporal dimension of the oilscape.

Meanwhile, the material dimension of oil extraction and its industrial traces have become deeply inscribed in Emiliano Zapata's living environment. The presence and the material impact of the oil industry have left visible, audible, and tangible traces everywhere in the surrounding territory where they are perceived by the community members with all their senses. The impact of the extractive industry has invaded the local environment and can therefore be considered an integral part of the physical appearance of Emiliano Zapata. Numerous industry-related incidents, accidents, and environmental spills have shaped the space in terms of risks and hazards associated with anxiety and concern about potential dangers.

The community members have adjusted their lifestyles, economic strategies, and behaviors to meet the demands of the oil industry and its challenges by using long-term adaptation mechanisms. To do this, they used the infrastructure provided by the oil industry, such as the roads and the bridge over the nearby river, which gave them access to the marketplaces of the cities in the area. The availability of new materials for house building is a result of commercialized agriculture and income opportunities created by casual labor. In addition, the residents of Emiliano Zapata began to partially integrate materials that were exclusively intended for industrial use into private buildings and public spaces in the community. Thus, they have taken advantage of the benefits offered by the oil industry through appropriation and repurposing. By adapting their housing and farming patterns over the long term, and as a short-term reaction by actively changing and repurposing the materialities of oil extraction, they have been taking part in the construction of the oilscape and continue to do so.

The relationship between company and community has determined the social dynamics of the oilscape since the beginning of the extraction in Emiliano Zapata. PEMEX was and still is perceived by many as a mighty "dragon," as an entity who can harm but also bring wealth to the community. Thus, the relationship was and still is highly ambivalent. The community members responded to the uncertainties caused by this ambivalence and the dominance of PEMEX by establishing contacts with PEMEX personnel or by opening businesses targeting PEMEX employees as customers. Land conflicts related to expropriation have also created internal tensions, and the presence of the company has reordered the social patterns when migrants from other communities seeking economic opportunities settled in close proximity to the oil field and established the San Andrés colony. These challenges were addressed by the community members by preparing claims against the company and using legal mechanisms such as the official parcelization of the territory via the government programs PROCEDE and FANAR. When the new company, Oleorey, took over some former PEMEX installations, the community members began negotiations with the firm, but faced a new set of uncertainties as accountabilities were not always clear.

The energy reform also threatened the use of the fracking technology on the ejido territory. It triggered new uncertainties and fears about environmental and health hazards, but also brought other actors, such as NGO activists, researchers, and media representatives to the oilscape. In some ways, the situation under the conditions of the energy reform reproduced well known patterns of marginalization and hegemony which are discussed in studies of environmental justice in extractive projects (see, e.g., Cotton 2016; Gedicks 2001; Perreault 2018). However, changing social dynamics challenged existing power structures and new actors became manifest in new forms of actions, such as the expression of contestation through protest. The sociocultural processes in the oilscape have constantly changed over time and created different uncertainties, which then have been reflected in the development of certain social patterns.

Due to the energy reform, the oilscape is now at a turning point in the process of oil extraction, with key parameters of social and material dimensions changing. This is most evident in the changing company-community relationships, and in the revival of old installations or ways of operating equipment that were used differently in the past, such as the gas flare. While old uncertainties such as infrastructure decay or the questionable stance of community members against the undisputed dominance of PEMEX are being resolved, new uncertainties are emerging. They become visible in aspects such as the confusing situation of accountability between the companies or the potential environmental hazards posed by fracking application.

The metaphor of a time bomb hits two types of uncertainties in the oilscape of Emiliano Zapata. On one hand, it represents the fear of accidents and the anxiety triggered by the toxic pollution of the living environment (see Auyero and Swistun 2008: 358; Kirsch 2014: 144). On the other hand, it stands for the uncertainty resulting from the particular temporal characteristics of oil, related to the promises of development and economic growth, while at the same time crises and decline are predictable (see Ferry and Limbert 2008: 3; Reyna and Behrends 2011: 5; Rogers 2015a: 367). For the residents of Emiliano Zapata, this led to a situation in which they adjusted their living conditions to the immediate risks in their environment, as well as to the dynamics of economic crises and upswings over time. The community members are therefore constantly challenged to reshape and renegotiate their strategies to mitigate the explosive unpredictability of the future (see Cooper and Pratten 2015: 1). As a result, they take part in shaping the physical surroundings and the socioeconomic patterns that determine the composition and appearance of the oilscape in which they live. The community members developed a variety of mechanisms for short-time coping and long-term adaptation of socioeconomic patterns and cultural norms (see Oliver-Smith 2013: 277).

By adapting economic practices, housing styles, and certain social norms, the sociocultural patterns in Emiliano Zapata have also changed. Comparable developments have been shown for other cases such as by Cancian for a community in Chiapas in the 1970s (1994), or by Colin Filer for a mining community in Papua New Guinea (1990). I argue that these processes do not necessarily only foster social disintegration (see Filer 1990) and the "decline of community" (see Cancian 1994) but are also mechanisms for dealing with the challenges of uncertainties and even for enabling the "continuation of community" without which they would have to perish. Therefore, I consider them necessary strategies to allow the continuity of Emiliano Zapata as a community, even though it has been massively transformed by every aspect of oil extraction. The same process can be observed in other environments where intensive oil extraction takes place (see, e.g., Cepek 2012; Fentiman 1996; Krøijer 2019) and the formation of an oilscape occurs.

Concluding Remarks on the Theoretical Frame of Oilscape and Time Bomb

The social time-bomb effect on landowning communities associated with mining described by Filer (1990) continues to be a suitable description of what happens in localities with a major extraction project all over the world. Resource extraction triggers social disintegration and major transformations of the living environment. Filer's analysis of this phenomenon is now more than thirty years old, but it nevertheless remains an adequate explanation of what happens in local communities around the world. The metaphor of the time bomb image encompasses the uncertainty and anxiety of living in a space determined by oil extraction. I consider such a space an oilscape, which emerges around an oil production site, where the extraction has inscribed itself over time in the material manifestation, social texture, and behavior of its residents. Its size is determined by the spatial extent of the extraction site. In addition to the material dimension, the temporal and specific social dynamics of the site are also taken into account. It therefore falls short of considering the "broader spatialities of oil including spaces of consumption and security" (Rogers 2015a: 372), which have been called for by Douglas Rogers as an "important diversification of the kinds of locations in which oil's materiality is being theorized" (2015: 372). This spatial focus on the extraction site could make it difficult to transfer the concept to places where oil is processed and boomtowns exist, because oilscapes could also be considered spaces where oil extraction has inscribed itself in the material manifestation and the social texture over time.

The oilscape is thus a space that has no specific territorial boundaries. Decisions, personnel, and material flows, as well as migratory movements also play a role. The borders of the oilscape are permeable, but the analytical focus provided by the concept of scapes reflects a certain perspective of the actors on an issue—other examples are mines (Ey and Sherval 2016), coal (Portal 2018) or even water (Karpouzoglou anf Vij 2017). The analysis in this book therefore represents a contribution to the literature on the anthropology of oil and resource extraction by presenting a new view of the broader category of "landscapes of extraction" (see e.g., Grund 2016; Halvaksz 2008; Liesch 2014; Wheeler 2014) in the form of timescapes (see e.g., Adam 1998; Lanzano 2018), or minescapes (see Ey and Sherval 2015). The analysis is therefore meant to represent a certain perspective on oil and gas extraction from an actor-centered point of view. When looking at such spaces, it is crucial to understand complex individual cases in detail to show how social and cultural dimensions affect people's lives to varying degrees (Weszkalnys 2013: 267). While the idea of the oilscape is indeed transferable to other contexts, it should be further developed in future research when applying to other cases.

Several scholars have discussed uncertainty as an accompanying factor of extraction (e.g., Appel 2012b; Auyero and Swistun 2008; Pijpers 2018; Weszkalnys 2014; Witte 2018), but only a closer analytical look at the specific conditions of oil and gas extraction allows for a comprehensive understanding of them. This study has shown how uncertainty arises from each of the individual dimensions, making it an intrinsic constant of the oilscape. Although the community members of Emiliano Zapata deal with them in different ways, the uncertainties are elementary in nature and cannot be eliminated. Rather, they reflect the oilscape, especially in sociocultural patterns, and must be considered a fundamental characteristic. I argue that these uncertainties are associated with oil extraction more generally, as other studies have pointed out, even if they do not deal specifically with uncertainties but with environmental hazards or economic risks (see, e.g., Cartwright 2013; DeCesare and Auyero 2017; Dyer 2002; Stedman et al. 2012; Vásquez 2014). Hence, the uncertainty would be an essential feature of the oilscape. However, it is important to keep in mind that the specific situation of oil extraction in Mexico has contributed to a special intensity and type of uncertainty in Emiliano Zapata due to technological, historical, national, and regional circumstances.

The location and history of the community in the complex of the development of the Mexican oil industry entail some particularities that affect, for example, the strategies used to respond uncertainties. Yet there are many examples from other oil extracting countries where global processes such as the rise of neoliberal and thus extractivist policies have had similar effects on the intensifying local inequalities, and thus foster similar uncertainties (see, e.g., Arsel, Hogenboom, and Pellegrini 2016; Bebbington and Bury 2013; Svampa 2019). Meanwhile, the more recent wave of post-neoextractivism, especially in Latin America (see, e.g., Burchardt and Dietz 2014; Davidov 2013; McNeish 2018), is changing the national policies, but not always the social reality at the extraction sites (see Revette 2017). The oilscape could serve as an analytic tool to further explore and compare such contexts. Furthermore, the concept is not necessarily limited to extractive areas, but could also be modified and applied to spaces where oil and gas are processed. The materialities of a processing site are undoubtedly different from those of an extraction site, but there are striking similarities due to the high degree of industrialization required for oil extraction, for example, compared to certain forms of mining (see Penfield 2019). The temporal dimension of processing sites can also be considered similar, but it is even more closely related to the boom-bust cycle described in classical boomtown literature (see, e.g., England and Albrecht 1984; Gramling and Brabant 1986; Moen 1981). The sociocultural dimension, however, would be particularly interesting to analyze, especially with regard to the constellation of actors and the understanding of labor relations. Topics like the distinction between work and labor, which also plays a role in Emiliano Zapata, and the constitution of local identity could be further explored through the extension of the concept to processing sites.

In the case of Emiliano Zapata, the extraction and processing activities are spatially decoupled and also physically separated from the daily activities of the residents. Nevertheless, due to its geographical location and the power structures in the political space, the community is part of these processes. Emiliano Zapata's community members live in close proximity to the national oil wealth, but hardly benefit from it—a situation often described in environmental justice literature (see Gedicks 2001; Malin et al. 2018; Mohai, Pellow, and Roberts 2009; Perreault 2018). Their community is located right next to the oil deposit, and a dense net of pipelines transporting crude oil and other substances to the processing site crisscrosses the ground beneath the houses and parcels of its members. Because they live only on the periphery but not at the center of the wealth associated with it, they do not benefit from infrastructural development, as is the case in the booming oil cities of the world. Similar cases of communities not sharing the wealth generated by extractive industries are found specifically in the Global South (see Appel 2012a; 2012b; Cepek 2012; Fentiman

1996), but also in the Western countries such as the United States (Perry 2012; Willow and Wylie 2014; Willow et al. 2014) or the UK (Bradshaw and Waite 2017; Cotton 2016; Smartt Gullion 2015; Williams et al. 2017; Whitton et al 2018). In the context of such unjust distribution patterns, the issue of political participation mechanisms was widely discussed among scholars working on environmental justice issues, such as free prior and informed consent (FPIC) and consultation mechanisms. However, the discussion has shown that these mechanisms are only partially able to compensate for existing inequalities and thus entail new uncertainties (Owen and Kemp 2014; Schilling-Vacaflor and Flemmer 2015).

The fact that the residents of Emiliano Zapata were not the main beneficiaries of oil wealth not only contributed to the emergence of economic challenges, but to some extent also reduced dependence on the oil industry. This factor is described by Marta Conde and Philippe Le Billon as "mine dependency" and refers to the relationship of the community in question to the extractive sector (2017: 686). The strongest dependency can be observed in special "mining towns" created specifically to house the miners (see Scott and Bennett 2015). But in other cases as well, communities that are heavily dependent on the extractive industry face difficulties when they are forced to find alternative livelihoods as the industry retreats and sometimes even abandons (see e.g., Andrews-Speed et al. 2005; Bowen 2019; Fisher 2007; Hilson and Yakovleva 2007). In the case of Emiliano Zapata, although the oil crisis presented new challenges to the community members, it did not have the same severe impact as in a typical oil town (see, e.g., Bowen 2019; Limbert 2010). For this reason, Emiliano Zapata's story is not a typical boomtown story. There is no spiraling process of local economic and demographic growth induced by the discovery of a resource, ending with a predictable bust when the resource runs out or loses value on the market, which leads to a severe crisis and possibly even depopulation of the city (Gramling and Brabant 1986: 179–80). In Emiliano Zapata, the agricultural activities continue and enable a diversification of income sources, which allows for more crisis resilience than in typical boomtowns. Although oil in Emiliano Zapata is inextricably linked to notions of the past, present, and future, the position of the community on the verge of oil wealth was also accompanied by a set of special circumstances that fostered a certain resilience in the face of industrial decline. These include, for example, the preservation of agricultural activities and land ownership in the sense of the ejido.

The community members, in their role as rural peasants, were never the intended beneficiaries of the wealth generated by the Mexican oil industry and thus never enjoyed the full benefit of its distribution. On the other hand, they were consequently never as dependent on the industrial development as typical oil towns and their inhabitants. Therefore, the community members are in some ways better equipped to deal with risks, changes, and uncertainties, as time has repeatedly shown.

The Time Bomb Reloaded?

On 1 December 2018, Mexico's political landscape changed drastically when the new President Manual López Obrador (referred to as AMLO) was sworn in. He has won the presidential election with 53 percent of the vote on 3 July 2018, when he promised a historic "fourth transformation" for Mexico.[1] His victory ended the dominance of the established PRI and PAN parties (the former had been governing Mexico for seventy years, only to be defeated by the latter for the first time in the year 2000), and for many Mexicans, it indeed represented a turning point in history (Breglia 2013: 219; Pedroza 2019: 2). For instance, AMLO promised to pacify the country and reduce inequality by fighting institutionalized drug crime and curbing corruption. He also announced the cancellation of controversial megaprojects such as the Texcoco airport through a vote in a public consultation, which unsettled foreign investors. But the peso has so far remained stable. At the same time, the AMLO administration announced measures to increase revenues from natural resources, including the weakened oil sector, and revealed plans to reappropriate some of the rents captured by mafia-esque structures that had emerged within the internal organization of PEMEX. One of AMLO's first attempts to stop stealing in the hydrocarbon industries was called the "huachicalero problem," which manifests as massive theft of oil from pipelines. This problem, which had become a major issue in the country, led to fuel supply disruptions for large parts of the country in 2019 (see Cunningham 2019; Nájar 2019; Pedroza 2019: 7; Redacción BBC News Mundo 2019). As part of his effort to make energy sovereignty the centerpiece of his administration's agenda, AMLO announced plans to reform and rebuild PEMEX by building a multibillion-dollar refinery in his home state of Tabasco in June 2019. Yet foreign analysts are skeptical about the potential success of this endeavor (Viscidi and Parish Flannery 2019).

Furthermore, AMLO announced that he would abandon fracking in the country, pointing to the environmental consequences such as suspected water shortage. However, the prohibition has not been implemented in national law. Under his government, the Comisión Nacional de Hidrocarburos (CNH)-approved Pemex Exploración y Producción (PEP)'s exploration plan for the Humapa oil field in Tampico-Misantla, a non-conventional source that would be extracted with fracking technology (Ordaz

2019; Schmidt 2019). AMLO then indeed banned the use of fracking for environmental reasons, despite the fact that it had already been assigned to Haliburton, a company that wanted to apply the new technology in Mexico. Environmentalists and activists concerned about fracking remain skeptical. The AMCF warned that CNH and PEMEX would ignore this order because of the earlier approval of the plan (Monroy and García 2019; Solís 2019).

Emiliano Zapata made it into national news again when the newspaper *SinEmbargo* published an article about the negative implications of the energy reform for indigenous people and campesinos. It pointed out that the modification of legislation under the reform included a change in land use rights and a lack of implementation of the right to prior consultation with the affected rural population. Emiliano Zapata thereby appeared as a negative example, already exploited by the oil industry under PEMEX without much hope of improving the situation (Morales 2019).

AMLO's assumption of office was accompanied by a variety of expectations. To date, there is general uncertainty about the final course of AMLO's government or its accomplishments on the issues initially announced. This holds particularly true for the promises to restructure the energy sector, which includes a possible prohibition of environmentally risky technologies like fracking, as well as for the general course of established and future oil extraction projects (Pedroza 2019: 1). Given the pressure the COVID-19 pandemic put on the national economy and the great potential that the CNH sees in national fracking deposits, the question whether fracking should be completely banned started to enter the public discussion again in 2020 (BNamericas 2020). Contrary to the presidents' promises to not apply fracking in new projects, PEMEX announced to invest heavily into projects that require fracking, during 2022 (Alcalá 2021). Again, the community members of Emiliano Zapata are thus provided with a new set of uncertainties regarding the future development of the oilscape they are living in and are therefore once more challenged to renegotiate the mechanisms for dealing with them.

Note

1. AMLO was referring to independence in the 1810s as the first transformation, the reformative period in the late 1850s as the second, and the revolution of the 1910s being the third (Pedroza 2019: 2).

References

Adam, Barbara. 1998. *Timescapes of Modernity: The Environment and Invisible Hazards*. London: Routledge. http://dx.doi.org/10.4324/9780203981382.
Administrador Regeneración. 2015a. "Petroleras Contaminan El Agua de Veracruz Con Fracking." [Oil companies contaminate Veracruz water with fracking] *Regeneración*, 3 June. Retrieved 21 December 2020 from https://regeneracion.mx/petroleras-contaminan-el-agua-de-veracruz-con-fracking/.
———. 2015b. "Nace Corason contra el fracking en la Huasteca y el Totonacapan." [Corason founded against fracking in the Huasteca and Totonacapan] *Regeneración*, June 27. Retrieved 21 December 2020 from https://regeneracion.mx/nace-corason-contra-el-fracking-en-la-huasteca-y-el-totonacapan/.
Alcalá, Pedro. 2021. "Is Fracking Getting the Green Light in Mexico?". Mexico Business News, September 22. Retrieved 03 May 2022 from https://mexicobusiness.news/oilandgas/news/fracking-getting-green-light-mexico.
Aguilar León, Irvin. 2018. "Extracción de petróleo y transformaciones socioterritoriales Comunidad Emiliano Zapata Veracruz, Mexico." [Oil extraction and socioterretorial transformations in the Comunidad Emiliano Zapata Veracruz, Mexico] *Regions & Cohesion* 8(1): 25–53.
Aguilar Madera, Carlos Gilberto. 2014. "El shale gas y el fracking." [Shale gas and fracking] *CIENCIA UANL* 17(67): 6–36.
Alaszewski, Andy. 2015. "Anthropology and Risk: Insights into Uncertainty, Danger and Blame from Other Cultures – A Review Essay." *Health, Risk & Society* 17(3–4): 205–25.
Alvarez, Jorge, and Fabian Valencia. 2015. *Made in Mexico: Energy Reform and Manufacturing Growth*. IMF working paper 15/45. Washington, DC: IMF.
AMCF (Alianza Mexicana Contra el Fracking). 2019. "Nueva investigación detalla la dimensión de fracking en México." [New detailed investigation about the dimensions of fracking in Mexico] *Alianza Mexicana Contra el Fracking*, 24 January. Retrieved 5 April 2022 from https://www.nofrackingmexico.org/nueva-investigacion-detalla-la-dimension-de-fracking-en-mexico/
Anand, Nikhil. 2011. "Pressure." *Cultural Anthropology* 26: 542–64.
Anand, Nikhil, Akhil Gupta, and Hannah Appel, ed. 2018. *The Promise of Infrastructure*. Durham, NC: Duke University Press.
Andrews-Speed, Philip, Guo Ma, Bingjia Shao, and Chenglin Liao. 2005. "Economic Responses to the Closure of Small-Scale Coal Mines in Chongqing, China." *Resources Policy* 30(1): 39–54. http://doi.org/10.1016/j.resourpol.2004.12.002.

Ánimas Vargas, Leticia. 2015. "Se organizan contra fracking en límites entre Puebla y Veracruz. Municipios." [They are organizing against fracking at the border between Puebla and Veracruz] *Municipios*, September 16. Retrieved 21 December 2020 from http://municipiospuebla.com.mx/nota/2015-09-16/interiores/se-organizan-contra-fracking-en-l%C3%ADmites-entre-puebla-y-veracruz.

Appadurai, Arjun. 1990. "Disjuncture and Difference in the Global Cultural Economy." *Theory, Culture & Society* 7(2–3): 295–310. http://doi.org/10.1177/026327690007002017.

Appel, Hannah C. 2012a. "Walls and White Elephants: Oil Extraction, Responsibility, and Infrastructural Violence in Equatorial Guinea." *Ethnography* 13(4): 439–65. http://doi.org/10.1177/1466138111435741.

———. 2012b. "Offshore Work: Oil, Modularity, and the How of Capitalism in Equatorial Guinea." *American Ethnologist* 39(4): 692–709. http://doi.org/10.1111/j.1548-1425.2012.01389.x.

Appel, Hannah, Arthur Mason, and Michael Watts ed. 2015a. *Subterranean Estates: Life Worlds of Oil and Gas*. Ithaca, NY: Cornell University Press.

———. 2015b. "Introduction: Oil Talk." In *Subterranean Estates: Life Worlds of Oil and Gas*, ed. Hannah Appel, Arthur Mason, and Michael Watts, 1–26. Ithaca: Cornell University Press.

Appel, Hannah, Nikhil Anand, and Akhil Gupta. 2018. "Introduction: Temporality, Politics, and the Promise of Infrastructure." In *The Promise of Infrastructure*, ed. Nikhil Anand, Akhil Gupta, and Hannah Appel, 1–40. Durham, NC: Duke University Press.

Apter, Andrew H. 2005. *The Pan-African Nation: Oil and the Spectacle of Culture in Nigeria*. Chicago: University of Chicago Press.

Archambault, Julie Soleil. 2015. "Rhythms of Uncertainty and the Pleasures of Anticipation." In *Ethnographies of Uncertainty in Africa*, ed. Elizabeth Cooper and David Pratten, 129–48. New York: Palgrave Macmillan.

Arsel, Murat; Barbara Hogenboom, and Lorenzo Pellegrini. 2016. "The Extractive Imperative and the Boom in Environmental Conflicts at the End of the Progressive Cycle in Latin America." *The Extractive Industries and Society* 3(4): 877–79. http://doi.org/10.1016/j.exis.2016.10.013.

Ashmoore, Olivia, Darrick Evensen, Chris Clarke, Jennifer Krakower, and Jeremy Simon. 2016. "Regional Newspaper Coverage of Shale Gas Development across Ohio, New York, and Pennsylvania: Similarities, Differences, and Lessons." *Energy Research & Social Science* 11: 119–32. http://doi.org/10.1016/j.erss.2015.09.005.

Auty, Richard M. 1993. *Sustaining Development in Mineral Economies: The Resource Curse Thesis*. London: Routledge. http://site.ebrary.com/lib/alltitles/docDetail.action?docID=10060585.

Auyero, Javier, and Debora Swistun. 2008. "The Social Production of Toxic Uncertainty." *American Sociological Review* 73(3): 357–79. http://doi.org/10.1177/000312240807300301.

Banks, Glenn. 1996. "Compensation for Mining: Benefit or Time-Bomb? The Porgera Gold Mine." In *Resources, Nations, and Indigenous Peoples: Case Studies from Australasia, Melanesia, and Southeast Asia*, ed. Richard Howitt, John Connell, and Philip Hirsch, 223–35. Oxford: Oxford University Press.

Baptista, João A. 2018. "The Road of Progress: Individualisation and Interaction Agency in Southeast Angola." *Ethnos* 83(3): 521–43. http://doi.org/10.1080/0 0141844.2016.1150312.
Barragán, José. 2019. "Comisariado Ejidal en México" [The Comisariado Ejidal in Mexico]. *Mexico Enciclopedia Jurídica Online*. https://mexico.leyderecho.org/comisariado-ejidal/
Barry, Andrew. 2013. *Material Politics: Disputes along the Pipeline*. RGS-IBG Book Series. Oxford: Wiley-Blackwell.
Bavinck, Maarten, and Erik M. Lorenzo Pellegrini, eds. 2014. *Conflicts over Natural Resources in the Global South*. London: CRC Press. http://dx.doi.org/10.1201/b16498.
Bear, Laura. 2014. "Doubt, Conflict, Mediation: The Anthropology of Modern Time." *Journal of the Royal Anthropological Institute* 20: 3–30. http://doi.org/10.1111/1467-9655.12091.
———. 2016. "Time as Technique." *Annual Review of Anthropology* 45(1): 487–502. http://doi.org/10.1146/annurev-anthro-102313-030159.
Bebbington, Anthony and Jeffrey Bury. 2013. *Subterranean Struggles: New Dynamics of Mining, Oil, and Gas in Latin America*. Peter T. Flawn Endowment in Natural Resource Management and Conservation. Austin: Univeristy of Texas Press.
Beckmann, Nadine. 2015. "The Quest for Trust in the Face of Uncertainty: Managing Pregnancy Outcomes in Zanzibar." In *Ethnographies of Uncertainty in Africa*, ed. Elizabeth Cooper and David Pratten, 59–83. Anthropology, Change and Development. Basingstoke, Hampshire: Palgrave Macmillan. https://doi.org/10.1057/9781137350831_4.
Beer, Bettina. 2014. "Boholano Olfaction." *The Senses and Society* 9(2): 151–73. http://doi.org/10.2752/174589314x13953118734788.
Behrends, Andrea. 2008. "Fighting for Oil When There Is No Oil Yet." *Focaal* 2008 (52): 39–56. http://doi.org/10.3167/fcl.2008.520103.
Behrends, Andrea, and Nikolaus Schareika. 2010. "Significations of Oil in Africa: What (More) Can Anthropologists Contribute to the Study of Oil?" *Suomen Antropologi* 35(1): 83–86. https://eref.uni-bayreuth.de/54681/.
Behrends, Andrea, and Remadji Hoinathy. 2017. "The Devil's Money: A Multi-Level Approach to Acceleration and Turbulence in Oil-Producing Southern Chad." *Social Analysis* 61(3): 56–72. http://doi.org/10.3167/sa.2017.610304.
Behrends, Andrea, Günther Schlee, and Stephen P. Reyna. 2011. *Crude Domination: An Anthropology of Oil*. Dislocations v. 9. New York: Berghahn Books. http://site.ebrary.com/lib/alltitles/docDetail.action?docID=10744985.
Behrends, Andrea, Sung-Joon Park, and Richard Rottenburg, eds. 2014. *Travelling Models in African Conflict Resolution: Translating Technologies of Social Ordering*. Africa-Europe Group for Interdisciplinary Studies, vol. 13. Boston: Brill.
Bender, Barbara. 2002. "Time and Landscape." *Current Anthropology* 43(S4): S103–S112. http://doi.org/10.1086/339561.
Benquet, Francis Mestries. 2003. "Crisis cafetalera y migración internacional en Veracruz." *Migraciones Internacionales Universidad Autónoma Metropolitana-Azcapotzalco* 2(2): 122–48.

Bertels, Ursula. 1993. *Das Fliegerspiel in Mexiko: Historische Entwicklung und gegenwärtige Erscheinungsformen*. [*The ceremony oft he Voladores in Mexico. Development and current forms*] Ethnologische Studien 24. Münster: Lit Verlag.
Bille Larsen, Peter. 2017. "Oil Territorialities, Social Life, and Legitimacy in the Peruvian Amazon." *Economic Anthropology* 4(1): 50–64. http://doi.org/10.1002/sea2.12072.
Black, Brian. 2000. *Petrolia: The Landscape of America's First Oil Boom*. Creating the North American Landscape. Baltimore, MD: Johns Hopkins University Press.
BNamericas. 2020. "Regulator Urges Mexico Govt to Reconsider Fracking Ban." BNamericas, December 18. Retrieved 03 May 2022 from https://www.bnamericas.com/en/news/regulator-urges-mexico-govt-to-reconsider-fracking-ban.
Bourdieu, Pierre. 1985. "The Social Space and the Genesis of Groups." *Social Science Information* 24(2): 195–220. http://doi.org/10.1177/053901885024002001.
———. 2018. "Social Space and the Genesis of Appropriated Physical Space." *International Journal of Urban and Regional Research* 42(1): 106–14. http://doi.org/10.1111/1468-2427.12534.
Bowen, Dawn S. 2019. "In the Shadow of the Refinery: An American Oil Company Town on the Caribbean Island of Aruba." *Journal of Cultural Geography* 36(1): 49–77. http://doi.org/10.1080/08873631.2018.1502398.
Bradshaw, Michael, and Catherine Waite. 2017. "Learning from Lancashire: Exploring the Contours of the Shale Gas Conflict in England." *Global Environmental Change* 47: 28–36. http://doi.org/10.1016/j.gloenvcha.2017.08.005.
Brasier, Kathryn J., Diane K. McLaughlin, Danielle Rhubart, Richard C. Stedman, Matthew R. Filteau, and Jeffrey Jacquet. 2013. "Research Articles: Risk Perceptions of Natural Gas Development in the Marcellus Shale." *Environmental Practice* 15(2): 108–22. http://doi.org/10.1017/s1466046613000021.
Breglia, Lisa. 2013. *Living with Oil: Promises, Peaks, and Declines on Mexicos Gulf Coast*. Austin: University of Texas Press.
Brown, Jonathan C. 1993. *Oil and Revolution in Mexico*. Berkeley: University of California Press. http://ark.cdlib.org/ark:/13030/ft3q2nb28s/.
Brown, Jonathan C., and Alan Knight, eds. 1992. *The Mexican Petroleum Industry in the Twentieth Century*. Austin: University of Texas Press.
Brown, Ralph B., Shawn F. Dorins, and Richard S. Krannich. 2005. "The Boom-Bust-Recovery Cycle: Dynamics of Change in Community Satisfaction and Social Integration in Delta, Utah." *Rural Sociology* 70(1): 28–49. http://doi.org/10.1526/0036011053294673.
Buck-Morss, Susan. 1992. "Aesthetics and Anaesthetics: Walter Benjamin's Artwork Essay Reconsidered." *October* 62: 3–41. http://doi.org/10.2307/778700.
Burchardt, Hans-Jürgen, and Kristina Dietz. 2014. "(Neo-)Extractivism: A New Challenge for Development Theory from Latin America." *Third World Quarterly* 35(3): 468–86. http://doi.org/10.1080/01436597.2014.893488.
Burtynski, Edward. 2009. *Australian Minescapes*. Welshpool: Western Australian Museum.
Calkins, Sandra. 2016. *Who Knows Tomorrow? Uncertainty in North-Eastern Sudan*. New York: Berghahn Books. http://fid.berghahnbooksonline.com/title/CalkinsWho.

Cancian, Frank. 1994. *The Decline of Community in Zinacantán: Economy, Public Life, and Social Stratification, 1960–1987*. Stanford, CA: Stanford University Press.

Cárdenas Gracia, Jaime Fernando. 2009. *En defensa del petróleo*. [In defense of the oil] Mexico City: Universidad Nacional Autónoma de México (UNAM).

CartoCrítica. 2019. "Actualidad de la fracturación hidráulica en México 2019." [Current hydraulic fracturing in Mexico 2019] *Carto Crítica: Investigación, mapas y datos para la sociedad civil*, 24 January. Retrieved 21 December 2020 from http://cartocritica.org.mx/2019/actualidad-de-la-fracturacion-hidraulica-en-mexico/.

Carreón Blaine, Emilie Ana. 2016. "Del hule al chapopote en la plástica mexica. Una revisión historiográfica" [From Rubber to Asphalt in Mexica Plastic Arts. A Historiographical Review]. *Trace 70, CECMA*: 9–44.

Cartwright, Elizabeth. 2013. "Eco-Risk and the Case of Fracking." In *Cultures of Energy*, ed. Sarah Strauss, Stephanie Rupp, and Thomas Love, 201–12. Walnut Creek, CA: Left Coast Press.

Castañeda Dower, Paul, and Tobias Pfutze. 2013. Specificity of Control: The Case of Mexico's Ejido Reform. *Journal of Economic Behavior & Organization* 91: 13–33.

Castro Alvarez, Fernando, Peter Marsters, Diego Ponce de León Barido, and Daniel M. Kammen. 2018. "Sustainability Lessons from Shale Development in the United States for Mexico and Other Emerging Unconventional Oil and Gas Developers." *Renewable and Sustainable Energy Reviews* 82: 1320–32. http://doi.org/10.1016/j.rser.2017.08.082.

CDI (Comisión Nacional para el Desarrollo de los Pueblos Indígenas). 2010. *Catálogo de Localidades Indígenas* [Indigenous Localities Catalog]. http://www.cdi.gob.mx/localidades2010-gobmx/.

Cepek, Michael. 2012. "The Loss of Oil: Constituting Disaster in Amazonian Ecuador." *The Journal of Latin American and Caribbean Anthropology* 17(3): 393–412. http://doi.org/10.1111/j.1935-4940.2012.01250.x.

Checa-Artasu, Martín, and Irvin Aguilar León. 2013. "Industria petrolera y conflictos socioambientales en la región del Totonacapan a través de la historia oral: el caso del municipio de Papantla, Veracruz." [Oil industry and socio-environmental conflicts in the Totonacapan region through oral history: the case of the municipality of Papantla, Veracruz]. Paper II Congreso Universitario de Historia Oral, Universidad Autónoma de la Ciudad de México, Mexico City, 6–8 November 2013.

Checa-Artasu, Martín M., and Regina Hernández Franyuti. 2016. *El petróleo en México y sus impactos sobre el territorio* [Oil in Mexico and its impacts on the territory]. Mexico City: Instituto de Investigaciones Dr. José María Luis Mora.

Chenaut, Victoria. 2010 *Los totonacas en Veracruz: población, familia y sociedad. Atlas del Patrimonio natural, histórico y cultural de Veracruz* [The Totonacs in Veracruz: population, family and society. Atlas of the natural, historical and cultural heritage of Veracruz]. Veracruz: Gobierno del Estado de Veracruz/Universidad Veracruzana.

———. 2017. "Impactos sociales y ambientales de la explotación de hidrocarburos en el municipio de Papantla, Veracruz (México)." *e-cadernos ces*. 28: 94–117.

Clarke, Christopher E., Philip S. Hart, Jonathon P. Schuldt, Darrick T.N. Evensen, Hilary S. Boudet, Jeffrey B. Jacquet, and Richard C. Stedman. 2015. "Public

Opinion on Energy Development: The Interplay of Issue Framing, Top-of-Mind Associations, and Political Ideology." *Energy Policy* 81: 131–40. http://doi.org/10.1016/j.enpol.2015.02.019.

Cochrane, Glynn. 2017. *Anthropology in the Mining Industry: Community Relations After Bougainville's Civil War.* Cham: Springer International Publishing. https://ebookcentral.proquest.com/lib/gbv/detail.action?docID=4787553.

Conde, Marta, and Philippe Le Billon. 2017. "Why Do Some Communities Resist Mining Projects While Others Do Not?" *The Extractive Industries and Society* 4(3): 681–97. http://doi.org/10.1016/j.exis.2017.04.009.

CONAPO (Consejo Nacional de Población). 2006. *Indíces de Marginalisación 2005.* http://www.conapo.gob.mx/work/models/CONAPO/indices_margina/margina2005/IM2005_principal.pdf.

Cooper, Elizabeth, and David Pratten, eds. 2015. *Ethnographies of Uncertainty in Africa.* Anthropology, Change and Development. Basingstoke, Hampshire: Palgrave Macmillan.

Coronil, Fernando. 1997. *The Magical State: Nature, Money, and Modernity in Venezuela.* Chicago: University of Chicago Press. http://www.loc.gov/catdir/description/uchi051/97008000.html.

Cotton, Matthew. 2016. "Fair Fracking? Ethics and Environmental Justice in United Kingdom Shale Gas Policy and Planning." *Local Environment* 22(2): 185–202. http://doi.org/10.1080/13549839.2016.1186613.

Cox, Rubert. 2018. "Anthropology of Senses." In *The International Encyclopedia of Anthropology*, ed. Hilary Callan, 1–12. Hoboken, NJ: Wiley-Blackwell.

Cross, Jamie. 2011. "Detachment as a Corporate Ethic: Materializing CSR in the Diamond Supply Chain." *Focaal* 60(60):34-46. http://doi.org/10.3167/fcl.2011.600104.

Cruz, Leticia. 2018. "En Veracruz, 60.5% de pozos de fracking del país: CNDH-UNAM." [In Veracruz, 60.5% of the country's fracking wells are in Veracruz: CNDH-UNAM]. *Imagen del Golfo*, 27 May. Retrieved 21 December 2020 from https://www.imagendelgolfo.mx/noticiasveracruz/xalapa/41224787/en-veracruz-60-5-percentage-de-pozos-de-fracking-del-pa-s-cndh-unam.html.

Cunningham, Nicholas. 2019. "Fuel Feuds in Mexico." *NACLA Report on the Americas* 51(2): 119–22. http://doi.org/10.1080/10714839.2019.1617466.

Czarnecki, Lukasz, and Delfino Vargas Chanes. 2018. "Welfare Regime, Neoliberal Transformation, and Social Exclusion in Mexico, 1980–2015." In *Social Welfare Responses in a Neoliberal Era*, ed. Mia Arp Fallov and Cory Blad, 72–87. Leiden: Brill.

D'Angelo, Lorenzo, and Robert J. Pijpers. 2018. "Mining Temporalities: An Overview." *The Extractive Industries and Society* 5(2): 215–22. http://doi.org/10.1016/j.exis.2018.02.005.

Dalakogulu, Dimitris. 2012. "'The Road from Capitalism to Capitalism': Infrastructures of (Post)Socialism in Albania." *Mobilities* 7(4): 571–86. http://doi.org/10.1080/17450101.2012.718939.

Dalakogulu, Dimitris, and Penny Harvey. 2012. "Roads and Anthropology: Ethnographic Perspectives on Space, Time and (Im)Mobility." *Mobilities* 7(4): 459–65. http://doi.org/10.1080/17450101.2012.718426.

Dávila Lárraga, Laura G. 2016. *How Does Prospera Work? Best Practices in the Implementation of Conditional Cash Transfer Programs in Latin America and the Caribbean.* IDB Inter-American Development Bank.

Davidov, Veronica. 2013. "Mining Versus Oil Extraction: Divergent and Differentiated Environmental Subjectivities in 'Post-Neoliberal' Ecuador." *The Journal of Latin American and Caribbean Anthropology* 18(3): 485–504. http://doi.org/10.1111/jlca.12043.

Davidson, Roger, and Gayle Davis. 2012. *Sexual State.* Edinburgh: Edinburgh University Press.

DeCesare, Donna, and Javier Auyero. 2017. "Patience, Protest, and Resignation in Contaminated Communities: Five Case Studies." *NACLA Report on the Americas* 49(4): 462–69. http://doi.org/10.1080/10714839.2017.1409375.

de la Fuente, Aroa, Juan C. Guerrero, Edmundo del Pozo, and Óscar Arredondo. 2016. *El sector de hidrocarburos en la Reforma Energética: retrocesos y perspectivas.* Mexico City: Fundar, Centro de Análisis e Investigación, A.C.

Delgado, Elvin. 2018. "Fracking Vaca Muerta: Socioeconomic Implications of Shale Gas Extraction in Northern Patagonia, Argentina." *Journal of Latin American Geography* 17(3): 102–31. https://www.jstor.org/stable/48619222.

de L'Estoile, Benoît. 2014. "'Money Is Good, but a Friend Is Better': Uncertainty, Organisation to the Future, and 'the Economy.'" In *Crisis, Value, and Hope: Rethinking the Economy*, ed. Leslie Aiello, 62–73. Chicago: University of Chicago Press.

del Palacio Langer, Ana Julia. 2015. "Agrarian Reform, Oil Expropriation, and the Making of National Property in Postrevolutionary Mexico." Ph.D. dissertation. New York: Columbia University.

———. 2016. "Jaime Merino: The Oil Cacique of Poza Rica, Veracruz, 1941–1959." *The Extractive Industries and Society* 3(2): 426–34.

de Montmollin, Peter. 2018. *Legal Uncertainties Cloud Mexico Energy Sector's Consultations of Indigenous Stakeholders.* NGI`s Mexico Gas Price Index, April 20.

de Rijke, Kim. 2013. "Hydraulically Fractured: Unconventional Gas and Anthropology." *Anthropology Today* 29(2): 13–17. http://doi.org/10.1111/1467-8322.12017.

Diehl, Richard A..2004. *The Olmecs: America's First Civilization.* London: Thames & Hudson.

DiMuzio, Timothy. 2010. "The Real Resource Curse and the Imperialism of Development." *Faculty of Arts—Papers (Archive)*, 94–97. https://ro.uow.edu.au/artspapers/585.

Di Nunzio, Marco. 2015. "Embracing Uncertainty: Young People on the Move in Addis Ababa's Inner City." In *Ethnographies of Uncertainty in Africa*, ed. Elizabeth Cooper and David Pratten, 149–72. New York: Palgrave Macmillan.

Dolan, Catherine, and Dinah Rajak, eds. 2016. *The Anthropology of Corporate Social Responsibility.* Dislocations 18. New York, NY: Berghahn Books.

Dyer, Christopher L. 2002. "Punctuated Entropy as Culture-Induced Change: The Case of the Exxon Valdez Oil Spill." In *Catastrophe and Culture: The Anthropology of Disaster*, ed. Susanna M. Hoffman and Anthony Oliver-Smith, 159–85. Santa Fe: School for Advanced Research Press.

Edelstein, Michael R. [1988] 2018. *Contaminated Communities: The Social and Psychological Impacts of Residential Toxic Exposure.* Boulder, CO: Westview Press.

Eiss, Paul K. 2008. "Beyond the Object." *Anthropological Theory* 8(1): 79–97. http://doi.org/10.1177/1463499607087496.
Ejatlas. 2017. "Gas fracking en la Huasteca y Totonacapan. Resistencia de la coordinadora Corason, Mexico." *Mauricio González and JMA*, 30 December. Retrieved 21 December 2020 from https://ejatlas.org/conflict/gas-fracking-en-huautla-hidalgo-mexico.
Engels, Bettina, and Kristina Dietz, eds. 2017. *Contested Extractivism, Society and the State: Struggles over Mining and Land*. Development, Justice and Citizenship. London: Palgrave Macmillan UK.
England, J. Lynn, and Stan L. Albrecht. 1984. "Boomtowns and Social Disruption." *Rural Sociology* 49(2): 230–46. https://eric.ed.gov/?id=EJ300275.
Espig, Martin, and Kim de Rijke. 2018. "Energy, Anthropology and Ethnography: On the Challenges of Studying Unconventional Gas Developments in Australia." *Energy Research & Social Science* 45: 214–23. http://doi.org/10.1016/j.erss.2018.05.004.
Ey, Melina, and Meg Sherval. 2015. "Exploring the Minescape: Engaging with the Complexity of the Extractive Sector." *Area* 48(2): 176–82. http://doi.org/10.1111/area.12245.
Faas, A. J. 2016. "Continuity and Change in the Applied Anthropology of Risk, Hazards, and Disasters." *Annals of Anthropological Practice* 40(1): 6–13. http://doi.org/10.1111/napa.12083.
Fabricant, Nicole, Bret Gustafson, and Laura Weiss. 2017. "Fossil Fuels and Toxic Landscapes." *NACLA Report on the Americas* 49(4): 385–86. http://doi.org/10.1080/10714839.2017.1409003.
Fabricant, Nicole, and Nancy Postero. 2019. "Performing Indigeneity in Bolivia: The Struggle over the TIPNIS." In *Indigenous Life Projects and Extractivism: Ethnographies from South America*, ed. Cecilie Vindal Ødegaard and Juan Javier Rivera Andía, 245–76. New York: Springer Science and Business Media.
Feodoroff, Timothé, Jennifer Franco, and Ana Maria Rey Martinez. 2013. "Old Story, New Threat: Fracking and the Global Land Grab." 16. TNI *Agrarian Justice Programme Briefing Paper*.
Fentiman, Alicia. 1996. "The Anthropology of Oil: The Impact of the Oil Industry on a Fishing Community in the Niger Delta." *Social Justice* 23 4(66): 87–99. http://www.jstor.org/stable/29766976.
Ferguson, James. 2005. "Seeing like an Oil Company: Space, Security, and Global Capital in Neoliberal Africa." *American Anthropologist* 107(3): 377–82. http://doi.org/10.1525/aa.2005.107.3.377.
Ferrari, Luca. 2014. "Pico del petróleo convencional y costos del petróleo no convencional (fracking)." [Peak of the costs of conventional oil and unconventional oil (fracking)]. In *Impacto social y ambiental del fracking, México*, ed. Benjamín Robles Montoya, 23–39. Senado de la República, Instituto Belisario Domínguez LXII Legislatura.
Ferry, Elizabeth E., and Mandana E. Limbert. 2008. "Introduction." In *Timely Assets: The Politics of Resources and Their Temporalities*, ed. Elizabeth E. Ferry and Mandana E. Limbert, 3–24. Santa Fe, NM: School of Advanced Research Press.

Filer, Colin. 1990. "The Bougainville Rebellion, the Mining Industry and the Process of Social Disintegration in Papua New Guinea." *Canberra Anthropology* 13(1): 1–39. http://doi.org/10.1080/03149099009508487.

Finewood, Michael H., and Laura J. Stroup. 2012. "Fracking and the Neoliberalization of the Hydro-Social Cycle in Pennsylvania's Marcellus Shale." *Journal of Contemporary Water Research & Education* 147(1): 72–79. http://doi.org/10.1111/j.1936-704x.2012.03104.x.

Firat, Bilge. 2016. "'The Most Eastern of the West, the Most Western of the East': Energy-Transport Infrastructures and Regional Politics of the Periphery in Turkey." *Economic Anthropology* 3(1): 81–93. http://doi.org/10.1002/sea2.12046.

Fisher, Eleanor. 2007. "Occupying the Margins: Labour Integration and Social Exclusion in Artisanal Mining in Tanzania." *Development and Change* 38(4): 735–60. http://doi.org/10.1111/j.1467-7660.2007.00431.x.

Flagler, Edward K. 2007. "Comercio y ferias de trueque: España y los indios de Nuevo México." [Trade and barter fairs: Spain and the Indians in New Mexico]. *Revista Española de Antropología Americana* 37(1): 51–65.

Frederick, Jake. 2016. *Riot!: Tobacco, Reform, and Violence in Eighteenth-Century Papantla, Mexico*. Sussex: Sussex Academic Press.

Freudenburg, William R. 1981. "Women and Men in an Energy Boom Town: Adjustment, Alienation, and Adaptation." *Rural Sociology* 46: 220–44.

Fry, Matthew, and Elvin Delgado. 2018. "Petro-Geographies and Hydrocarbon Realities in Latin America." *Journal of Latin American Geography* 17(3): 10–14. http://doi.org/10.1353/lag.2018.0039.

García-Chiang, Armando. 2018. "Corporate Social Responsibility in the Mexican Oil Industry: Social Impact Assessment as a Tool for Local Development." *International Journal of Corporate Social Responsibility* 3, article 15: 1–8.

García-Chiang, Armando, and Jaime-Ramón Rodríguez. 2008. "Responsabilidad Social en la empresa: La región Marina noreste de Pemex Exploración y Producción." [Corporate Social Responsibility: The Northeastern Marine Region of Pemex Exploration and Production]. *Equilibrio Económico*, IX, 4(1): 17–40.

García Martínez, Ariel. 2012. "Juventud indígena en el Totonacapan Veracruzano" [Indigenous youth in Totonacapan Veracruz]. Revista LiminaR. Estudios sociales y humanísticos 10(1) San Cristóbal de Las Casas, Chiapas, México: 75–88.

Garner, Paul. 2011. *British Lions and Mexican Eagles: Business, Politics, and Empire in the Career of Weetman Pearson in Mexico, 1889–1919*. Stanford: Stanford University Press.

Gedicks, Al. 2001. *Resource Rebels: Native Challenges to Mining and Oil Corporations*. Cambridge, MA: South End Press.

Gelber, Elizabeth. 2015. "Black Oil Business: Rogue Pipelines, Hydrocarbon Dealers, and the 'Economics' of Oil Theft." In *Subterranean Estates: Life Worlds of Oil and Gas*, ed. Arthur Mason, Hannah Appel, and Michael Watts, 274–90. Ithaca, NY: Cornell University Press.

Gerali, Francesco. 2013. "Environment, Economy, Politics and Technology: A Brief Analysis on Mexican Petroleum up to Early 20th Century." *History of Oil Industry Journal* 13: 237–60.

Gerali, Francesco and Paolo Riguzzi. 2013. "Los inicios de la actividad petrolera en México, 1863-1874: una nueva cronología y elementos de balance" [The beginnings of oil activity in Mexico, 1863–1874: a new chronology and balance sheet elements]. Boletin del Archivo Historico de Petroleros Mexicanos: 63–89.

Geurts, Kathryn L. 2002. *Culture and the Senses: Bodily Ways of Knowing in an African Community*. Ethnographic studies in subjectivity 3. Berkeley: University of California Press. http://www.jstor.org/stable/10.1525/j.ctt1pnrfv.

Gilberthorpe, Emma. 2006. "'It's Raining Money': Anthropology, Film and Resource Extraction in Papua New Guinea." *Anthropology in Action* 13(3):13–21. http://doi.org/10.3167/aia.2006.130303.

———. 2007. "Fasu Solidarity: A Case Study of Kin Networks, Land Tenure and Oil Extraction in Kutubu, Papua New Guinea." *American Anthropologist* 109(1): 109–19.

———. 2014. "The Money Rain Phenomenon: Papua New Guinea Oil and the Resource Curse." In *Natural Resource Extraction and Indigenous Livelihoods: Development Challenges in an Era of Globalisation*, ed. Emma Gilberthorpe and Gavin M. Hilson, 90–108. London: Routledge.

Gilberthorpe, Emma, and Gavin M. Hilson, eds. 2014. *Natural Resource Extraction and Indigenous Livelihoods: Development Challenges in an Era of Globalisation*. London: Routledge.

Gilberthorpe, Emma, and Elissaios Papyrakis. 2015. "The Extractive Industries and Development: The Resource Curse at the Micro, Meso and Macro Levels." *The Extractive Industries and Society* 2(2): 381–90. http://doi.org/10.1016/j.exis.2015.02.008.

Gilberthorpe, Emma, and Dinah Rajak. 2017. "The Anthropology of Extraction: Critical Perspectives on the Resource Curse." *The Journal of Development Studies* 53(2): 186–204. https://doi.org/10.1080/00220388.2016.1160064.

Gledhill, John. 2011. "The People's Oil: Nationalism, Globalization and the Possibility of Another Country in Brazil, Mexico and Venezuela." In *Crude Domination: An Anthropology of Oil*, ed. Andrea Behrends, Stephen P. Reyna, and Günther Schlee, 165–89. Oxford: Berghahn Books.

Gómez, Christian. 2015. "La Jornada: Pemex Rehúsa Pagar Daños En Veracruz Por Fugas De Hidrocarburos . . . Y Ya Llegó El Fracking." [La Jornada: Pemex Refuses To Pay Damages In Veracruz For Hydrocarbon Leaks . . . And Fracking Has Arrived]. *La Jornada*, 17 November. Retrieved 21 December 2020 from https://www.jornada.com.mx/2015/11/17/estados/034n1est.

Gonzáles Jácome, Alba. 2007. "Conversación social y cultural: De los agrosistemas tradicionales a los alternativos en México." [Social and cultural conversation: From traditional to alternative agrosystems in Mexico] In *Los nuevos caminos de la agricultura: procesos de conversión y perspectivas*, ed. Alba Gonzáles Jácome and Francisco D. Gurri García, 59–97. Madrid: Universidad Iberoamericana.

González Minchaca, Damaris. 2011. "El municipio en México" [The municipality in Mexico]. *Revista República Jurídica Administrativa* 2(3). https://revistas-colaboracion.juridicas.unam.mx/index.php/republica-juridica-admin/article/view/437/397.

Gónzales Rocha, Mercedes. 1993. "El poder de la ausencia: Mujeres y migración an una comunidad de Los Altos de Jalisco." [The power of absence: Women and migration in a community of Los Altos de Jalisco]. In *Las realidades regionales de la crisis nacional*, ed. J. S. Tapia, 317–34. Zamora, Michoacán: El Colegio de Michoacán.

Govers, Cora. 2006. *Performing the Community: Representation, Ritual and Reciprocity in the Totonac Highlands of Mexico*. Münster: LIT.

Gramling, Bob, and Sarah Brabant. 1986. "Boomtowns and Offshore Energy Impact Assessment." *Sociological Perspectives* 29(2): 177–201. http://doi.org/10.2307/1388958.

Grove, David C. 2014. *Discovering the Olmecs: An Unconventional History*. Austin: University of Texas Press.

Grund, Lisa K. 2016. "The Tales and Trails of a Tuwama: Makushi Perceptions of Land Use and Disputes over Resources in the South Pakaraima Mountains, Guyana." *The Extractive Industries and Society* 3(3): 669–75. http://doi.org/10.1016/j.exis.2016.01.001.

Haarstad, Håvard. 2012. "Extracting Justice? Critical Themes and Challenges in Latin American Natural Resource Governance." In *New Political Spaces in Latin American Natural Resource Governance*, ed. Håvard Haarstad, 1–16. Studies of the Americas. New York: Palgrave Macmillan.

Haller, Tobias, ed. 2007. *Fossil Fuels, Oil Companies, and Indigenous Peoples: Strategies of Multinational Oil Companies, States, and Ethnic Minorities; Impact on Environment, Livelihoods, and Cultural Change*. Action anthropology 1. Vienna: Lit Verlag.

Halvaksz, Jamon A. 2008. "Whose Closure? Appearances, Temporality, and Mineral Extraction in Papua New Guinea." *Journal of the Royal Anthropological Institute* 14(1): 21–37. http://doi.org/10.1111/j.1467-9655.2007.00476.x.

Han, Clara. 2018. "Precarity, Precariousness, and Vulnerability." *Annual Review of Anthropology* 47(1): 331–43. http://doi.org/10.1146/annurev-anthro-102116-041644.

Harma, Risto F. 2009. "Child Labor in Nigeria." In *The World of Child Labor: An Historical and Regional Survey*, ed. Hugh D. Hindman, 224–28. New York: Routledge.

Harvey, Penny, and Hannah Knox. 2012. "The Enchantments of Infrastructure." *Mobilities* 7(4): 521–36. http://doi.org/10.1080/17450101.2012.718935.

Hassan, Robert. 2010. "Globalization and the 'Temporal Turn': Recent Trends and Issues in Time Studies." *Korean Journal of Policy Studies* 25(2): 83–102.

Hays, Jake, Michael McCawley, and Seth B. C. Shonkoff. 2017. "Public Health Implications of Environmental Noise Associated with Unconventional Oil and Gas Development." *Science of The Total Environment* 580: 448–56. http://doi.org/10.1016/j.scitotenv.2016.11.118.

Hernández Borbolla, Manuel. 2014. "Comunidades resienten primeros efectos del 'fracking' en México." [Communities feel first effects of fracking in Mexico]. *Huffington Post*, 15 October.

Hernandez Cervantes, Aleida, and Anna Zalik. 2018. "Canadian Capital and the Denationalization of the Mexican Energy Sector: A Geojuridical Approach." *Journal of Latin American Geography* 17(3): 42–72. http://doi.org/10.1353/lag.2018.0041.

Hernández Ibarzábal, José A. 2017. "Gas Security in the Land of Insecurity: Governance Challenges of Shale Gas Development in Mexico." *Journal of Energy & Natural Resources Law* 35(4): 363–76. http://doi.org/10.1080/02646811.2017.1358001.

High, Mette Marie and Sean Field. 2020. "Oil, Oil, Who Wants Some Oil? Part 1: Reflections on Oil Infrastructures at a Time of Negative Oil Prices." *Center for Energy Ethics*, 27 May. https://energyethics.st-andrews.ac.uk/blog/oil-oil-who-wants-some-oil-reflections-on-oil-infrastructures-at-a-time-of-negative-oil-price/.

Hilson, Gavin Michael, and Natalia Yakovleva. 2007. "Strained Relations: A Critical Analysis of the Mining Conflict in Prestea, Ghana." *Political Geography* 26(1): 98–119. http://doi.org/10.1016/j.polgeo.2006.09.001.

Hoffmann, Odile, and Emilia Velázquez Hernández, eds. 1994. *Las llanuras costeras de Veracruz: La lenta construcción de regiones. [The Coastal Plains of Veracruz: The Slow Construction of Regions]*. Xalapa: Ediciones Marcué.

Hoffman, Susanna M., and Anthony Oliver-Smith, eds. 2002. *Catastrophe & Culture: The Anthropology of Disaster*. School of American Research Advanced Seminar Series. Santa Fe, NM: School of American Research Press.

Hofmeister, Sabine. 1997. "Nature's Temporalities: Consequences for Environmental Politics." *Time & Society* 6(2–3): 309–21. http://doi.org/10.1177/0961463x97006002011.

Howes, David. 2005. "Introduction" and "Forming Perceptions." In *Empire of the Senses: The Sensory Culture Reader*, ed. David Howes, 1–21, 399–403. Oxford: Berg.

Hudgins, Anastasia, and Amanda Poole. 2014. "Framing Fracking: Private Property, Common Resources, and Regimes of Governance." *Journal of Political Ecology* 21(1): 303–19. http://doi.org/10.2458/v21i1.21138.

Huesca-Pérez, María Elena, Claudia Sheinbaum-Pardo, and Johann Köppel. 2018. "From Global to Local: Impact Assessment and Social Implications Related to Wind Energy Projects in Oaxaca, Mexico". *Impact Assessment and Project Appraisal* 36(6): 479–493. https://doi.org/10.1080/14615517.2018.1506856.

Ingold, Tim. 2011. *The Perception of the Environment: Essays on Livelihood, Dwelling and Skill*. Reissued with new preface. London: Routledge.

Jacka, Jerry K. 2018. "The Anthropology of Mining: The Social and Environmental Impacts of Resource Extraction in the Mineral Age." *Annual Review of Anthropology* 47(1): 61–77. http://doi.org/10.1146/annurev-anthro-102317-050156.

Jorritsma, Marie. 2012. "'Don't Frack with Our Karoo': Water, Landscape, and Congregational Song in Kroonvale, South Africa." *Safundi* 13(3–4): 373–91. http://doi.org/10.1080/17533171.2012.715420.

Kama, Kärg. 2020. "Resource-Making Controversies: Knowledge, Anticipatory Politics and Economization of Unconventional Fossil Fuels." *Progress in Human Geography* 44(2): 333–56.

Kaposy, Tim. 2017. "Petroleum`s Longue Durée: Writing Oil`s Temporalities into History." In *Petrocultures: Oil, Politics, Culture*, ed. Sheena Wilson, Adam Carlson, and Imre Szeman, 389–405. Québec: McGill-Queen's University Press.

Karpouzoglou, Timothy, and Sumit Vij. 2017. "Waterscape: A Perspective for Understanding the Contested Geography of Water." *Wiley Interdisciplinary Reviews: Water* 4(3): e1210. http://doi.org/10.1002/wat2.1210.

Kasburg, Carola. 1992. *Die Totonaken von El Tajín: Beharrung und Wandel über vier Jahrzehnte* [The Totonaks of El Tajín: Persistence and Change over Four Decades]. Ethnologische Studien 22. Münster: Lit Verlag.

Khalidi, Rashid. 2010. "The Middle East: Geostrategy and Oil." In *The Energy Reader*, ed. Laura Nader, 271–81. Oxford: Wiley-Blackwell.

Kirsch, Stuart. 2014. *Mining Capitalism: The Relationship between Corporations and Their Critics*. Oakland, CA: University of California Press.

Klare, Michael T. 2002. *Resource Wars: The New Landscape of Global Conflict*. New York: Henry Holt and Company.

Kourí, Emilio H. 2004. *A Pueblo Divided: Business, Property, and Community in Papantla, Mexico*. Stanford, CA: Stanford University Press.

Krøijer, Stine. 2019. "In the Spirit of Oil: Unintended Flows and Leaky Lives in Northeastern Ecuador." In *Indigenous Life Projects and Extractivism: Ethnographies from South America*, ed. Cecilie Vindal Ødegaard and Juan J. Rivera Andía, 95–118. Approaches to Social Inequality and Difference. Cham: Springer International Publishing. https://doi.org/10.1007/978-3-319-93435-8_4.

Lanzano, Cristiano. 2018. "Gold Digging and the Politics of Time: Changing Timescapes of Artisanal Mining in West Africa." *The Extractive Industries and Society* 5(2): 253–59. http://doi.org/10.1016/j.exis.2018.02.006.

Larkin, Brian. 2013. "The Politics and Poetics of Infrastructure." *Annual Review of Anthropology* 42(1): 327–43. http://doi.org/10.1146/annurev-anthro-092412-155522.

Lastiri, Xanath. 2015. "Papantla Despierta, Y En Su Patio Hay Fracking; ¿quién Lo Hizo Sin Nosotros? Reclama." [Papantla awakens, and in your backyard there's fracking; Who decided this without Us? Time to reclaim]. *SinEmbargo MX*, 22 November. Retrieved 21 December 2020 from https://www.sinembargo.mx/22-11-2015/1558554.

Le Billon, Philippe, ed. 2005. *The Geopolitics of Resource Wars: Resource Dependence, Governance and Violence*. Case studies in geopolitics. London: Frank Cass.

Lefebvre, Henri. 1991. "The Production of Space." In *The People, Place, and Space Reader*, ed. Gieseking, Jen Jack, William Mangold, Cindi Katz, Setha Low, and Susan Saegert, 289–94. New York: Routledge.

Leonard, Lori. 2016. *Life in the Time of Oil: A Pipeline and Poverty in Chad*. Indianapolis, IN: Indiana University Press.

Li, Gege. 2020. "Surreal Californian Oilscape Wins Climate Change Photography Award." *New Scientist*, 25 November. Retrieved 5 October 2021 from https://www.newscientist.com/article/mg24833102-000-surreal-californian-oilscape-wins-climate-change-photography-award/#ixzz78sMuXCpG.

Licona Valencia, Ernesto. 2014. "Un sistema de intercambio híbrido: el mercado/tianguis La Purísima, Tehuacán-Puebla, México." [A hybrid exchange system: La Purísima market/tianguis, Tehuacán-Puebla, Mexico]. *Antipoda* 18: 137–63.

Liesch, Matthew. 2014. "Spatial Boundaries and Industrial Landscapes at Keweenaw National Historical Park." *The Extractive Industries and Society* 1(2): 303–11. http://doi.org/10.1016/j.exis.2014.08.007.

Limbert, Mandana. 2008. "Depleted Futures: Anticipating the End of Oil in Oman." In *Timely Assets: The Politics of Resources and Their Temporalities*, ed. Elizabeth E.

Ferry and Mandana E. Limbert, 25–74. Santa Fe, NM: School of Advanced Research Press.

———. 2010. *In the Time of Oil*. Stanford, CA: Stanford University Press. http://dx.doi.org/10.1515/9780804774604.

López Vallejo; Francisco Javier. 2020. *Entre la vainilla y el petroleo, tenencia, industria petrolera y reparto en las tierras de Papantla: El caso de la hacienda petrolera Palma Sola, 1880–1936*. [Between vanilla and oil, tenure, oil industry and land distribution in Papantla: The case of the oil hacienda Palma Sola, 1880-1936.] Licenciatura Thesis Historia, Universidad Nacional Autónoma de México (UNAM).

Love, Thomas. 2008. "Anthropology and the Fossil Fuel Era." *Anthropology Today* 24(2): 3–4. http://doi.org/10.1111/j.1467-8322.2008.00568.x.

Lovins, Amory B. 2010. "Winning the Oil Endgame." In *The Energy Reader*, ed. Laura Nader, 282–86. Oxford: Wiley-Blackwell.

Löw, Martina. 2008. "The Constitution of Space." *European Journal of Social Theory* 11(1): 25–49. http://doi.org/10.1177/1368431007085286.

Low, Setha. 2009. "Toward an Anthropological Theory of Space and Place." *Special Issue on Signification and Space. Semiotica* 175(1–4): 21–37. http://doi.org/10.1515/semi.2009.041.

———. 2014. "Spatialized Culture: An Engaged Anthropological Approach to Space and Place." In *The People, Place, and Space Reader*, ed. Jen Jack Gieseking, William Mangold, Cindi Katz, Setha Low, and Susan Saegert, 34–39. New York: Routledge.

Malin, Stephanie A., Tara Opsal, Tara O'Connor Shelley, and Peter M. Hall. 2018. "The Right to Resist or a Case of Injustice? Meta-Power in the Oil and Gas Fields." *Social Forces* 97(4): 1811–38. http://doi.org/10.1093/sf/soy094.

Masferrer Kahn, Elio. 2004. *Totonacos -Pueblos indígenas del México contemporáneo*. [Totonacos - Indigenous peoples of contemporary Mexico]. Mexico City: CDI Comisión Nacional para el Desarrollo de los Pueblos Indígenas.

Mason, Arthur, Hannah Appel, and Michael Watts, eds. 2015. *Subterranean Estates: Life Worlds of Oil and Gas*. Ithaca, NY: Cornell University Press.

Maurer, Noel. 2011. "The Empire Struck Back: Sanctions and Compensation in the Mexican Oil Expropriation of 1938". *The Journal of Economic History* 71(03): 590–615. https://doi.org/10.1017/S0022050711001859.

May, Jon, and Nigel J. Thrift, eds. 2001. *Timespace: Geographies of Temporality*. Critical Geographies 13. London: Routledge. http://www.loc.gov/catdir/enhancements/fy0649/00045742-d.html.

McNeish, John-Andrew. 2018. "Resource Extraction and Conflict in Latin America." *Colombia Internacional* 93(93): 3–16. http://doi.org/10.7440/colombiaint93.2018.01.

Melly, Caroline. 2013. "Ethnography on the Road: Infrastructural Vision and the Unruly Present in Contemporary Dakar." *Africa* 83(3): 385–402. http://doi.org/10.1017/s0001972013000235.

Merino Acuña, Roger. 2015. "The Politics of Extractive Governance: Indigenous Peoples and Socio-Environmental Conflicts." *Extractive Industries and Society* 2(1): 85–92. http://doi.org/10.1016/j.exis.2014.11.007

Milano, Flavia, and Irene Irazábal Briceño. 2018. *Extractive Sector and Civil Society: When the Work of Communities, Governments and Industries Leads to Development.* Inter-American Development Bank. http://dx.doi.org/10.18235/0001363.

Mitchell, Timothy. 2011. *Carbon Democracy: Political Power in the Age of Oil.* London: Verso. http://www.loc.gov/catdir/enhancements/fy1312/2011277420-b.html.

Moen, Elizabeth. 1981. "Women in Energy Boom Towns." *Psychology of Women Quarterly* 6(1): 99–112. http://doi.org/10.1111/j.1471-6402.1981.tb01063.x.

Mohai, Paul, David Pellow, and J. T. Roberts. 2009. "Environmental Justice." *Annual Review of Environment and Resources* 34(1): 405–30. http://doi.org/10.1146/annurev-environ-082508-094348.

Monreal Ávila, Ricardo. 2008. "El petróleo en la historia y en la cultura de México." [Petroleum in the history and culture of Mexico]. In *El petróleo en la historia y en la cultura de México*, ed. José Alfonso Suárez del Real Aguilera, 69–90. Mexico City: Grupo parlamentario del PRD.

Monroy, Jorge, and Karol García. 2019. "AMLO Prohíbe Fracking Aprobado Por La CNH Para Campo Humapa." [AMLO prohibits fracking approved by CNH for Humapa Field]. *El Economista*, 27 June. Retrieved 21 December 2020 from https://www.eleconomista.com.mx/empresas/AMLO-prohibe-fracking-aprobado-por-la-CNH-para-campo-Humapa-20190627-0032.html.

Morales, Flavia. 2019. "Indígenas cuentan cómo Pemex arruinó su paraíso y la Reforma Energética los despojó de tierra." [Indigenous people tell how Pemex ruined their paradise and the Energy Reform dispossessed them of land]. *SinEmbargo*, 1 February. Retrieved 21 December 2020 from https://www.sinembargo.mx/01-02-2019/3529766.

Mottura, David. 2017. "El Petrolero, Prisionero De La Virilidad." [The oil-worker, prisoner of virility]. *Observatorio Petrolero Sur*, 23 October. Retrieved 21 December 2020 from https://opsur.org.ar/2017/10/23/el-petrolero-prisionero-de-la-virilidad/.

Munn, Nancy D. 1992. "The Cultural Anthropology of Time: A Critical Essay." *Annual Review of Anthropology* 21(1): 93–123. http://doi.org/10.1146/annurev.an.21.100192.000521.

Nájar, Alberto. 2019. "'Huachicoleo' En México: Las Consecuencias Económicas Del Desabasto Por El Combate Al Robo De Combustible." [Huachicoleo' in Mexico: the economic consequences of fuel theft fighting fuel shortages]. *BBC News Mundo*, 11 January. Retrieved 21 December2020 from https://www.bbc.com/mundo/noticias-america-latina-46834506.

Nash, June C. 1979. *We Eat the Mines and the Mines Eat Us: Dependency and Exploitation in Bolivian Tin Mines.* New York: Columbia University Press.

Nejapa García, Miriam Karina. 2018. "Conflictos socioterritoriales a causa de la industria petrolera, el caso del AC San Andrés Veracruz." [Socio-territorial conflicts due to the oil industry, the case of AC San Andres Veracruz]. Licenciatura Thesis, Division of Social Science and Humanities, Universidad Autónoma Metropolitana Unidad Iztapalapa.

Nolte, Detlef, and Almut Schilling-Vacaflor. 2012. "Introduction: The Times They Are a Changin': Constitutional Transformations in Latin America since the

1990s." In *Constitutionalism in Latin America: Promises and Practices*, ed. Detlef Nolte and Almut Schilling-Vacaflor, 3–30 London: Ashgate.
Nueva Ley de Hidrocarburos. 2014. *Articulo 96*. http://www.diputados.gob.mx/LeyesBiblio/ref/lhidro/LHidro_orig_11ago14.pdf.
Nueva Ley de Hidrocarburos. 2014. *Articulo 118*. http://www.diputados.gob.mx/LeyesBiblio/ref/lhidro/LHidro_orig_11ago14.pdf.
Nuijten, Monique. 2003. *Power, Community and the State: The Political Anthropology of Organisation in Mexico*. London [i.a.]: Pluto Press.
O'Connor, Rebecca, and Lisa Viscidi. 2015. "Mexico's Energy Reform: Bridging the Skills Gap." *Energy Policy Brief. Inter-American Dialogue*. https://prealblog.files.wordpress.com/2015/06/mexicosenergyreform-version-2.pdf.
O'Faircheallaigh, Ciaran. 2013. "Extractive Industries and Indigenous Peoples: A Changing Dynamic?" *Journal of Rural Studies* 30: 20–30. http://doi.org/10.1016/j.jrurstud.2012.11.003.
Oliver-Smith, Anthony. 1996. "Anthropological Research on Hazards and Disasters." *Annual Review of Anthropology* 25(1): 303–28. http://doi.org/10.1146/annurev.anthro.25.1.303.
——— . 2013. "Disaster Risk Reduction and Climate Change Adaptation: The View from Applied Anthropology." Human Organization 72(4): 275–82. https://doi.org/10.17730/humo.72.4.j7u8054266386822.
Omeje, Kenneth C. 2008. *Extractive Economies and Conflicts in the Global South: Multi-Regional Perspectives on Rentier Politics*. Aldershot: Ashgate.
Olmedo Carranza, Bernardo. 2009. *Crisis en el campo mexicano [Crisis in the Mexican countryside]*. Mexico City: Universidad Nacional Autónoma de México (UNAM), Instituto de Investigaciones Económicas.
Olvera Ribera, Alberto. 1989. "La Evolución de la Conciencia Obrera den Poza Rica 1932–1959." [The evolution of workers' consciousness in Poza Rica 1932-1959]. In *Veracruz un tiempo para contar . . .*, ed. Mirna Benítez, Carmen Blázquez, Abel Juárez, and Gerna Lozano y Nathal, 35–58. Xalapa: Colección Regiones de México Universidad Veracruzana, Instituto Nacional de Antropología e Historia.
——— . 1992. "The Rise and Fall of Union Democracy at Poza Rica, 1932–1940." In *The Mexican Petroleum Industry in the Twentieth Century*, ed. Jonathan C. Brown and Alan Knight. Austin, 63–89: University of Texas Press.
Ordaz, Yeshua. 2019. "CNH aprueba plan de trabajo para Pemex con fracking." *Milenio*, 25 June. Retrieved 21 December 2020 from https://www.milenio.com/negocios/pemex-contara-plan-usaran-fracking-cnh.
Owen, John R., and Deanna Kemp. 2014. "'Free Prior and Informed Consent', Social Complexity and the Mining Industry: Establishing a Knowledge Base." *Resources Policy* 41: 91–100. http://doi.org/10.1016/j.resourpol.2014.03.006.
Palermo, Hernán M. 2017. *La Producción De La Masculinidad En El Trabajo Petrolero. [The production of masculinity in the petroleum sector]*. Sociedad. Buenos Aires: Editorial Biblos.
Parry, Jonathan. 2018. "Introduction." In *Industrial Labor on the Margins of Capitalism: Precarity, Class and the Neoliberal Subject*, edited by Chris Hann and Jonathan Parry, 1–38. Max Planck Studies in Anthropology and Economy Ser v.4. New York, NY: Berghahn Books Incorporated.

Pauli, Julia. 2000. *Das geplante Kind [The planned child]*. Hamburg: LIT.

———. 2007a. "'Que vivan mejor aparte': Migración, estructura familiar y género en una comunidad del México central" [Que vivan mejor aparte: migration, family structure and gender in a community in Central Mexico]. In *Familias mexicanas en transición: Unas miradas antropológicas*, ed. David L. Robichaux, 87–116. Mexico City: Universidad Iberoamericana

———. 2007b. "Zwölf-Monats-Schwangerschaften: Internationale Migration, reproduktive Konflikte und weibliche Autonomie in einer zentralmexikanischen Gemeinde." [Twelve-month pregnancies: international migration, reproductive conflict, and female autonomy in a Central Mexican community]. *Tsantsa. Zeitschrift der schweizerischen ethnologischen Gesellschaft* 12: 71–81.

Pearson, Thomas W. 2013. "Frac Sand Mining in Wisconsin: Understanding Emerging Conflicts and Community Organizing." *CAFÉ* 35(1): 30–40. http://doi.org/10.1111/cuag.12003.

Pedersen, Morten A., and Morten Nielsen. 2013. "Trans-Temporal Hinges: Reflections on an Ethnographic Study of Chinese Infrastructural Projects in Mozambique and Mongolia." *Social Analysis* 57(1): 122–42.

• Pedroza, Luicy. 2019. "AMLO's First 100 Days: Mixed Signals." *GIGA Focus Latin America* 2: 1–12.

PEMEX (Petróleos Mexicanos). 2010. Social Responsibility Report 2010. Mexico City: PEMEX

Peña, Miguel, and Magdalena Lizardo. 2017. "Extractive Industry in the Dominican Republic: A History of Growth, Regression and Recovery." *The Extractive Industries and Society* 5(3): 218–27. http://doi.org/10.1016/j.exis.2017.03.005.

Penfield, Amy. 2018. *Extractive Pluralities: The Intersection of Oil Wealth and Informal Gold Mining in Venezuelan Amazonia*. Indigenous Life Projects and Extractivism. New York: Springer International Publishing. http://dx.doi.org/10.1007/978-3-319-93435-8_3.

Perreault, Tom. 2018. "Energy, Extractivism and Hydrocarbon Geographies in Contemporary Latin America." *Journal of Latin American Geography* 17(3): 235–52. http://doi.org/10.1353/lag.2018.0048.

Perry, Simona L. 2012. "Development, Land Use, and Collective Trauma: The Marcellus Shale Gas Boom in Rural Pennsylvania." *CAFÉ* 34(1): 81–92. http://doi.org/10.1111/j.2153-9561.2012.01066.x.

Pijpers, Robert J. 2016. "Mining, Expectations and Turbulent Times: Locating Accelerated Change in Rural Sierra Leone." *History and Anthropology* 27(5): 504–20. http://doi.org/10.1080/02757206.2016.1222524.

———. 2018. "Navigating Uncertainty: Large-Scale Mining and Micro-Politics in Sierra Leone." Ph.D. dissertation. Oslo: University of Oslo.

Pijpers, Robert J., and Thomas H. Eriksen, eds. 2019. *Mining Encounters: Extractive Industries in an Overheated World*. London: Pluto Press.

Popke, Jeff, and Rebecca M. Torres. 2013. "Neoliberalization, Transnational Migration, and the Varied Landscape of Economic Subjectivity in the Totonacapan Region of Veracruz." *Annals of the Association of American Geographers* 103(1): 211–29. http://doi.org/10.1080/00045608.2011.652871.

Portal, Claire. 2018. "Geodiversity and Anthropocene Landscapes: New Perceptions and Aesthetic Renewal of Some European 'Coalscapes.'" *Environment, Space, Place* 10(1): 89–110.

Press, Daniel, and Steven C. Minta. 2000. "The Smell of Nature: Olfaction, Knowledge and the Environment." *Ethics, Place & Environment* 3(2): 173–86. http://doi.org/10.1080/713665886.

Quintal Avilés; Ella F. 1986. "La sección 30 sel STPRM (Poza Rica)" [The section 30 in the STPRM (Poza Rica)]. *Los sindicatos nacionales en el Mexico contemporaneo* 1: 289–328.

———. 1994. "Antropología de una ciudad obrera." *Estudios Demográficos y Urbanos* 9(2): 429–37. https://estudiosdemograficosyurbanos.colmex.mx/index.php/edu/article/view/917/910.

Rabe, Barry G., and Christopher Borick. 2013. "Conventional Politics for Unconventional Drilling? Lessons from Pennsylvania's Early Move into Fracking Policy Development." *Review of Policy Research* 30(3): 321–40. http://doi.org/10.1111/ropr.12018.

Ramírez, Érika. 2015. "Fracking: abren más de 900 pozos en seis estados." [Fracking: more than 900 wells opened in six states]. *Voltaire.net*, 13 July. Retrieved 21 December 2020 from https://www.voltairenet.org/article188145.html.

Redacción BBC News Mundo. 2019. "Significado de huachicolero: ¿por qué llaman así a los ladrones de combustible en México?" [Meaning of huachicolero: why do they call fuel thieves in Mexico that name?]. *BBC News Mundo*, 11 January. Retrieved 21 December 2020 from https://www.bbc.com/mundo/noticias-america-latina-46831943.

Redacción el Heraldo. 2018. "El llano papanteco en pleno vuelo" [The Papanteco plain in full flight]. *El Heraldo*, 10 October. Retrieved 21 December 2020 from http://elheraldodepozarica.com.mx/estado/papantla/65475-el-llano-papanteco-en-pleno-vuelo.html/.

Redacción Proceso. 2017. "Ordenan a Pemex informar sobre beneficiarios de programa de apoyo al medio ambiente" [Pemex ordered to inform on beneficiaries of environmental support program]. *Proceso*, 5 July. Retrieved 21 December 2020 from https://www.proceso.com.mx/493678/ordenan-a-pemex-informar-beneficiarios-programa-apoyo-al-medio-ambiente

Reina, Elena. 2016. "La UNAM deja fuera al 91% de los aspirantes externos." [UNAM leaves out 91% of external applicants.] *El País*, 19 July. Retrieved 21 December 2020 from https://elpais.com/internacional/2016/07/19/mexico/1468940807_182231.html

Reno, Joshua. 2011. "Beyond Risk: Emplacement and the Production of Environmental Evidence." *American Ethnologist* 38(3): 516–30. http://doi.org/10.1111/j.1548-1425.2011.01320.x.

Reporte Proyecto IICA-RAN. 2012. *Cuaderno de Alternativas de Desarrollo y Retos del Núcleo Agrario "Emiliano Zapata"* [Development Alternatives and Challenges of the Agrarian Nucleus „Emiliano Zapata"]. Papantla de Olarte. Veracruz.

Revette, Anna C. 2017. "This Time It's Different: Lithium Extraction, Cultural Politics and Development in Bolivia." *Third World Quarterly* 38(1): 149–68. http://doi.org/10.1080/01436597.2015.1131118.

Reyna, Stephen P. 2007. "The Traveling Model that Would Not Travel: Oil, Empire, and Patrimonialism in Contemporary Chad." *Social Analysis* 51(3): 78–102. http://doi.org/10.3167/sa.2007.510304.

Reyna, Stephen, and Andrea Behrends. 2011. "The Crazy Curse and Crude Domination: Toward an Anthropology of Oil." In *Crude Domination: An Anthropology of Oil*, ed. Andrea Behrends, Stephen P. Reyna and Günther Schlee, 3–30. Oxford: Berghahn Books.

Reynolds Whyte, Susan, and Godfrey Etyang Siu. 2015. "Contingency: Interpersonal and Historical Dependencies in HIV Care." In *Ethnographies of Uncertainty in Africa*, ed. Elizabeth Cooper and David Pratten, 19–35. New York: Palgrave Macmillan.

Richardson, Tanya, and Gisa Weszkalnys. 2014. "Introduction: Resource Materialities." *Anthropological Quarterly* 87(1): 5–30. http://doi.org/10.1353/anq.2014.0007.

Riffo, Lorena. 2017. "Fracking and Resistance in the Land of Fire: Struggles over Fracking in Northern Patagonia, Argentina, Highlight the Need to Decommodify and Democratize Energy Resources and Seek Alternatives." *NACLA Report on the Americas* 49(4): 470–75.

Rincón Gallardo, Gilberto. 2004. "Anti-Discrimination Legislation and Policies in Mexico." In *Social Inclusion and Economic Development in Latin America*, ed. Mayra Buvinic, Jaqueline Mazza, and Ruthanne Deutsch, 87–94. Inter-American Development Bank.

Ringel, Felix. 2016. "Neue Gegenwärtigkeit in Hoyerswerda: Zur Anthropologie und Zukunft Ostdeutschlands." [New Presence in Hoyerswerda: on the anthropology and future of East Germany]. In *Der Osten: Neue sozialwissenschaftliche Perspektiven auf einen komplexen Gegenstand jenseits von Verurteilung und Verklärung*, ed. Sandra Matthaeus and Daniel Kubiak, 141–67. Wiesbaden: Springer Fachmedien.

Rippy, Merrill. 1972. *Oil and the Mexican Revolution*. Leiden: Brill.

Rodman, Margaret. 1992. "Empowering Place: Multilocality and Multivocality." *American Anthropologist* 94(3): 640–56.

Rogers, Douglas. 2015a. "Oil and Anthropology." *Annual Review of Anthropology* 44(1): 365–80. http://doi.org/10.1146/annurev-anthro-102214-014136.

———. 2015b. *The Depths of Russia. Oil Power and Culture After Socialism*. Ithaca, NY: Cornell University Press.

Ross, Michael L. 1999. "The Political Economy of the Resource Curse." *World Politics* 51(2): 297–322. http://doi.org/10.1017/S0043887100008200.

———. 2001. "Does Oil Hinder Democracy?" *World Politics* 53(3): 325–61. http://doi.org/10.1353/wp.2001.0011.

Salas Landa, Mónica. 2016. "Crude Residues: The Workings of Failing Oil Infrastructure in Poza Rica, Veracruz, Mexico." *Environment and Planning* 48(4): 718–35. http://doi.org/10.1177/0308518X15594618.

Salman, Ton, and Marjo de Theije. 2017. "Analysing Conflicts around Small-Scale Gold Mining in the Amazon: The Contribution of a Multi-Temporal Model." *The Extractive Industries and Society* 4(3): 586–94.

Sánchez Campos, Paul A. 2016. "Whatever Happened to the Mexican Oil Bonanza? The Challenges of Mexico's New OilFund." *Natural Resources Journal* 56(2): 291–312.
Santiago, Myrna I. 2006. *The Ecology of Oil: Environment, Labor, and the Mexican Revolution, 1900–1938*. Studies in Environment and History. Cambridge: Cambridge University Press.
———. 2016. "Oil and Environment in Mexico." In *Oxford Research Encyclopedia of Latin American History*. Retrieved 3 March 2019 from http://oxfordre.com/view/10.1093/acrefore/9780199366439.001.0001/acrefore-9780199366439-e-319.
Santoyo Torres, Mario Antonio. 2009. "La mano negra: poder regional y estado en México (Veracruz, 1928–1943)." [The Black Hand: regional power and state in Mexico (Veracruz, 1928-1943)]. In *La Revolución Mexicana en Veracruz Díaz*, ed. Bernardo García and David Skerrit Gardner, 443–70. antología: 518. Veracruz: SEV.
Savino, Lucas. 2016. "Landscapes of Contrast: The Neo-Extractivist State and Indigenous Peoples in 'Post-Neoliberal' Argentina." *The Extractive Industries and Society* 3(2): 404–15. http://doi.org/10.1016/j.exis.2016.02.011.
Sawyer, Suzana. 2004. *Crude Chronicles*. Durham, NC: Duke University Press.
———. 2012. *The Politics of Resource Extraction: Indigenous Peoples, Multinational Corporations, and the State*. Hampshire: Palgrave Macmillan.
Schafft, Kai A., Yetkin Borlu, and Leland Glenna. 2013. "The Relationship between Marcellus Shale Gas Development in Pennsylvania and Local Perceptions of Risk and Opportunity." *Rural Sociology* 78(2): 143–66. http://doi.org/10.1111/ruso.12004.
Schilling-Vacaflor, Almut and Riccarda Flemmer. 2015. "Conflict Transformation through Prior Consultation? Lessons from Peru." *Journal of Latin American Studies* 47(4): 811–39. http://doi.org/10.1017/S0022216X15000826.
Schmidt, Gerold. 2019. "Fracking trotz gegenteiliger Versprechen von AMLO?" [Fracking Despite AMLO's Promises to the Contrary?]. *Nachrichtenpool Lateinamerika*, 21 February. Retrieved 21 December 2020 from https://www.npla.de/poonal/fracking-trotz-gegenteiliger-versprechen-von-amlo/.
Schmidt, Peer. 2007. "Die Erfindung Des Campesino: Die Deagrarisierung im Mexiko des 20. Jahrhunderts" [The invention of the Campesino: The deagrarization in Mexico of the 20th century] *Geschichte und Gesellschaft* 33 (4): 515–45. https://doi.org/10.13109/gege.2007.33.4.515.
Schöneich, Svenja. 2014. "From Global Decisions and Local Changes: The Ceremonial Dance of the Voladores Becomes UNESCO Intangible Cultural Heritage." *ethno* 36(1–2): 447–66. http://doi.org/10.7202/1037617ar.
Schritt, Jannik. 2018. "Crude Controversies: Disputes along Niger's Petro-Infrastructure." *History and Anthropology* 29(5): 645–69. http://doi.org/10.1080/02757206.2018.1445625.
———. 2019. "Well-Oiled Protest: Adding Fuel to Political Conflicts in Niger." *African Studies Review* 62(2): 49–71. http://doi.org/10.1017/asr.2018.19.
Scott, Rebecca, and Elizabeth Bennett. 2014. "Branding Resources: Extractive Communities, Industrial Brandscapes and Themed Environments." *Work Employment & Society* 29(2): 278–94. http://doi.org/10.1177/0950017013519844.

Seco, Raquel. 2013. "Un parche para los 'descolgados' del sistema universitario en México." *El País*, 21 June. Retrieved 21 December 2020 from https://elpais.com/sociedad/2013/06/21/actualidad/1371777937_225272.html.

Seelke, Clare Ribando, M. Angeles Villarreal, Michael Ratner, and Phillip Brown. 2015. "Mexico's Oil and Gas Sector: Background, Reform Efforts, and Implications for the United States." *Congressional Report, Congressional Research Service* Retrieved 21 December 2020 from .https://sgp.fas.org/crs/row/R43313.pdf.

SEFIPLAN (Secretaría de Finanzas y Planeación del Estado de Veracruz). 2016 Sistema de Información Municipal: Papantla. *CUADERNILLOS MUNICIPALES, 2016* http://ceieg.veracruz.gob.mx/wp-content/uploads/sites/21/2016/05/Papantla.pdf.

Serna, Ana María. 2008. "Extranjeros, petróleo y revolución en el norte de Veracruz, 1910–1920." [Foreigners, petroleum and revolution in northern Veracruz, 1910-1920]. *Dimensión Antropológica* 43: 17–55. https://www.revistas.inah.gob.mx/index.php/dimension/article/view/1542.

———. 2012. *Resources for Reform: Oil and Neoliberalism in Argentina*. Stanford, CA: Stanford University Press. http://site.ebrary.com/lib/uniregensburg/Doc?id=10571088.

Sígler, Édgar. 2016. "Chicontepec: la gran derrota de Pemex." [Chicontepec: Pemex's great defeat]. *Expansion*, 22 June. Retrieved 21 December 2020 from https://expansion.mx/empresas/2016/06/21/chicontepec-la-gran-derrota-de-pemex.

Silva Ontiveros, Letizia, Paul G. Munro, Melo Zurita, and Maria de Lourdes. 2018. "Proyectos De Muerte: Energy Justice Conflicts on Mexico's Unconventional Gas Frontier." *The Extractive Industries and Society* 5(4): 481–89. http://doi.org/10.1016/j.exis.2018.06.010.

Simonelli, Jeanne. 2014. "Home Rule and Natural Gas Development in New York: Civil Fracking Rights." *Journal of Political Ecology* 21(1): 258. http://doi.org/10.2458/v21i1.21136.

Skerrit Gardner, David. 1994. "Tres culturas: Un nuevo espacio régional (el caso de la colonia francesa de Jicaltepec-San Rafael)." [Three cultures: A new regional space (the case of the French colony of Jicaltepec-San Rafael]. In *Las llanuras costera de Veracruz: La lenta construcción de regiones*, ed. Odile Hoffmann and Emilia Velázquez Hernández, 161–92. Xalapa: Ediciones Marcué.

Smartt Gullion, Jessica. 2015. *Fracking the Neighborhood: Reluctant Activists and Natural Gas Drilling*. Urban and Industrial Environments. Cambridge, MA: MIT Press.

Smith, Derek A., Peter H. Herlihy, John H. Kelly, and Aida R. Viera. 2009. "The Certification and Privatization of Indigenous Lands in Mexico." *Journal of Latin American Geography* 8(2): 175–207. http://www.jstor.org/stable/25765267.

Smith, James H. 2015. "May It Never End: Price Wars, Networks, and Temporality in the '3Ts' Mining Trade of the Eastern D.R. Congo." *HAU: Journal of Ethnographic Theory* 5(1): 1–34.

Smith Rolston, Jessica. 2013. "Specters of Syndromes and the Everyday Lives of Wyoming Energy Workers." In *Cultures of Energy: Power, Practices, Technologies*, ed. Sarah Strauss, Stephanie Rupp, and Thomas Love, 213–26. Walnut Creek: Left Coast Press.

Solís, Arturo. 2019. "AMLO rechaza producir más gas con fracking porque 'no tendríamos agua.'" *Forbes México*, 18 July. Retrieved 21 December 2020 from https://www.forbes.com.mx/amlo-rechaza-producir-mas-gas-con-fracking-porque-no-tendriamos-agua/.

Stammler, Florian, and Vladislav Peskov. 2008. "Building a 'Culture of Dialogue' Among Stakeholders in North-West Russian Oil Extraction." *Europe-Asia Studies* 60(5): 831–49. http://doi.org/10.1080/09668130802085182.

Stedman, Richard C., Jeffrey B. Jacquet, Matthew R. Filteau, Fern K. Willits, Kathryn J. Brasier, and Diane K. McLaughlin. 2012. "Environmental Reviews and Case Studies: Marcellus Shale Gas Development and New Boomtown Research: Views of New York and Pennsylvania Residents." *Environmental Practice* 14(4): 382–93. http://doi.org/10.1017/S1466046612000403.

Stewart, Pamela J., and Andrew Strathern, eds. 2003. *Landscape, Memory and History: Anthropological Perspectives*. Anthropology, Culture, and Society. London: Pluto Press. http://www.jstor.org/stable/10.2307/j.ctt18fsck3

Stojanovski, Ognen. 2012. "Handcuffed: An Assessment of PEMEX's Performance a Strategy." In *Oil and Governance: State-Owned Enterprises and the World Energy Supply*, ed. David G. Victor, David R. Hults, and Mark C. Thurber, 280–333. Cambridge: Cambridge University Press.

Stoller, Paul. 1989. *The Taste of Ethnographic Things: The Senses in Anthropology*. Contemporary Ethnography Series. Philadelphia: University of Pennsylvania Press. http://www.jstor.org/stable/10.2307/j.ctt3fhjx9.

Storck Karl-Ludwig. 1986. "Die mexikanische Hacienda am Beispiel des Beckens von Oaxaca, Mexiko: Ein Beitrag zur Begriffsbestimmung" [The Mexican Hacienda — The Example of the Oaxaca Basin, Mexico. A Contribution towards the Terminological Definition]. *Erdkunde* 40(4): 271–82.

Strauss, Sarah, Stephanie Rupp, and Thomas Love, ed. 2013. *Cultures of Energy: Power, Practices, Technologies*.Walnut Creek: Left Coast Press.

Suárez Ávila, Alberto Abad. 2017. *The Rule of Law and Mexico`s Energy Reform: The Implementation of the Energy Reform and Socio-Environmental Conflicts regarding Hydrocarbons in Mexico*. James A. Baker III Institute for Public Policy of Rice University.

Svampa, Maristella. 2015. "Commodities Consensus: Neoextractivism and Enclosure of the Commons in Latin America." *South Atlantic Quarterly* 114(1): 65–82. http://doi.org/10.1215/00382876-2831290.

———. 2019. *Neo-Extractivism in Latin America:* Cambridge: Cambridge University Press. http://dx.doi.org/10.1017/9781108752589.

Torry, William I., William A. Anderson, Donald Bain, Harry J. Otway, Randall Baker, Frances D'Souza, Philip O'Keefe et al. 1979. "Anthropological Studies in Hazardous Environments: Past Trends and New Horizons." *Current Anthropology* 20(3): 517–40. http://www.jstor.org/stable/2742110.

Uwem, E. Ite. 2019. "Sustainability Assurance and Evaluation for Effective Corporate Social Responsibility Communication." SPE Nigeria Annual International Conference and Exhibition, Lagos, Nigeria, August 2019. https://doi.org/10.2118/198776-MS.

Valderrama Rouy, Pablo. 2005. "The Totonac." In *Native Peoples of the Gulf Coast of Mexico*, ed. Alan R. Sandstrom and Enrique Hugo García Valencia, 187–210. Tuscon: University of Arizona Press.

Vázquez Castillo, María Teresa. 2004. *Land Privatization in Mexico: Urbanization, Formation of Regions, and Globalization in Ejidos*. New York: Routledge.

Velázquez Hernández, Emilia. 1995. *Cuando los arrieros perdieron sus caminos. La conformación regional del Totonacapan* [When the muleteers lost their roads. The regional conformation of Totonacapan]. Zamora, Michoacán: El Colegio de Michoacán, (Colección Investigaciones).

von Schnitzler, Antina. 2008. "Citizenship Prepaid: Water, Calculability, and Techno-Politics in South Africa." *Journal of Southern African Studies* 34(4): 899–917. http://doi.org/10.1080/03057070802456821.

Valdivia, Gabriela. 2008. "Governing Relations between People and Things: Citizenship, Territory, and the Political Economy of Petroleum in Ecuador." *Political Geography* 27(4): 456–77. http://doi.org/10.1016/j.polgeo.2008.03.007.

Vásquez, Patricia I. 2014. *Oil Sparks in the Amazon*. Athens: University of Georgia Press. https://library.oapen.org/handle/20.500.12657/30559.

Vidal Cano, Estefany. 2016. "La Mediación y El Uso Ocupacional Superficial En Materia de Hidrocarburos Derivado de La Reforma Energética En México" [Mediation and surface occupational use in hydrocarbon matters derived from the Energy Reform in Mexico]. *Revista Iberoamericana de Producción Académica y Gestión Educativa* 3(5): 1–27

Vigh, Henrik. 2006. *Navigating Terrains of War: Youth and Soldiering in Guinea Bissau*. Methodology and History in Anthropology 13. New York: Berghahn Books.

Vindal Ødegaard, Cecilie, and Juan J. Rivera Andía, eds. 2019. *Indigenous Life Projects and Extractivism: Ethnographies from South America*. Approaches to Social Inequality and Difference. Cham: Springer International Publishing.

Viscidi, Lisa, and Jason Fargo. 2015. *Local Conflicts and Natural Resources: A Balancing Act for Latin American Governments*. The Dialogue. Energy Working Papers.

Viscidi, Lisa, and Nathaniel Parish Flannery. 2019. "Mexico's Problematic Energy Policy." *The Dialogue—Leadership for the Americas*, 7 June. Retrieved 21 December 2020 from https://www.thedialogue.org/analysis/mexicos-problematic-energy-policy/

Watts, Michael. 2005. "Righteous Oil? Human Rights, the Oil Complex and Corporate Social Responsibility." *Annual Review of Environment and Resources* 30(1): 373–407. http://doi.org/10.1146/annurev.energy.30.050504.144456.

———. 2011. "Blood Oil: The Anatomy of a Petro-insurgency in the Niger Delta." In *Crude Domination: An Anthropology of Oil*, ed. Andrea Behrends, Stephen P. Reyna, and Günther Schlee, 49–80. Oxford: Berghahn Books.

———. 2012. "A Tale of Two Gulfs: Life, Death, and Dispossession along Two Oil Frontiers." *American Quarterly* 64(3): 437–67. http://www.jstor.org/stable/23273530.

Welker, Marina. 2014. *Enacting the Corporation: An American Mining Firm in Post-Authoritarian Indonesia*. Berkeley: University of California Press. http://www.jstor.org/stable/10.1525/j.ctt5vjzm0.

Weszkalnys, Gisa. 2013. "Oil's Magic: Contestation and Materiality." In *Cultures of Energy: Anthropological Perspectives on Powering the Planet*, ed. Sarah Strauss, Stephanie Rupp, and Thomas Love. Walnut Creek, CA: Left Coast Press Inc.

———. 2014. "Anticipating Oil: The Temporal Politics of a Disaster Yet to Come." *The Sociological Review* 62(1_suppl): 211–35. http://doi.org/10.1111/1467-954x.12130.

———. 2016. "A Doubtful Hope: Resource Affect in a Future Oil Economy." *Journal of the Royal Anthropological Institute* 22(S1): 127–46. http://doi.org/10.1111/1467-9655.12397.

Wheeler, Rebecca. 2014. "Mining Memories in a Rural Community: Landscape, Temporality and Place Identity." *Journal of Rural Studies* 36: 22–32. http://doi.org/10.1016/j.jrurstud.2014.06.005.

Whiteman, Gail, and Katy Mamen. 2002. *Meaningful Consultation and Participation in the Mining Sector?: A Review of the Consultation and Participation of Indigenous Peoples within the International Mining Sector*. Ottawa: North-South Institute.

Whitmarsh, Lorraine, Nick Nash, Paul Upham, Alyson Lloyd, James P. Verdon, and J.-Michael Kendall. 2015. "UK Public Perceptions of Shale Gas Hydraulic Fracturing: The Role of Audience, Message and Contextual Factors on Risk Perceptions and Policy Support." *Applied Energy* 160: 419–30. http://doi.org/10.1016/j.apenergy.2015.09.004.

Whitton, John, Matthew Cotton, Ioan M. Charnley-Parry, and Kathryn Brasier, eds. 2018. *Governing Shale Gas: Development, Citizen Participation and Decision Making in the US, Canada, Australia and Europe*. Routledge Studies in Energy Policy. London: Routledge.

Williams, Laurence, Phil Macnaghten, Richard Davies, and Sarah Curtis. 2017. "Framing 'Fracking': Exploring Public Perceptions of Hydraulic Fracturing in the United Kingdom." *Public Understanding of Science (Bristol, England)* 26(1): 89–104. http://doi.org/10.1177/0963662515595159.

Willow, Anna J., and Sara Wylie. 2014. "Politics, Ecology, and the New Anthropology of Energy: Exploring the Emerging Frontiers of Hydraulic Fracking." *Journal of Political Ecology* 21(1): 222–36. http://doi.org/10.2458/v21i1.21134.

Willow, Anna J., Rebecca Zak, Danielle Vilaplana, and David Sheeley. 2014. "The Contested Landscape of Unconventional Energy Development: A Report from Ohio's Shale Gas Country." *Journal Environmental Studies and Sciences* 4(1): 56–64. http://doi.org/10.1007/s13412-013-0159-3.

Wilson, Sheena, Adam Carlson, and Imre Szeman. 2017. "On Petrocultures: Or, Why We Need to Understand Oil to Understand Everything Else." In *Petrocultures: Oil, Politics, Culture*, ed. Sheena Wilson, Adam Carlson, and Imre Szeman, 3–19. London: McGill-Queen's University Press.

Witte, Annika 2018. "An Uncertain Future—Anticipating Oil in Uganda." Ph.D. dissertation. Göttingen: Göttingen University.

Wood, Duncan. 2010. "The Administration of Decline: Mexio's Looming Oil Crisis". *Law and Business Review of the Americas*. 16(4): 855–70. https://scholar.smu.edu/lbra/vol16/iss4/11

Yu, Chin-Hsien, Shih-Kai Huang, Ping Qin, and Xiaolan Chen. 2018. "Local Residents' Risk Perceptions in Response to Shale Gas Exploitation: Evidence from China." *Energy Policy* 113: 123–34. http://doi.org/10.1016/j.enpol.2017.10.004.

Zalik, Anna. 2008. "Oil Sovereignties: Ecology and Nationality in the Nigerian Delta and the Mexican Gulf!" In *Extractive Economies and Conflicts in the Global South: Multi-Regional Perspectives on Rentier Politics*, ed. Kenneth Omeje, 181–98. Aldershot: Ashgate Publishing, Ltd.

———. 2009. "Zones of Exclusion: Offshore Extraction, the Contestation of Space and Physical Displacement in the Nigerian Delta and the Mexican Gulf." *Antipode* 41(3): 557–82. http://doi.org/10.1111/j.1467-8330.2009.00687.x.

Index

Adam, Barbara, 34
Agencia de Seguridad, Energía e Ambiente (ASEA), 58–59
agencia municipal
agente municipal, 66–68, 82, 90, 166, 171–72
   community council, 65, 71
   secretary, 65
   surveillance committee, 66
   treasurer, 65
Anand, Nikhil, 27
anxiety, 3–4, 11, 15, 73, 92, 105, 115, 129, 184–86
Allianza Mexicanan contra el Fracking (AMCF), 59, 174, 191
agrarian counter reform, 56, 155, 179. *See also* neoliberal turn
agricultural crisis, 95
Alemán, Miguel, 52
Appadurai, Arjun, 5, 181
Appel, Hannah, 19, 27, 28
Área Contractual (AC), 61
Article 27 of the Mexican Constitution, 48–49, 51, 53, 55, 147. *See also* Mexican Constitution of 1917
asentamiento humano. See fundo legal
auditorio, 165–66, 180
Auyero, Javier, 38
Aztec people, 44

Banks, Glenn, 4
Behrends, Andrea, 19
Bender, Barbara, 34
Black, Brian, 6, 32
boom and bust cycle, 4, 24, 38, 105, 182–83, 188–89

boomtown, 24, 31, 88, 104, 187–89. *See also* boom and bust cycle
Bourbon Reforms, 44
Breglia, Lisa, 4, 32, 41
British Mexican Railroad Company, 47
Buck-Morss, Susan, 108

Calles, Plutarco Elías, 48
Calderón, Felipe, 56–57
Camacho, Ávila, 52
campesino, 48, 51–52, 60, 70, 94, 122, 124–25, 153–54, 163, 165, 191
Cancian, Frank, 4, 186
Cancun, 96
Cantarell oilfield, 32, 42, 54
cantón de Papantla 42
Cárdenas, Lázaro, 49–50, 52
Carranza, Venustiano, 48
Cartwright, Elizabeth, 30
cash crops, 42, 123, 125, 139.
Cazones de Herreras, 50
chapopote, 44–45
Chumatlán, 50
citrus fruits, 60, 62, 65, 91, 95, 122. *See also* cash crop
Coahuitlán, 50
Coatzintla, 48, 50
Colonia San Andrés, 75, 85–86, 88, 138, 161–65
construction work, 81, 92, 94, 128, 167
contamination
   air, 3, 12, 29, 112, 124, 127
   climate effects, 110, 125
   soil, 3, 12, 29, 37, 112–13, 124–25, 127, 130
   water, 3, 12, 29, 112, 124, 127

comedor. See community kitchen
community kitchen, 11, 21, 64, 69, 83, 100, 114, 131, 135, 169
community store, 60, 65, 69, 71
communal education system
primaria, 68, 134, 164
telebachillerato, 69, 70, 93, 94
telesecundaria, 93
Comisión Nacional de Hidrocarburos (CNH), 190–91
Consejo Nacional de Población (CONAPO), 64
Comisión Nacional para el Desarrollo de los Pueblos Indígenas de México (CDI), 41
commercial agriculture, 22–23, 53, 184. *See also* cash crops
Compañía Mexicana de Petróleo El Águila SA, 47, 48
compensation, 2, 3, 4, 84, 86, 88, 91–92, 97, 99, 110, 132–36, 139, 140–42, 144, 154, 155, 159, 167–68, 178–79, 183
condueñazgo, 46–47
Conquista, 43, 45
contestation. *See* protest
corn, 42, 60, 62, 65, 70, 91, 95, 99, 120, 122, 145
Corporate Social Responsibility (CSR), 20, 132, 134, 136, 141, 147, 152, 169–71, 179
Coxquihui, 50
crisis del campo See under agricultural crisis
cuartel 128. *See also* military

damages
accidents, 10–11, 21–22, 38, 88, 91, 95, 100–1, 104, 126–27, 129, 132, 136, 139, 141–42, 152, 154–55, 161, 164, 166, 168–69, 179, 182–85
pollution, 38, 62, 79, 87–88, 91, 101, 103, 105, 110, 112–13, 123–30, 133, 136, 152, 182–85

seepage, 11, 84, 88, 91, 95, 99–100, 103–4, 109–12, 114, 118, 124, 126–27, 131, 133, 142, 146, 152, 154–55, 160, 166, 168, 177, 179
de Madrid, Miguel, 55
de Sahagun, Bernardino, 45
del Palacio Langer, Ana Julia, 51
DICONSA, 71

Echeverría, Luis, 53
economic crisis, 4, 12, 24, 38, 53–57, 74, 79, 93, 95, 100, 105, 142, 164, 175, 182, 189. *See also* oil crisis
Edelstein, Michael, 37
ejido organization
assembly, 50, 66, 98, 110, 155–57, 159–60, 162
comisariado, 50, 56, 64–66, 72
council, 65, 99, 133, 138–39, 155, 169
El Águila. *See under* Compañía Mexicana de Petróleo El Àguila SA
El Llano, 60–61, 71,
employment in the oil industry. See *petrolero*
Encuentro Regional Norte-Golfo por la Defensa del Agua y el Territorio Frente a los Proyectos de Muerte, 10, 174
Espinal, 50
ethnography of the senses, 108–10, 118, 184,
expropriation, 9, 43, 49, 51, 58, 87, 148, 155, 157–58, 184. *See also* nationalization of the oil sector
Ey, Melina, 5–6, 35, 182

FANAR, 157, 165, 180
faena (community service), 66, 72
farm hand, 65, 103, 120, *See also* part-time laborer
fracking, 2, 8–12, 14, 28–31, 59–60, 62–63, 67, 101–3, 173–79, 185, 190–91
Federal Civil Code, 58
fiesta patronal, 69, 164
Filer, Colin, 3, 88, 186

Filomeno Mata, 50
Foreign investment in Mexico. *See* neoliberal politics in Mexico
fossil fuels, 19, 29–30, 52, 101
Fox, Vicente, 56
free prior and informed consent (FPIC), 189
fundo legal. See human settlement area
Furber, Percy 47
Furbero oilfield, 47

gas flare, 2, 11, 22, 108, 110–13, 115–16, 124, 158, 166, 171–73, 176, 185
Gilberthorpe, Emma, 18, 19
Global South, 10, 188
Graffiti, 2, 10, 174,
Gulf Coast, 44–45, 47, 87, 123
Gupta, Akhil, 27
Gutiérrez Zamora, 50, 54, 62

hacienda, 46, 77–78, 103
Hacienda San Andrés, 77
highway, 80, 86, 119, 134, 136
Honduras, 131
human settlement area, 64, 80–81, 109, 157–58
Humapa oil field, 190
Huasteca, 19, 44
hydraulic fracturing *See under* fracking

Illnesses, 37, 110, 124
indemnification, 51–52, 147, 155–60, 164, 167, 178. *See also* compensation
indigenous (Totonac) traditions
  family, 77, 150–51
  language, 81, 149–51, 183
  settlement patterns, 46, 88, 103,
  traditional clothing, 81–82
infrastructure(es)
  concept of, 26–28
  pipelines, 5, 25–29, 35, 37, 56, 76, 81–86, 88, 90, 98, 102, 104, 107–9, 112–13, 115–19, 124–29, 132, 136–39, 142, 148, 152–54, 161, 179, 182–83, 188, 190

public buildings, 6, 26, 28, 35, 37, 49, 54, 66, 68, 108, 114, 125, 131, 133, 135–36, 141, 148, 161
transport, 5, 26, 35, 37, 49, 54, 64, 68, 87, 93, 98, 114, 121, 125, 128–29, 137, 141, 148, 161, 182–83
ingeniero, 25, 76, 94–95, 105, 109, 117, 153–54
Inter-American Development Bank, 134
ILO convention, 59
International Labor Organization (ILO), 59
International Monetary Fund, 55
Instituto Nacional de Estadística y Geografía (INEGI), 62, 71, 164

jornaleros See part-time laborers

land conflicts, 50, 144, 148, 163–64, 184
landless peasants, 49, 70, 76, 90, 161
Llanura Costera, 42, 71
licencia social, 170. *See also* Corporate Social Responsibility (CSR)
López Obrador, Manuel, 15, 190
Low, Setha, 33

Macatlán, 50
Mason, Arthur, 19, 29
Mateos, López, 53
maize. *See* corn
Mesoamerica, 44
Mexican Constitution of 1917, 42, 47–49, 51, 55, 57–58
Mexican energy reform of 2013/14, 2, 9–10, 12, 14–16, 57, 59, 62–63, 67, 74–75, 96, 98, 101, 160, 165, 167, 171, 173, 175, 177–80, 183, 185, 191
Mexican Revolution, 8, 49–51, 67, 70–71, 93
Mexican oil boom (oil bonanza), 9, 49, 53–54, 57, 67
Mexico City, 10, 14, 106, 138, 174
military, 78, 80
milpa, See also small-scale farming, 43, 45–46, 62, 70, 77, 87, 120, 121–25, 130

Mitchell, Timothy, 19
Monclova Pirineos Gas, 63
monoculture *See* commercial agriculture
Monterrey, 89, 96, 112, 121

nahuatl *See* Atztec people
nationalization of the oil sector, 8, 49, 51, 67, 147
neoliberal politics in Mexico, 54–57, 62, 173, 188
Nueva Ley de Hidrocarburos 2014 *See* Mexican energy reform of 2013/14
municipality of Papantla, 42, 50–51, 57, 60–62

Obregón Álvaro, 48
obrero, 153–54. *See also* oil workers
oil crisis, 1, 4, 11, 41, 54, 88, 104, 129, 141, 179, 189
oil curse, 20–21, 23
oil shock of 1973, 53
oil theft (*huachicalero*), 190
oil worker, 2, 25, 47–48, 51–52, 55, 67, 76, 82, 85, 87, 94–95, 102, 126, 146–48, 150–54, 160, 164, 169
Oleorey SA de CV, 63, 96–100, 106, 115, 166, 167–72, 179, 184
Oliver-Smith, Anthony, 13, 74
Olmec people, 44
oranges 1, 61, 91, 99, 110, 120–24, 140, 145, 164. *See also* citrus fruits
organized crime, 2, 57, 61, 190

Paleocanal de Chicontepec, 42
Papantla de Olarte 42–48, 54, 65–66, 71, 78–79, 122, 154
Partido Acción Nacional (PAN), 56
Partido Revolucionario Institucional (PRI), 56, 94
part-time laborer 76–77, 81, 91–92, 94–95, 99, 122, 126, 128, 131, 153–54, 168, 180
peak oil, 29, 67
Pemex Corporate Industrial Safety and Environmental Protection Division, 133

Pemex Exploración y Producción (PEP), 63, 190
post-neoextractivism, 188
Procaruría Agraria, 158
PROCEDE, 56, 155–57, 180, 184
Programa de Apoyo a la Comunidad y Medio Ambiente (PACMA), 134
Peña Nieto, Enrique, 9, 57
petrolero. *See* oil worker
Petroleum Exporting Countries (OPEC), 53
Portillo, López, 55
postrevolutionary turmoil, 78–79, *See also* Mexican Revolution
Poza Rica de Hidalgo, 2, 49–50, 52, 54, 57, 66, 85, 93–94, 97, 114, 119, 121–22, 147, 152–54, 162, 168, 170–71
Poza Rica oilfield, 9, 48–49, 54
Precolonial Mexico, 44
Programa de Certificación de Derechos Ejidales y Titualción de Solares Urbano (PROCEDE). 56, 155–57, 180, 184. *See also* agrarian counter reform
PROSPERA, 64
protest, 2, 9–10, 30, 47, 59, 102, 139, 171–74, 176–79, 185
Puebla 42, 32, 161

quemazón, 85–88, 117, 161

Rajak, Dinah, 13, 18
Registro Agrario Nacional (RAN), 66
remittances 22, 61, 65, 104, 106, 128, 183
resistance. *See* protest
Reyna, Stephen, 19
Reynosa, 96, 121
Rivera Maya, 96
river Cazones 43
river Papaloapan, 43
river Remolino 1, 79, 172
Rogers, Douglas, 14, 186
Ross, Michael, 20

Salinas de Gortari, Carlos, 55
Santa Rosa, 79

Santiago, Myrna, 6, 19, 32
Scape(s)
  concept, 3, 5, 32–36, 181, 187
  minescape, 5–7, 35, 182, 187
Schlee, Günther, 19
Secretaría de Energía (SENER), 59
Secretaría del Desarrollo Social (SEDESOL), 64
Secretaría de Medio Ambiente y Recursos Naturales (SERMANAT), 58
shale gas. *See under* fracking
Sherval, Meg, 5–6, 35, 182
Sindicato de Trabajadores Petroleros de la República Mexicana (STPRM), 48, 51, 54, 94, 154. *See also* oil workers
small-scale farming, 16, 51, 53, 65, 70, 94, 130, 139. *See also campesino*
social impact assessments. *See* Mexican energy reform of 2013/14
social impact studies. *See* Mexican energy reform of 2013/14
space/spatiality, 22, 27–29, 31–36, 39, 74, 103, 105, 113, 138, 143, 178, 181. *See also* Scape(s)
Stewart, Pamela, 34
Strathern, Andrew, 34
Strikes, 20, 47–48, 51. *See also* oil worker
Swistun, Debora, 38

Tampico-Misantla, 190
Teenek people, 44

Tecolutla, 50
Tihuatlán, 50
Totonacapan, 42–50, 53, 60, 62, 77–78, 121, 123, 149
Totonac people, 44–45, 47, 50, 53, 70, 77, 176
  Migration, 22, 24, 61, 92, 95–96, 101, 104. *See also* remittances
turbinas, 115

United States of America (USA), 24, 30, 47, 53, 55, 189

vanilla, 41, 44–47, 53, 78–79, 87, 120, 122
vanilla trade. *See under* vanilla
Vásquez, Patricia, 32
Veracruz (state), 7, 9, 14, 21, 42, 44–45, 47, 62–63, 66–67, 72, 101, 121, 174
voladores de Papantla, 149, 180

Xalapa, 14

wage labor, 3–4, 53, 60–61, 65, 88, 91, 94, 119, 122–23, 153. *See also* part-time laborer
Watts, Michael, 19, 29
Weszkalnys, Gisa, 19, 26
World Bank, 55

Zapata, Emiliano (revolutionary), 7–8
Zedilla, Ernesto, 55
Zozocolco de Hidalgo, 50